Bugle Resounding

Shades of Blue and Gray Series

Louis S. Gerteis and Clayton E. Jewett, Series Editors
Herman Hattaway and Jon Wakelyn, Consulting Editors

The Shades of Blue and Gray Series offers Civil War studies for the modern reader—Civil War buff and scholar alike. Military history today addresses the relationship between society and warfare. Thus biographies and thematic studies that deal with civilians, soldiers, and political leaders are increasingly important to a larger public. This series includes books that will appeal to Civil War Roundtable groups, individuals, libraries, and academics with a special interest in this era of American history.

Bugle Resounding

Music and Musicians of the Civil War Era

Edited by
Bruce C. Kelley and Mark A. Snell

University of Missouri Press
Columbia

University of Missouri Press, Columbia, Missouri 65211
Printed and bound in the United States of America

First paperback printing, 2018

Library of Congress Cataloging-in-Publication Data

National Conference on Music of the Civil War Era.
Bugle resounding : music and musicians of the Civil War era / edited by Bruce C. Kelley and Mark A. Snell.
p. cm. — (Shades of blue and gray series)
Principally papers presented at the National Conference on Music of the Civil War Era in 2001 and 2002.
Includes index.
ISBN 978-0-8262-2153-7 (alk. paper)
1. Music—United States—19th century—History and criticism—Congresses. 2. United States—History—Civil War, 1861–1865—Songs and music—History and criticism—Congresses. I. Snell, Mark A. II. Kelley, Bruce C. III. Title. IV. Series.
ML200.4.N38 2004
780'.973'09034—dc22 2004010358

∞™ This paper meets the requirements of the American National Standard for Permanence of Paper for Printed Library Materials, Z39.48, 1984.

Typefaces: Goudy Handtooled and Simoncini Garamond

Contents

Preface

On January 1, 1863, Bugler Charles Reed of the Ninth Massachusetts Battery wrote in a letter to his mother, "I . . . made these old Virginia hills echo and resound with my good bugle."[1] The title of this work, *Bugle Resounding,* harkens back to that moment but also looks forward to what we hope will be a new era in research on music of the Civil War period. This volume is an outgrowth of the 2001 and 2002 National Conference on Music of the Civil War Era. These colloquiums were conceived by the editors of this book and were sponsored in part by the Department of Music at Shepherd University (then Shepherd College) and by the university's George Tyler Moore Center for the Study of the Civil War, and in part through the generosity of numerous private donors, and through grants by the West Virginia Humanities Council and by the Gettysburg Battlefield Preservation Association. In addition to the presentation of papers, the conferences also featured concerts, exhibits, and workshops. These conferences established, for the first time, an academic setting solely devoted to exploring the effects of the Civil War on music and musicians.

The United States in the mid-nineteenth century was musically vibrant. Rising industrialization, a growing middle class, and increasing concern for the founding (and funding) of *American* centers of art created a culture that was rich in musical capital. The importance of music to Americans of this period can be documented to some extent through piano production figures, participation trends in community bands and choirs, sales of sheet music, and the like. Some measure of American society's devotion to music can also be gleaned through a cursory glance at the letters, diaries, and memoirs of those

1. Eric A. Campbell, ed., *"A Grand Terrible Dramma": From Gettysburg to Petersburg: The Civil War Letters of Charles Wellington Reed* (New York: Fordham University Press, 2000), 63.

who experienced the Civil War. Beyond its importance to the people of its own time, however, is the fact that this music still influences our culture today, in the pervasive popularity of a number of songs from the era, the brass band tradition, and even to the historic roots of today's rock and jazz styles.

While there are numerous academic resources that examine the music and musicians of this era, the research is spread across a wide array of disciplines and is found in a great variety of journals, books, and papers. It is difficult to assimilate this diverse body of research, and few sources are dedicated solely to a rigorous and comprehensive investigation of the music and the musicians of the Civil War era. This anthology is an initial attempt to address that need.

The authors of the following essays represent many different disciplines and professional fields. Bringing together experts from so many different backgrounds does present some unique challenges. Terminology that is basic to one discipline or profession may not be as well defined for others. *Programmatic music,* for example, is a basic term used by music scholars, but its meaning may be unclear to traditional historians and laymen. In general, we have decided to err on the side of caution when using terminology that may not be generally understood across academic disciplines. Some allowances must also be made for differences in writing styles. Although the editors have attempted to unify the essays contained in this volume, we were not unmindful of the fact that our writers come from a variety of academic disciplines and professional backgrounds—indeed, we regard this as one of the strengths of this collection.

Nine papers were selected from among the many excellent presentations at the conferences, and one new essay, the first, was written specifically for this book. The essays contained herein represent the forefront of scholarship in music of the Civil War era. The first essay in this volume reviews the current state of research on this topic and attempts to organize existing research into several distinct categories. In the second essay, Deane L. Root, expanding on his keynote address at the second conference, examines the idea of "community" and describes how music of the Civil War era, specifically the music of Stephen Foster, often created multiple meanings for members of diverse communities. Then, Lenora Cuccia examines the portrayal of women in popular music of the war, examining such roles as mother, sweetheart, and "gutsy gal." In the next essay, Richard C. Spicer describes the colorful history of the New Hampshire Third Regimental Band and the Hilton Head Post Band. After that, David B. Thompson's essay takes a look at a relatively forgotten category of music: piano works by Confederate composers. Walter L. Powell's essay examines the war retrospectively through "The Silver Horn," one of the last songs written by the prolific composer Henry Clay Work. Next, Kirsten M. Schultz documents the production, use, and contents of Confederate "songsters"—songbooks of lyrics—one of the few academic essays to fully examine this unique source of music. In the next essay, Michael Saffle examines the vibrant contributions of Irish Americans to music of the war era. Then, Eric A. Campbell focuses on the life of an extraordinary field musician, the bugler Charles Reed, who won the Medal of Honor at the Battle of Gettysburg. Campbell's research segues neatly into the final essay, which describes how the Battle of Gettysburg was depicted in popular music up to 1913, the fiftieth anniversary of that momentous fight.

Each of the preceding essays makes a significant contribution to research in the music of this era. They are also representative of the wide diversity of research that is available on this topic. It is our hope that this volume will encourage more interdisciplinary research on a subject that has relevance for both its own time and for ours.

A project of this magnitude is not possible without the significant help of numerous people. We would like to thank specifically Denise Messinger, program assistant at the George Tyler Moore Center for the Study of the Civil War, who helped untiringly both with the conferences and with the production of this collection of essays. We would also like to thank the volunteers who helped with the conferences: Tom White, Al Pejack, Ron French, and Lori Kaylor, staff members of the George Tyler Moore Center for the Study of the Civil War; the brothers of the Shepherd University chapter of Phi Mu Alpha (the National Music Honors Fraternity); Robert Farmer, a Shepherd University art major; Peggy Miller, administrative assistant for the Shepherd University Department of Music; Anders Henriksson and Mark McCoy, chairs of the Department of History and Department of Music, respectively; and Dow Benedict, dean of the School of Arts and Humanities at Shepherd. Finally, we would like to thank pianist Helen Beedle, who came to the rescue during the first conference when the scheduled performer for the Friday evening concert failed to show; Helen graciously stepped in—on very short notice—and performed magnificently.

Bruce C. Kelley and Mark A. Snell
April 21, 2004
Shepherd University

Bugle Resounding

"Old Times There Are Not Forgotten"

An Overview of Music of the Civil War Era

Bruce C. Kelley

On June 3, 1862, the diarist Mary Boykin Chesnut wrote:

> I sat down at my window in the beautiful moonlight and tried hard for pleasant thoughts. A man began to play on the flute with piano accompaniment; first "Ever of Thee I Am Kindly Dreaming"; then "Long, Long, Weary Day." At first I found it but a complement to the beautiful scene, and it was soothing to my wrought-up nerves; but Von Weber's "Last Waltz" was too much. Suddenly I broke down. Heavens, what a bitter cry! Such floods of tears! The wonder is there was any of me left.[1]

The raw power and emotion of the American Civil War seared our national conscience and transformed American culture. It is estimated that one in sixteen men of military age died in the North, and one in five in the South.[2] The economic, political, and social effects of the war and its aftermath likewise transformed the nation's music to such an extent that its role in the conflict remains to this day a topic of passionate interest. Reenactors on authentic or reproduction period instruments currently perform music of the Civil War at numerous festivals, and hundreds of thousands of Web sites are devoted to the

1. Mary Boykin Chesnut, *A Diary from Dixie,* ed. Ben Ames William (New York: D. Appleton, 1905; reprint, Boston: Houghton Mifflin, 1961), 232 (page references are to reprint edition).

2. Maris A. Vinovskis, "Have Social Historians Lost the Civil War?" in *Toward a Social History of the American Civil War: Exploratory Essays,* ed. Maris Vinovskis (Cambridge: Cambridge University Press, 1990), 1–30.

subject or mention it in some way.[3] At the time this essay was written (2003), sixteen CDs featuring Civil War music and fifty-three books on the topic were commercially available at a large book retailer (compared, for example, to six CDs and sixteen books on music of World War II). It is obvious that the music of this period has a sustaining popularity.

While there are numerous academic resources that examine the music and musicians of this era, the research is spread across a wide array of disciplines and is found in a great variety of journals, books, and papers. It is difficult to assimilate this diverse body of research, and few sources are dedicated solely to a rigorous and comprehensive investigation of the music and musicians of the Civil War era. Thus, to provide a context for the following essays, this essay examines some of the existing research on music of this period. This is by no means an easy task, for America in the 1860s had a rich, diverse, and multifaceted musical culture. Research on music of the Civil War era can be broadly organized into ten categories:

Music Personalities. The antebellum United States was a place of great promise for musicians. How were the personal and professional lives of performers and composers changed by the war?

European Art Music. The American Civil War occurred during the middle of the Romantic period in European music history. How did the American public receive this music? In what venues or for what occasions was it performed? Did the war have an impact on this music's performance or reception?

Popular Song and Dance. Song and dance provided much-needed reprieve from the horrors of war, both in the field and at home. What were the topics of these songs? How did popular music portray the enemy? Are collections of the music still available to the general consumer today?

Music and Culture. Music is an integral part of American culture. What societal values did the music of the Civil War exhibit? Did the music of that period have a cultural significance beyond what we would understand today? What roles did specific ethnic and geographical communities play?

3. A major Internet search engine turned up more than 954,000 Web pages that contained the phrase "Civil War music."

African American Music and Musicians. The war affected African Americans to a greater extent than any other societal or cultural group. How was this experience manifested in music? In what ways did the music reflect the values of society toward blacks, both slave and free? What contributions did African American composers, musicians, instrument-makers, and publishers make to the musical world at large?

Military and Civilian Bands. The wind band (and fife and drum corps) may be the most persistent musical symbol of this era. What was the developmental history of these ensembles? What types of literature were performed, and what types of instruments did they use? What historical roles did individual bands play?

Innovations. The nineteenth century was a period of technological and pedagogical innovation. How did this carry over to the development, design, and construction of musical instruments? What kinds of method books or new pedagogical studies were developed during this era?

Music Publishing. Publishing firms in the North and South rushed to print music for their respective causes (and sometimes for both causes). Who were the major publishers of the era? What was their history and the extent of their work?

Collection and Description. Musical artifacts from the Civil War era have been gathered in numerous public and private collections. Where are these collections, and what does analysis of the collections reveal?

New Beginnings. The Civil War caused mass movements of both soldiers and civilians. What was the musical effect of the cultural intermingling that resulted? What new styles would emerge from this musical cross-fertilization?

These categories, while not always distinct, serve as reference points for reviewing the current state of scholarship.

MUSICAL PERSONALITIES

On Monday, April 8, 1861, the following announcement was made in the amusements section of the *New York Times:*

> Mr. Gottschalk's return to the City during the coming week is already the theme of general conversation. This superb artist has written

> so many new compositions lately, that his programmes will present a rare degree of freshness. We shall also have an opportunity of hearing Miss Carlotta Patti to great advantage in these entertainments. This remarkable young singer has created a great success wherever she has appeared, and for the concert-room is pronounced superior to her sister Adalina.

The excitement created by the Confederate attack on Fort Sumter four days later undoubtedly eclipsed Louis Gottschalk's return to New York (and Adalina's career would surpass by far that of her sister Carlotta), but America in the 1860s was nonetheless a time of great promise for musicians. Communities supported traveling opera companies, symphonic orchestras, and theaters, while American-born performers were beginning to compete artistically with their European counterparts. Composers found an outlet for their work in a growing publishing industry, and amateur musicians sang in church, joined singing societies, and participated in community bands. As war approached, some musicians became wholeheartedly devoted to one cause or the other, but many simply attempted to survive the war as best they could, maintaining their hard-earned careers in the face of uncertain times and—especially in the South—physical dislocation.

Because it is impractical to review the full body of research that has examined the lives and careers of Civil War musicians, this essay therefore will focus primarily on five musicians: John Hill Hewitt, George Root, Thomas Greene Wiggins, Patrick Gilmore, and Clara Louise Kellogg. Their lives provide an intimate, informative, sometimes entertaining, and sometimes harrowing view of the war's impact on musicians, and at the same time, they serve as illustrations for describing the wide diversity that occurs in the quality and quantity of research in this area.

John Hill Hewitt (1801–1890) was a prolific writer of both music and prose. He was born in New York but spent most of his life in the South. He believed slavery was morally wrong and was pro-Union prior to the war, but Lincoln's call for troops to invade the South changed his loyalties. He volunteered for the Confederate army at the outbreak of hostilities but was rejected due to his lack of military experience and his age (he was sixty years old at the time). Although unable to wear the uniform of his new nation, Hewitt "served" by writing numerous plays and managing theaters in Richmond and

Augusta. He composed five musical stage works during the war (the most popular being *The Vivandiere*) and wrote over three hundred songs. Some of these proved popular in both the North and the South, including "Somebody's Darling" and "All Quiet along the Potomac Tonight." Hewitt is the best known of the Southern composers—he is the only one, for example, to receive a full chapter in Richard Harwell's *Confederate Music.* Other sources that investigate this composer include an article by Lee Orr and a dissertation by Coy Huggins, both titled "John Hill Hewitt: Bard of the Confederacy," John Tasker Howard's "The Hewitt Family in American Music," and William Winden's dissertation, "The Life and Music Theatre Works of John Hill Hewitt." In addition, Lee Orr and Lynn Bertrand have compiled and analyzed Hewitt's compositions in their book *The Collected Works of John Hill Hewitt.* Generally speaking, Hewitt's influence on music of the Civil War era, his role in the war, and its impact on his music and career have been well documented. There are few significant resources, however, that detail the careers of other Confederate composers.[4]

George Root (1820–1895) achieved a considerable reputation writing songs for the Union cause. He was also a prominent music educator and a partner in the publishing firm of Root and Cady, which was founded by Chauncey Cady and George's brother Ebenezer in 1858. Root composed a number of cantatas and many parlor songs prior to the war, and he was the first composer to respond when the war broke out: "The First Gun Is Fired! May God Protect the Right!" was issued on April 15, 1861, just three days after Fort Sumter was fired upon. He wrote over thirty war anthems, including such well-

4. Richard Harwell, *Confederate Music* (Chapel Hill: University of North Carolina Press, 1950); N. Lee Orr, "John Hill Hewitt: Bard of the Confederacy," *American Music Research Center Journal* 4 (1994): 31–75; Coy Elliot Huggins, "John Hill Hewitt: Bard of the Confederacy" (Ph.D. diss., Florida State University, 1964); John Tasker Howard, "The Hewitt Family in American Music," *Musical Quarterly* 17 (1931): 25–39; William Craig Winden, "The Life and Music Theatre Works of John Hill Hewitt" (Ph.D. diss., University of Illinois, 1972); N. Lee Orr and Lynn Wood Bertrand, *The Collected Works of John Hill Hewitt* (New York: Garland Press, 1994). Regarding other Confederate composers, Theodore von La Hache, for example, wrote over six hundred compositions, including several works in honor of the Confederacy, yet the only consequential work on his life is a dissertation by Warren C. Fields, "The Life and Works of Theodore von La Hache" (Ph.D. diss., University of Iowa, 1973).

known songs as "The Vacant Chair," "The Battle Cry of Freedom," "Just before the Battle, Mother," and "Tramp! Tramp! Tramp! or the Prisoner's Hope." His autobiography, *The Story of a Musical Life,* dedicates one chapter to a description of his war years. It is interesting for its first-person view of the role of music in the war, and it contains vignettes about some of his best-known songs. Although a few sources, such as Dena Epstein's *Music Publishing in Chicago before 1871: The Firm of Root and Cady, 1858–1871,* P. H. Carder's "George Frederick Root, Pioneer Music Educator: His Contributions to Mass Instruction in Music," and Deane L. Root's *American Popular Stage Music, 1860–1880,* discuss Root in some detail, amazingly no biography has yet been written about this important American composer.[5]

Perhaps no composer or performer exemplifies the upheaval, discord, and contradictions of the Civil War era as well as Thomas Greene Wiggins (1849–1908). Wiggins (also known as Thomas Bethune, or "Blind Tom") was blind from birth and was a slave of James N. Bethune. He was identified as a musical prodigy by the age of four and was performing concerts throughout the state of Georgia by the time of his eighth birthday. His programs included a variety of works by European masters such as Bach, Beethoven, and Liszt, but he also performed his own compositions and often amazed audiences with improvisations on popular operatic tunes. He had a phenomenal musical memory and could perform difficult pieces after one hearing. During the war he performed concerts under the direction of the Bethunes to raise money for the Confederacy. Wiggins, of course, became a free man after the war, but in 1865 he was put into the custody of the Bethunes because he was reportedly unable to care for himself.

Scholarship regarding this composer has been as full of discord and contradiction as the composer's life. Early scholarship, brushed with prejudice, considered Blind Tom to be a phenomenon of nature—a

5. George Frederick Root, *The Story of a Musical Life* (Cincinnati: John Church, 1891; reprint, New York: AMS, 1971); Dena Epstein, *Music Publishing in Chicago before 1871: The Firm of Root and Cady, 1858–1871,* Detroit Studies in Music Bibliography 14 (Detroit: Information Coordinators, 1969); P. H. Carder, "George Frederick Root, Pioneer Music Educator: His Contributions to Mass Instruction in Music" (Ph.D. diss., University of Maryland, 1971); Deane L. Root, *American Popular Stage Music, 1860–1880* (Ann Arbor, Mich.: UMI Research Press, 1981).

self-taught and mentally deficient musical genius—in short, a savant. As late as 1967, Norborne T. Robinson's article "Blind Tom: Musical Prodigy," for example, claimed that Wiggins was "Blind, mentally deficient almost to the point of idiocy." More recent scholarship has challenged a number of the myths surrounding the education and career of Thomas Wiggins, showing that he augmented his considerable natural ability with formal training in performance and music theory from a number of instructors, and a daily practice regimen that sometimes lasted eight hours.[6]

Patrick S. Gilmore (1829–1892) was born in Ireland and moved to Boston in 1849. He held a number of positions as a bandleader in Massachusetts and in 1858 established his own band. By 1860, his band had become so popular that it played for both the Democratic and Republican presidential conventions. During the Civil War the band was attached to the Twenty-fourth Massachusetts Infantry Regiment, and Gilmore was charged with organizing and training all the Massachusetts brigade bands. He was later assigned to administer all the bands of the Department of the Gulf, and in this capacity Gilmore organized the first of the "monster" concerts that would cement his national reputation. He assembled for the 1864 inauguration of the governor of Louisiana an ensemble consisting of a five-hundred-piece band, a six-thousand-voice chorus, fifty cannons, and forty soldiers to strike anvils. Gilmore composed a number of Civil War songs, including "Freedom on the Old Plantation," "The Spirit of the North," and "God Save the Union," and he is credited with writing the still-popular "When Johnny Comes Marching Home," although this

6. Norburne T. Robinson, "Blind Tom: Musical Prodigy," *Georgia Historical Quarterly* 51 (1967): 336–58. Geneva H. Southall has written numerous monographs on Wiggins, including *Blind Tom, the Black Pianist-Composer (1849–1908)* (Lanham, Md.: Scarecrow Press, 1999); *Blind Tom: The Post–Civil War Enslavement of a Black Musical Genius,* vol. 1 (Minneapolis: Challenge Productions, 1979); *The Continuing "Enslavement" of Blind Tom, the Black Pianist Composer (1865–1887),* vol. 2 (Minneapolis: Challenge Productions, 1983); and "Blind Tom: A Misrepresented and Neglected Composer-Pianist," *The Black Perspective in Music* 3, no. 2 (May 1975): 141–59. Other works about this composer and performer include Dominique-Rene Lerma, "Black-American Pianists: Another Incomplete Story," *Sonorities in Black Music* 3 (1980): 22–28; E. M. Thornton, "The Mystery of Blind Tom," *Georgia Review* 15 (1961): 395; E. Abbott, "The Miraculous Case of Blind Tom," *Etude* 58 (1940): 517; A. Tutein, "The Phenomenon of 'Blind Tom,'" *Etude* 37 (1918): 91; and J. Becket, "Blind Tom as He Is To-day," *Ladies' Home Journal* 15, no. 10 (1898): 13.

authorship has been called into question. He was the quintessential performer, conductor, promoter, impresario, and showman. Marwood Darlington's *Irish Orpheus: The Life of Patrick S. Gilmore, Bandmaster Extraordinary,* contains a chapter on Gilmore's Civil War activities and a separate (albeit short) chapter on the concert in New Orleans. A number of articles have also examined Gilmore's importance to the development of the brass band tradition in the United States and his influence on Sousa, and Gilmore's service record and performance tours are well documented. How Gilmore personally reacted to the war and how this giant figure of the era influenced music and musicians outside the realm of the brass band is less well documented. For example, Camillo Urso, a violin prodigy who performed with Gilmore in Boston in 1863, attempted to direct her own monster concert in San Francisco in 1870.[7] While Gilmore's career has attracted significant scholarship, few authors have investigated the careers of other bandmasters in the Union and Confederate armies, who served with equal selflessness, if with less fanfare.[8]

Clara Louise Kellogg (1842–1916) was a professional soloist and later manager of her own opera company. A native South Carolinian, Kellogg sought advanced vocal training in the North and in 1861 successfully debuted at the New York Academy of Music. Kellogg's memoirs, published in 1913, describe how she endured the draft riots in New York City and also how opera productions were adjusted to entertain audiences and turn profits during the war:

7. Marwood Darlington, *Irish Orpheus: The Life of Patrick S. Gilmore, Bandmaster Extraordinary* (Philadelphia: Oliver-Maney-Klein, 1950). Other articles focusing on Patrick Gilmore include Stephen P. Gilmore, "Patrick Sarsfield Gilmore: America's Prototypical Impresario," *Journal of Band Research* 34, no. 1 (fall 1998): 69–100; Frank J. Cipolla, "Patrick S. Gilmore: The Boston Years and Beyond," in *Kongressbericht Abony/Ungarn 1994,* ed. Wolfgang Suppan (Tutzing, Germany: Hans Schneider, 1996), 183–87; Jere Humphreys, "Strike Up the Band! The Legacy of Patrick S. Gilmore," *Music Educators Journal* 74, no. 2 (October 1987): 22–26; and G. R. Leighton, "Bandmaster Gilmore," *American Mercury* 30 (1933): 172. On Camillo Urso, see Betsy G. Miller, "A Lady Gives a Monster Concert," *Bulletin of the Society for American Music* 26, no. 1 (spring 2000): 1, 6–8.

8. Some notable exceptions include pages 31–43 in Stuart Feder, *Charles Ives: "My Father's Song": A Psychoanalytic Biography* (New Haven, Conn.: Yale University Press, 1992); James Richard Gay, "The Wind Music of Felix Vinatieri, Dakota Territory Bandmaster" (DMA doc., University of Northern Colorado, 1982); and James P. Cassaro, "Other Musical Chadwicks: John M. and George M. of Central New York," *Notes: Quarterly Journal of the Music Library Association* 54, no. 2 (1997): 388–418.

> Then Maretzek bethought himself of *La Figlia del Reggimento,* a military opera, very light and infectious, that might easily catch the wave of public sentiment at the moment. We put it on in a rush. I played the Daughter and we crowded into the performance every bit of martial feeling we could muster. I learned to play the drum, and we introduced all sorts of military business and bugle calls, and altogether contrived to create a warlike atmosphere. We were determined to make a success of it; but we were also genuinely moved by the contagious glow that pervaded the country and the times, and to this combined mood of patriotism and expediency we sacrificed many artistic details. For example, we were barbarous enough to put in sundry American national airs and we had the assistance of real Zouaves to lend colour; and this reminds me that about the same period Isabella Hinckley even sang *The Star Spangled Banner* in the middle of a performance of *Il Barbiere.*[9]

Kellogg's career is covered in June Ottenberg's *Opera Odyssey: Toward a History of Opera in Nineteenth-Century America,* and Kellogg is mentioned in most general texts on American opera or American music, but her memoirs remain unfortunately the only comprehensive resource on her remarkable life.[10]

The lives of Civil War–era musicians provide compelling testimony of the war's impact on their careers. Unfortunately, many musicians have received only cursory examination. The war's gripping reality surely touched the life of every musician who lived through it, and their experiences deserve to be fully documented.

EUROPEAN ART MUSIC

A rather unique view of America during the Civil War can be seen through the eyes of the young Russian composer Nikolay Rimsky-Korsakov, who served on an Imperial Russian Navy ship stationed on

9. Clara Louise Kellogg, *Memoirs of an American Prima Donna* (New York: Putnam, 1913; reprint, New York: Da Capo Press, 1978), 56 (page references are to reprint edition).

10. June C. Ottenberg, *Opera Odyssey: Toward a History of Opera in Nineteenth-Century America,* Contributions to the Study of Music and Dance 32 (Westport, Conn.: Greenwood Press, 1994).

the east coast of the United States from October 1863 to April 1864. His autobiography is long on details about his visit to Niagara Falls but shorter in commentary about the war: "During the whole of our stay in the United States, the Americans were engaged in their Civil War. The Northern and Southern states fought over the question of slave-holding. We followed the course of events with deep interest, though we kept exclusively within the Northern territory, which fought under President Lincoln for the emancipation of the Negroes."[11] European art music has always been an integral part of American life and culture. Scholars have sought to discover the breadth and depth of this popularity and to determine its impact on American culture through issues such as patronage, opera production and performance, and the reception of specific European composers.

Research on art music of the 1860s, more than any other area described in this essay, has tended to diminish the historical impact of the war. For example, Richard Hihn's dissertation "Boston, Dwight, and Pianists of Nineteenth Century America: The European Connection" chronicled European influences on prominent American pianists in Boston through 1865 but makes no reference to how the Civil War may have affected this influence.[12] *Cultivating Music in America: Women Patrons and Activists since 1860,* a series of essays edited by Ralph P. Locke and Cyrilla Barr, describes the formation of a number of symphonies and artistic organizations through the first significant wave of patronage that occurred in the United States in the mid-nineteenth century, but none of the essays in the book directly document the war's philanthropic impact on artistic societies—even though at least one other researcher has claimed that "the great watershed that hastened the destruction or delayed the founding of more orchestras was the Civil War."[13] John Dizikes's *Opera in America: A Cultural History* divides the history of American opera into six "acts."

11. Margery Stomne Selden, "The Musical Midshipman," *Officer Review* 26, no. 10 (July 1987): 3–5.

12. Richard Randall Hihn, "Boston, Dwight, and Pianists of Nineteenth Century America: The European Connection" (DMA doc., University of Colorado, 1984).

13. Ralph P. Locke and Cyrilla Barr, eds., *Cultivating Music in America: Women Patrons and Activists since 1860* (Berkeley and Los Angeles: University of California Press, 1997). The dissenting opinion can be found in D. T. Potter, "Creating the Legend: Mozart's Music in America, 1786–1861," *Proteus: A Journal of Ideas* 8, no. 2 (fall 1991): 16–22.

The second act, "Expansion," covers the years 1836–1863, while the third act, "Monopoly," covers the years 1863–1903. Limited references to the war can be found in the narrative—he does mention, for example, that the war had so diminished concert attendance in Chicago that theater managers were forced to reduce the size of both the chorus and the orchestra in an attempt to break even—but in general the text sidesteps any significant discussion about the war.[14] The effect of the war on opera, however, was not insignificant. As Ottenberg described:

> By the early 1860s the imminence of the Civil War cast a pall over most theatrical and musical life. In Charleston all interest was focused on the political situation, as South Carolina seceded, and the theater was forgotten. Adelina Patti chose the moment to head for Europe while Clara Louise Kellogg, also at the beginning of her career, chose to stay here, but noted that the times were hard for opera and remained so throughout the war. . . . In general, managers, stars, and troupes had retreated to Europe for the duration of the Civil War, realizing that the country's entire attention was riveted on this painful internal battle with little time for musical diversions. The war's physical damage was of course greatest in the South, where operatic centers such as Richmond, Charleston, and New Orleans suffered heavily under fire, bombardment, or blockade.[15]

Opera was exceedingly popular during this period, however. Arias and overtures were transcribed for wind ensembles, and opera was performed coast to coast, from the sophisticated cities of the East and South all the way to San Francisco. George Martin attempted to account for the popularity of Verdi's operas in San Francisco during the war, concluding that "In a period of Civil War, men and women perhaps heard in Verdi's pessimism a reflection of their own melancholy and of the death they felt around them; and in his melodramas they thrilled to his call to make something fine of dying."[16]

14. John Dizikes, *Opera in America: A Cultural History* (New Haven: Yale University Press, 1993).

15. Ottenberg, *Opera Odyssey,* 111, 117.

16. George Whitney Martin, *Verdi at the Golden Gate: Opera and San Francisco in the Gold Rush Years* (Berkeley and Los Angeles: University of California Press, 1993), 210.

Harlan Jennings discovered through an analysis of concert programs that the initial restraint on theatrical activities caused by the war was temporary in St. Louis, which maintained a regular concert season throughout the latter years of the war. Jennings also determined that Mozart operas, with the notable exception of *Don Giovanni,* were not generally as popular with the people of St. Louis during the war as were operas by other European composers such as Bellini and Gounod. D. T. Potter came to a similar conclusion but noted that while Mozart's music (with the exception of a few sacred works) was not overwhelmingly popular in the antebellum United States, as the war approached, some of his more whimsical works became fashionable, providing brief moments of respite from the gathering tensions of war. The Richmond 1861 concert season, for example, contained selections from *The Magic Flute* and *The Marriage of Figaro.* J. Bunker Clark examined the popularity of Johann Sebastian Bach during the 1860s and found that the Civil War period saw an important rise in consciousness of Bach's organ music, due primarily to the work of John Knowles Paine (1839–1906). Clark's essay unfortunately gives few details on how the war may have affected Paine's touring schedule or influenced (negatively or positively) the spread of Bach's music.[17]

While the importance of classical music to Americans in the middle of the nineteenth century is well documented, too many of these inquiries minimize or ignore the cultural, economic, and artistic influences of the war. The conflict certainly must have changed the ways Americans received and disseminated classical music, but these changes have not yet been thoroughly examined.

POPULAR SONG AND DANCE

Twenty-five-year-old Eliza Frances Andrews wrote the following diary entry in January 1865:

17. Harlan Jennings, "Mozart Opera in the American Heartland a Century Ago: A Look at Performances from St. Louis to Denver in the Nineteenth Century," *Proteus: A Journal of Ideas* 8, no. 2 (fall 1991): 23–28; Potter, "Creating the Legend"; J. Bunker Clark, "The Beginnings of Bach in America," in *American Musical Life in Context and Practice to 1865,* ed. James Heintze, Essays in American Music: Garland Reference Library of the Humanities no. 11583 (New York: Garland Press, 1994), 337–51.

> The party was delightful. Albany is so full of charming refugees and Confederate officers and their families that there is always plenty of good company, whatever else may be lacking. I danced three sets with Joe Godfrey, but I don't like the square dances very much. The Prince Imperial is too slow and stately, and so complicated that the men never know what to do with themselves. Even the Lancers are tame in comparison with a waltz or a gallop. I love the gallop and the *Deux Temps* better than any. We kept it up till two o'clock in the morning, and then walked home.[18]

Popular music played an extraordinarily important role during the Civil War. Song and dance provided a much-needed reprieve from the horrors of war, both in the field and at home. This music simultaneously spoke of love, death, and the complaints of army life. It glorified each nation's cause and vilified, caricatured, and stereotyped the enemy. Some of these songs and dances entered the national psyche so forcefully that they are still popular and available today.

A number of historians and musicologists have described and categorized popular songs of the period. A sampling of these titles includes Ernest Emurian's *Stories of Civil War Songs,* Willard and Porter Heaps's *The Singing Sixties: The Spirit of Civil War Days Drawn from the Music of the Times,* Kent Bowman's *Voices of Combat: A Century of Liberty and War Songs, 1765–1865,* June Sawyers's "The Blues and the Greys: Songs of the Civil War," and Lawrence Abel's *Singing the New Nation: How Music Shaped the Confederacy, 1861–1865.*[19] While these books and articles are worth studying individually, they come to the same general conclusion. In Sawyers's words, "Although the Civil War era had its share of syrupy arrangements and overwrought, sentimental ballads, it is the best of the songs that we remember and

18. Quoted in Allison Thompson, "Dancing on the Eve of Battle: Some Views about Social Dance during the American Civil War," *Country Dance and Song* 21 (March 1991): 19–25.

19. Ernest K. Emurian, *Stories of Civil War Songs* (Natick, Mass.: W. A. Wilde, 1960); Willard A. Heaps and Porter W. Heaps, *The Singing Sixties: The Spirit of Civil War Days Drawn from the Music of the Times* (Norman: University of Oklahoma Press, 1960); Kent Bowman, *Voices of Combat: A Century of Liberty and War Songs, 1765–1865* (New York: Greenwood Press, 1987); June Skinner Sawyers, "The Blues and the Greys: Songs of the Civil War," *Sing Out!* 36, no. 3 (November 1991–January 1992): 2–13; E. Lawrence Abel, *Singing the New Nation: How Music Shaped the Confederacy, 1861–1865* (Mechanicsburg, Pa.: Stackpole Books, 2000).

commemorate. . . . These 19th-century creations continue to address fundamental truths about life, about death and about the nature of war." If the sentiment of these songs was universal, so too was the musical style. Elizabeth Wallace analyzed stylistic characteristics in popular piano pieces by Gottschalk and La Hache and concluded that "Gottschalk the Federalist and La Hache the Confederate used the same kind of musical language to individually champion opposing causes. Except for the fact that the tunes were recognizable symbols of the warring factions, a listener might have mistaken which of the two men had composed the work."[20]

Caroline Moseley searched for the "recognizable symbols" inherent within the music of each side of the war and concluded that "perceptions of regional distinctiveness, North and South, fostered musical antagonism and hastened the American Civil War."[21] According to Moseley, Southern songs despised the greed of Northern merchants and their Puritan and Saxon heritage, while Southerners described themselves with images of chivalry, protectiveness, and the nobleness of perceived Norman ancestry. Southern humor tended to be ironic and self-directed, while Union humor mocked Southern chivalry and parodied the Southern lifestyle. Southern songs emphasized the preservation of their rights, while Northern songs emphasized preservation of the Union.

The pervasive popularity of this era's music has resulted in numerous reprintings of Civil war songs. Some collections were printed quite early—Brander Matthews's "The Songs of the War" was published in 1887, while both William Fagan's *Southern War Songs: Camp-Fire, Patriotic and Sentimental* and the Brainard's Sons publication *Songs of Dixie: A Collection of Camp Songs, Home Songs, Marching Songs, Plantation Songs* were printed in 1890. The most recent edition of Civil war songs to be published is Keith and Rusty McNeil's *Civil War Songbook: With Historical Commentary,* printed in 1999.[22]

20. Sawyers, "Blues," 8; Elizabeth Ann Wallace, "The Effect of War on the Lives and Work of Piano Composers and the Evolution of Compositional Technique in War-Related Piano Pieces from 1849 through the Second World War" (Ph.D. diss., Texas Tech University, 1990), 75.

21. Caroline Moseley, "Irrepressible Conflict: Differences between Northern and Southern Songs in the Civil War," *Journal of Popular Culture* 25, no. 2 (fall 1991): 45.

22. Brander Matthews, "The Songs of the War," *Century Magazine* 34, no. 4 (August 1887): 619–30; William Long Fagan, *Southern War Songs: Camp-Fire, Patriotic,*

The Civil War is known for its many memorable songs, but composers also kept a steady stream of dances and other popular instrumental pieces available to the public. Allison Thompson provides descriptive analysis of many of the social dances of the era in her article "Dancing on the Eve of Battle: Some Views about Social Dance during the American Civil War." She describes briefly how the dances were to be performed and examines the social context of dance and the mixed feelings evinced by many of those who continued to dance despite, or even because of, the horrors of the war. Thompson concludes, "The Civil War was a time of heightened emotions. Grief and sorrow for the slain warred with the natural desire of young people to embrace life even in the face of terrible bloodshed."[23] The popular songs and dances of the era provided solace for a people in the worst of circumstances. The history and meaning of many of the songs have been carefully studied, and there is a strong tradition of preserving and publishing some of the most popular songs from the era.

MUSIC AND CULTURE

Dwight's Journal, one of the most prominent music publications at the time of the Civil War, printed the following observation in an 1865 article titled "The Present State of Music": "What is thus begun in the circles of well-to-do 'society,' is emulated, by force of example, of ignorance, of false ambition, by the multitude. Even in the sphere of petty trade and handicraft, time is stolen and wrested from the hard necessity of toil, and money from small earning, to purchase at least for the daughters a piano, notes, music-teacher, above all in the hope of thereby counting among 'cultivated people.'"[24] Music was an essential element of both Northern and Southern culture. Not

and Sentimental (New York: M. T. Robinson, 1890); *Songs of Dixie: A Collection of Camp Songs, Home Songs, Marching Songs, Plantation Songs* (New York: S. Brainard's Sons, 1890); Keith McNeil and Rusty McNeil, eds., *Civil War Songbook: With Historical Commentary* (Riverside, Calif.: WEM Records, 1999).

23. Thompson, "Dancing," 24–25.

24. Quoted in Sheryl M. Mueller, "Concepts of Nineteenth-Century Piano Pedagogy in the United States" (Ph.D. diss., University of Colorado, 1995), 130.

only was musical accomplishment a signifier of culture, but also the music of the era provides insight regarding Americans' perceptions of themselves and the conflict in which they were caught, and it sheds light on the attitudes and prejudices of mid-nineteenth-century society. The intersection of music and culture has been explored in a variety of cross-disciplinary contexts, combining the study of music with fields such as geography, political science, and sociology.

A number of studies have examined the musical history of specific communities, and these sources provide a perspective on how the war influenced music education, industry, participation, and performances in locations throughout America. Ronald Cole found that the war had a significant impact on the concert traditions, sacred music, music societies, and local composers of Portland, Maine, and Ellen Knight documented that the war depleted local church choirs in Winchester, Massachusetts. Paul Leclair discovered that the prominence of military bands in Washington, D.C., combined with a broad interest in musical education and an appreciation of opera and theater to create an atmosphere of intensified artistic development during the war.[25]

Albert Stoutamire examined the war's impact on public and social music, theater, concerts, and church music in Richmond, Virginia, and found that "Local concert ventures increased in scope during 1860 and were continued into the Civil War period after travel restrictions had curtailed performances by visiting artists. All concert activity ceased early in 1862, but local performances were revived in the fall of 1863 under the leadership of newly arrived immigrants from New Orleans. Music was heard with theatre entertainments and at social functions throughout the war period." Kansas City was a focus of both prewar violence and wartime conflict, but it was also a center of musical activity. Theodore Albrecht concluded that the armed conflict along the Missouri-Kansas border slowed development of music in the city but that, even as the war ended, musical culture

25. Ronald F. Cole, "Music in Portland, Maine, from Colonial Times through the Nineteenth Century" (Ph.D. diss., Indiana University, 1975); Ellen Knight, "Music in Winchester, Massachusetts: A Community Portrait, 1830–1925," *American Music* 11, no. 3 (fall 1993): 263–82; Paul Leclair, "The Francis Scala Collection: Music in Washington, D.C., at the Time of the Civil War" (Ph.D. diss., Catholic University, 1973).

began a period of growth, culminating in the opening of the Coates Opera House in 1870. Donald Pugh examined music education, church music, music publications, professional organizations, opera, amateur musical societies, and social balls in Houston, Texas. He discovered that the blockade of Galveston caused many of its residents to flee to Houston, where they remained until the fall of the Confederacy. This rapid increase in population propelled Houston to prominence that would not diminish after the war. The war did postpone many educational and religious projects, since much of the money that would have gone to improve civic services was redirected into military support, but by war's end Houston had emerged as a cultural center along the Gulf Coast.[26]

The influence of the war on the contributions and historical roles of specific groups of people has also been a subject of interest to scholars. The war had a tremendous impact on African Americans; this aspect has been so richly explored that it constitutes a separate section of this essay. The war's effect on other ethnic cultures, however, remains rather less well known. One good example of research in this area is Theodore Albrecht's "More Than Polkas and Prosit," which examines the influence of German Americans on music in Texas. German music was well received and well liked in the state, and German musicians often became schoolteachers, finding that their appreciation for and knowledge of music was a respected element of primary education. The war dampened the activities of German Americans in Texas, however, for they were often accused of being pro-Union, and they were hesitant to gather in large groups lest they raise suspicion—even if they were simply making music. Indeed, the first U.S. flag placed at the Alamo after the surrender of the Confederacy was reportedly raised by a German musician, William Thielepape, who broke out wine and songbooks to celebrate the occasion. A less complete examination of the war's impact on ethnic communities is Aleksander Janta's *A History of Nineteenth Century American-Polish Music,* which provides brief descriptions of prominent Polish musicians of

26. Albert L. Stoutamire, "A History of Music in Richmond, Virginia, from 1742 to 1865" (Ph.D. diss., Florida State University, 1960), 244; Theodore Albrecht, "Music in Kansas City before the Civil War," in *Midwest Note-book* 1, no. 1 (May 1992): 3–6; Donald Wagner Pugh, "Music in Frontier Houston, 1836–1876" (DMA doc., University of Texas at Austin, 1970).

the era, although it often raises more questions than it answers. One example is the entry for Mathias Keller: "He composed over 100 songs, including some for the Civil War." Other entries follow this pattern in that nothing much is said about either the musician's output or role in the war itself.[27]

A number of scholars have examined women's role in the music of this era. Judith Tick's dissertation "Towards a History of American Women Composers before 1870" is perhaps the most comprehensive resource in this area; in it, she analyzes works such as Mrs. E. Blessey's "Continental Polka Mazurka," Margaret Weir's "Dixie Doodle," Alice Lane's "The Stars of Our Banner," and an anonymous Richmond woman's "God Will Defend the Right." She also provides detailed accounts of five early American composers, one of whom, Emily Parkhurst, was active during the Civil War, writing songs such as "The Union Medley" (1863), "New Emancipation Song" (1864), and "The Sanitary Fair Polka" (1864). Tick concludes that a number of changes occurred during the era that made it a period of transition for women, including the extension of musical accomplishment to include the composition of parlor songs and dances, the growth of a female subculture (symbolized by the ladies' magazine market), and the precedent set by prominent English women composers. Cheryl Jackson's "Women as Leaders of Collegiate Bands, 1850–1980" describes how the shortage of men during and after the war contributed to greater participation of women as bandleaders in the collegiate setting. Between 1850 and 1865 women directed bands at Moores Hill College (Miss Martha J. Haughton), Iowa Conference Seminary (Miss Alice M. Foulke), and Kansas State Agricultural College in Manhattan, Kansas (Mrs. Eliza C. Beckwith).[28]

Cultural research also has focused on specific pieces of music and historic events. Jari Villanueva's *Twenty-Four Notes That Tap Deep Emotions: The Story of America's Most Famous Bugle Call* is an excel-

27. Theodore Albrecht, "More Than Polkas and Prosit," in *Texas Humanist* 7, no. 6 (July–August 1985): 26–27, 41; Aleksander Janta, *A History of Nineteenth Century American-Polish Music, with Annotated Bibliography and Illustrations* (New York: Kosciuszko Press, 1982), 100.

28. Judith Tick, "Towards a History of American Women Composers before 1870" (Ph.D. diss., City University of New York, 1979); Cheryl Jackson, "Women as Leaders of Collegiate Bands, 1850–1980," in *College Music Society Symposium* 38 (1998): 118–25.

lent survey of the historical issues surrounding the creation and meaning of "Taps," and it debunks several myths surrounding the creation of this bugle call. Earlier, Leon Bly investigated the history and social context of the march and found that the Civil War played an important role in the development of the genre, marking the dividing line between the popularity of the slow march of the prewar years with the quick march, which was used for most military activities.[29]

Jean Thomas explored music associated with the sanitary fairs of the Civil War—fairs and bazaars to raise funds to improve medical care for the wounded—concluding that "The fairs offer compelling evidence of the contradictory currents so prevalent in American life during the Civil War: fervid patriotism, a strong sense of moral obligation, and high cultural aspirations on the one hand; rampant commercialism, lofty pretensions, and a denial of the realities of war on the other. The fairs served as purveyors of these dual aspects of American culture; their histories—both individual and collective—provide a rich contextual basis for the examination of musical life during the Civil War." Two authors have examined music associated with the presidential campaigns of 1860 and 1864. Cheryl Taranto compared political songsters for the presidential campaign of 1860 and claimed that these books offer a thoughtful and comprehensive look at the issues and personalities of the campaign because the texts of the songs acted to clarify and simplify campaign platforms. D. Pickens evaluated historical images in Republican campaign songs and concluded that in the 1860 and 1864 elections Republican songs advocated specifically for a national unity, replacing the themes of regional and ethnic loyalty that had been at the heart of the party's founding.[30]

The 1860s were a period of intense cultural upheaval, which is reflected in the music of this era. Music provides an important role in understanding the broader social context of the war. Cross-disciplinary

29. Jari Villanueva, *Twenty-Four Notes That Tap Deep Emotions: The Story of America's Most Famous Bugle Call* (Baltimore: JV Music, 2001); Leon Joseph Bly, "The March in American Society" (Ph.D. diss., University of Miami, 1977).

30. Jean Waters Thomas, "Music of the Great Sanitary Fairs: Culture and Charity in the American Civil War" (Ph.D. diss., University of Pittsburgh, 1989), 9; Cheryl T. Taranto, "Political Songsters for the Presidential Campaign of 1860" (Ph.D. diss., Louisiana State University, 1994); D. Pickens, "Historical Images in Republican Campaign Songs, 1860–1900," *Journal of Popular Culture* 15 (winter 1981): 165–74.

approaches to studying the music of this period offer fresh perspectives on how music was shaped by this conflict.

AFRICAN AMERICAN MUSIC AND MUSICIANS

On December 31, 1862, thousands of slaves and freed people attending a prayer meeting in the District of Columbia sang the following words to the tune of "John Brown's Body" as they awaited the enactment of the Emancipation Proclamation on January 1, 1863:

> The first of January next, eighteen sixty-three,
> So says the Proclamation, the slaves will all be free!
> To every kindly heart 'twill be the day of jubilee;
> For the bond shall all go free![31]

The American Civil War had a tremendous cultural impact on African Americans that was reflected through music by and about members of the race as well as in the values and prejudices such music displayed. In the introduction to *Feel the Spirit: Studies in Nineteenth-Century Afro-American Music,* editors George Russell Keck and Sherrill V. Martin concluded that

> Black Americans had actively contributed to the dramatic events leading to emancipation. During the war, they acted as soldiers and sailors, in addition to their service in military bands. Northern soldiers, journalists, and missionaries who came to the South during and immediately after the war discovered and recorded the rich musical and religious heritage of Southern blacks in newspapers, journals, and letters. The first publication of slave songs appeared in 1861; by 1867 collections of these songs were published. In their music the slaves documented their culture and consciousness, often including references to the war itself.[32]

31. Quoted in Sherrill V. Martin, "Music of Black Americans during the War Years, 1861–1865," in *Feel the Spirit: Studies in Nineteenth-Century Afro-American Music,* ed. George Russell Keck and Sherrill V. Martin, Contributions in Afro-American and African Studies 119 (Westport, Conn.: Greenwood Press, 1988), 4.

32. George Russell Keck and Sherrill V. Martin, eds., *Feel the Spirit: Studies in Nineteenth-Century Afro-American Music,* Contributions in Afro-American and African Studies 119 (Westport, Conn.: Greenwood Press, 1988), x.

Black composers, performers, publishers, promoters, and instrument makers played an important role in the musical history of mid-nineteenth-century America. The war and emancipation provided great opportunities for black musicians, for as Paul Cimbala described, they "continued to function in their traditional roles of repository of folk culture and lightning rod of community identity." Keith Wilson reiterated this idea in his book *Campfires of Freedom: The Camp Life of Black Soldiers during the Civil War* and stated that "Music was a vital element in black culture. On the slave plantation it had enriched the texture of life and acted as an important vehicle for survival. In the army, it served a similar function. It helped the black soldier place his military experience in a cultural continuum, and it eased his transition to freedom and citizenship. Around the campfire the soldiers created new songs for a new world."[33]

Histories of African American musicians have generally recognized the war as an important turning point. Eileen Southern's epic *The Music of Black Americans: A History,* for example, provides a comprehensive overview of African American music and musicians from the seventeenth century to the early 1980s. Although the scope of Southern's book necessitates a generalized treatment of the war, she does touch on subjects such as music in the Union army, music in the Confederate army, music in the contraband camp, and emancipation. Charles Wesley and Patricia Romero's text, *Negro Americans in the Civil War,* is representative of many general histories on African Americans of the period in that it provides brief vignettes about such songs as "Many Thousand Go," the "Marching Song of the First Arkansas Colored Regiment," and "They Look Like Men of War."[34]

The Civil War and subsequent emancipation of the slaves created a deep interest in the music of African Americans. This interest has been manifested by a willingness among researchers to seek out the history and transmission of music by and about African Americans.

33. Paul Cimbala, "Black Musicians from Slavery to Freedom: An Exploration of an African-American Folk Elite and Cultural Continuity in the Nineteenth-Century Rural South," *Journal of Negro History* 80, no. 1 (winter 1995): 15–29; Keith P. Wilson, *Campfires of Freedom: The Camp Life of Black Soldiers during the Civil War* (Kent, Ohio: Kent State University Press, 2002).

34. Eileen Southern, *The Music of Black Americans: A History,* 2d ed. (New York: Norton, 1983); Charles H. Wesley and Patricia W. Romero, *Negro Americans in the Civil War* (New York: Publishers, 1967).

Dena Epstein's *Sinful Tunes and Spirituals: Black Folk Music to the Civil War* examines secular and sacred black folk music from the Civil War era and documents the emergence of black folk music during the Civil War. This folk music was transmitted to American culture at large through such events as the Port Royal Experiment and the creation of black folk song compilations such as the *Slave Songs of the United States* (published in 1867). Epstein concludes, "A strong impetus to nineteenth-century transcriptions (defective as they were) was provided by the Civil War, which shattered the closed society in which the slaves had been confined. The dislocation of war brought slaves for the first time into large-scale contact with the world outside the plantations, and with strangers from the North who found the blacks and their music enormously appealing." Sherrill Martin's "Music of Black Americans during the War Years, 1861–1865" also argues that the war brought the music of both Northern and Southern blacks into the national consciousness. Black Americans were active participants in all events of the Civil War, earning for themselves the right to not only fight but to enlist in bands and attempt concert careers. The mingling of cultures as the war progressed into the South allowed Northerners to discover, experience, and record the rich musical heritage of the newly freed slaves.[35]

White transcribers usually attempted to faithfully notate what they heard in traditional black music but were often stymied by the specialized vocal techniques used in such music. Lucy McKim Garrison, after attempting to transcribe some of the music she heard from ex-slaves at Port Royal, wrote in 1862: "It is difficult to express the entire character of these negro ballads by mere musical notes and signs. The odd turns made in the throat; and the curious rhythmic effect produced by single voices chiming in at different irregular intervals, seem almost as impossible to place on score, as the singing of birds or the tones of an Aeolian harp." Epstein's "Black Spirituals: Their Emergence into Public Knowledge" points out the flawed transcriptions in early collections of black spirituals, especially those used

35. Dena J. Epstein, *Sinful Tunes and Spirituals: Black Folk Music to the Civil War,* Music in American Life series (Urbana: University of Illinois Press, 1977), 348; Martin, "Music of Black Americans," 1–16. See also Dena J. Epstein, "Documenting the History of Black Folk Music in the United States: A Librarian's Odyssey," *Fontes artis musicae* 23, no. 4 (October–December 1976): 151–57.

by the Fisk Jubilee Singers. She found that "The significance of these notated versions is that most comments on the spirituals until the advent of field recordings in the 1930s were based upon them, not upon live performances. . . . What is more, many of the concert arrangements sounded like it. A clear distinction between concert arrangements and authentic folk versions would not be made for many years. The limitations of musical notation were not widely recognized in the nineteenth century."[36] Robin Hough investigated Reverend Taylor's *A Collection of Revival Hymns and Plantation Melodies,* published in 1882 in Cincinnati by Marshall W. Taylor and W. C. Echols, and assessed the blending of Taylor's political agenda with the specific religious significances of the original slave songs, spirituals, or hymns. Hough argues that

> Taylor's book was designed to help heal the scars of the war by showing how, through mutual understanding, blacks and whites could lay claim to a common religious heritage and thus create a common political future. He intended to combine the best of the religious songs of the slaves with a sampling of the white revival hymns most popular among blacks at the time. Thus, ideally, the freedmen and religiously sensitive whites could view through music their recent, common past as a time in which God intervened directly in history to free the slaves through the agency of the Civil War.[37]

Ronald Radano examined the transcriptions of slave spirituals with a critical eye, theorizing that

> A racialized, sound-filled difference became the key reference point for white writers, whose essays and transcriptions offered ever newer ways of gesturing to a realm out of bounds. . . . For what white intellectuals gave up in their civilizing ambitions was precisely the transcendent freedom their embrace of slave difference had celebrated. Accordingly, the perceived purity and wholeness of the slave songs

36. Lucy McKim Garrison, "Songs of the Port Royal 'Contrabands,'" *Dwight's Journal of Music* 21 (November 8, 1862): 254–55, quoted in Dena J. Epstein, "Black Spirituals: Their Emergence into Public Knowledge," *Black Music Research Journal* 10, no. 1 (spring 1990): 58–66, 63.

37. Robin Hough, "Choirs of Angels Armed for War: Reverend Marshall W. Taylor's *A Collection of Revival Hymns and Plantation Melodies,*" in Keck and Martin, *Feel the Spirit,* 17–33.

> also signified what was missing in whiteness as a consequence of the civilization itself. Without reducing reform efforts to a callous solipsism, we can recognize the white claim to give voice to the slave as an act of ventriloquism, whose motivations were necessarily complicated and ambivalent. By embracing the ideals of romantic perfectibility associated with folklore and the spirituals, these reformers described qualities felt to be missing in themselves, to which they could only gesture in a series of desperate, imitative acts.[38]

White transcribers of black music were, according to Radano, incapable of creating true settings of black folk and sacred songs and unconsciously intertwined their own needs and attitudes about blacks into their transcriptions.

Several authors have analyzed music of the era for prejudicial images of blacks. Caroline Moseley's essay "When Will Dis Cruel War Be Ober?" finds persistent negative attitudes toward African Americans in popular songs and concludes, "The pervasive antiblack sentiment expressed in Civil War song would certainly not explain the adoption of the Fourteenth and Fifteenth Amendments. It may, however, help to explain the immediate reassertion of white supremacy in the post-Reconstruction South. It may also help to explain the sad tale of Northern acquiescence, and the collusive subversion of the nascent rights of freedmen." Sam Dennison concurs with Mosley in his book *Scandalize My Name: Black Imagery in American Popular Music.* Examining bias and racism as it appeared in popular songs such as "Dixie," "Kingdom Coming," "The Yellow Rose of Texas," "The Song of the Contrabands," "Wake Nicodemus," "Babylon Is Fallen!" "The Black Brigade," and many others, he concludes that almost all of the songs about blacks from this era are to some extent demeaning to the black image.[39]

African Americans made many significant contributions to American music beyond the influence of folk songs and spirituals. There have been surveys on the lives and careers of musicians such as tenor

38. Ronald Radano, "Denoting Difference: The Writing of the Slave Spirituals," *Critical Inquiry* 22 (spring 1996): 506–44.

39. Caroline Moseley, "'When Will Dis Cruel War Be Ober?' Attitudes toward Blacks in Popular Songs of the Civil War," *American Music* 2, no. 3 (fall 1984): 1–26; Sam Dennison, *Scandalize My Name: Black Imagery in American Popular Music,* Critical Studies in Black Life and Culture 13 (New York: Garland Press, 1982).

Thomas J. Bowers (1823–1885), soprano Nellie Brown Mitchell (1845–1924), and composer Joseph W. Postlewaite (1827–89). Richard Schwartz has claimed that the Civil War created significant opportunities for African American cornetists to develop performance technique, and he documented their innovations to the cornet's design and performance. Ann Sears examined the contributions black composers made to piano repertoire and concluded, "The pioneers who blazed the trail in the nineteenth century created works of lasting historical and musical worth. Far too long forgotten, this music is ripe for revival."[40]

There is strong research on African-American contributions to music of the war era, especially in relation to the documentation and transmission of black spirituals and folk songs. Unfortunately, other contributions to music made by African Americans have not always been clearly acknowledged, and remain less well documented.

MILITARY AND CIVILIAN BANDS

On the evening of the second day's fighting at the battle of Chancellorsville, the Union right flank was turned by Stonewall Jackson's forces. As the Union soldiers broke in panic under the assault, the band of the Fourteenth Connecticut was ordered forward to play. The regimental historian later wrote: "with shot and shell crashing all about them, . . . [they] played 'The Star-Spangled Banner,' 'The Red, White, and Blue,' and 'Yankee Doodle' and repeated them for fully

40. Ann Sears, "Keyboard Music by Nineteenth-Century Afro-American Composers," in Keck and Martin, *Feel the Spirit,* 155. See also Ronald Henry High, "Black Male Concert Singers of the Nineteenth Century: A Bibliographic Study," in Keck and Martin, *Feel the Spirit,* 117–34; Ronald Henry High, "Three African-American Tenors of the Nineteenth Century: Thomas J. Bowers, Wallace King, Sidney Woodward," *Journal of Singing* 54, no. 5 (May–June 1998): 19–25; Carolyne Lamar Jordan, "Black Female Concert Singers of the Nineteenth Century: Nellie Brown Mitchell and Marie Selika Williams," in Keck and Martin, *Feel the Spirit,* 35–48; Samuel A. Floyd, "A Black Composer in Nineteenth-Century St. Louis," *Nineteenth-Century Music* 4, no. 2 (1980): 121–33; and Samuel A. Floyd, "J. W. Postlewaite of St. Louis: A Search for His Identity," *The Black Perspective in Music* 6 (1978): 151–67; and Richard I. Schwartz, "The African American Contribution to the Cornet of the Nineteenth Century: Some Long-Lost Names," *Historic Brass Society Journal* 12 (2000): 61–88.

twenty minutes. They never played better. . . . Its effect upon the men was magical. . . . It was a remarkable circumstance that none of them were killed. I think one or two of them were slightly wounded by pieces of exploding shells." Civilian and military wind bands were an integral feature of social life during the Civil War and were perhaps the most pervasive musical symbol of that era. "I don't believe we can have an army without music," exclaimed Robert E. Lee after listening to a brass serenade in 1864. "A space of three years servitude and one year sick" was how George Ives, the youngest bandmaster in the Union army and father of the composer Charles Ives, characterized his own service as leader of the band of the First Connecticut Heavy Artillery Regiment.[41]

Research in this area has tended to focus on the personalities, duties, instrumentation, and music of the military bands. Examples of this include works such as Margaret and Robert Hazen's *The Music Men: An Illustrated History of Brass Bands in America, 1800–1920;* Robert Garofalo and Mark Elrod's *A Pictorial History of Civil War Era Musical Instruments and Military Bands;* Kenneth Olson's dissertation, "Yankee Bands of the Civil War," and his book *Music and Musket: Bands and Bandsmen of the American Civil War;* and Francis Lord and Arthur Wise's *Bands and Drummer Boys of the Civil War.*[42] These texts generally document the role of bands through photographs, illustrations, diaries, journals, and unit histories and provide analyses of band music and period instruments.

41. Charles D. Page, *History of the Fourteenth Regiment Connecticut Volunteer Infantry* (Meriden, Conn.: Horton Printing, 1906), 120–21, quoted in William Alfred Bufkin, "Union Bands of the Civil War (1862–1865): Instrumentation and Score Analysis" (Ph.D. diss., Louisiana State University, 1973), 89; Walter Clark, ed., *North Carolina Regiments, 1861–1865,* (Raleigh, N.C.: n.p., 1901) 2:397–400, quoted in Bell Irvin Wiley, *The Life of Johnny Reb: The Common Soldier of the Confederacy* (Baton Rouge: Louisiana State University Press, 1943; reprint, 1997), 157; Feder, *Charles Ives,* 43.

42. Margaret Hindle Hazen and Robert Hazen, *The Music Men: An Illustrated History of Brass Bands in America, 1800–1920* (Washington, D.C.: Smithsonian Institution, 1987); Robert Garofalo and Mark Elrod, *A Pictorial History of Civil War Era Musical Instruments and Military Bands* (Charleston, W.Va.: Pictorial Histories, 1985); Kenneth Olson, "Yankee Bands of the Civil War" (Ph.D. diss., University of Minnesota, 1971); Kenneth E. Olson, *Music and Musket: Bands and Bandsmen of the American Civil War* (Westport, Conn.: Greenwood Press, 1981); Francis A. Lord and Arthur Wise, *Bands and Drummer Boys of the Civil War* (New York: Da Capo Press, 1979).

Some of the research focuses more on the instruments than on the bandsmen themselves. William Bufkin's dissertation, "Union Bands of the Civil War (1862–65): Instrumentation and Score Analysis," for example, briefly investigates the lives and responsibilities of the field musicians and the regimental (later brigade) brass bands but primarily concentrates on describing the various instruments used by the musicians. He also analyzes several scores to demonstrate the arranging techniques used during the period. G. B. Lane's article "Brass Instruments Used in Confederate Military Service during the American Civil War" describes the contents and condition of two of the best surviving collections of instruments played by Confederate bands—the Museum of Old Salem in Winston-Salem, North Carolina, and the rehearsal room of the Stonewall Brigade Band in Staunton, Virginia.[43]

The histories of specific bands have also been of interest to researchers. Dwight Gardstrom explored the wartime contributions of the Fourth Minnesota Regimental Band and the field musicians of the Fourth Minnesota Infantry Volunteers, which served the entire war, despite the order to break up regimental bands in 1862. This document examines these musicians in detail, describing the musical background, ethnicity, age, occupations, organization, training, and financial support of the bandsmen. Gardstrom concludes, "The Fourth Regimental Brass Band of the Minnesota Infantry Volunteers was representative of the bands which comprised this historical high point of the brass band history. This Fourth Regimental Band served with their regiment during all of their engagements and even took up arms when necessary. They received special mention from Generals Sherman and Logan for gallant service performed at Allatoona. This band achieved the distinction of leading the whole column in the Grand Review at the end of the war."[44] Harry Hall described the activities of the Twenty-sixth Regimental Band from Salem, North Carolina. This remarkable band enlisted in March 1862 and fought with the Army of Northern Virginia from the Seven Days' Battle

43. Bufkin, "Union Bands"; G. B. Lane, "Brass Instruments Used in Confederate Military Service during the American Civil War," *Historic Brass Society Journal* 4 (1992): 71–86.

44. Dwight A. Gardstrom, "A History of the Fourth Regimental Band and Musicians of the Fourth Minnesota Infantry Volunteers during the War of the Great Rebellion, 1861–1865" (Ph.D. diss., University of Minnesota, 1989), 317.

through Gettysburg and the Wilderness campaign. On April 5, 1865, the band was captured after having been separated from the regiment four days earlier. The diary of cornetist Julius Augustus Leinbach poignantly recalled that event: "Striking a little by-road, we followed it until it took us into the main road and right into a squad of the enemy. We walked up to them and were taken in charge. Our instruments were taken from us and that seemed to be the bitterest experience of all. I had learned to love my B♭ cornet more than all the rest of my few possessions and to see it go into the hands of another and know that I would never see it again, was a very hard thing to endure."[45] While the lion's share of research has documented the activities of military bands, a few scholars have traced the histories of civilian bands of the period. Clayton Tiede's dissertation, "The Development of Minnesota Community Bands during the Nineteenth Century," specifically focuses on bands that were nonmilitary and noneastern. It discusses the role of civilian bands during such wartime activities as civic concerts, temperance celebrations, public works openings, and political rallies. Tiede argues that "The band sparked the civic functions, enticed the populace into the lecture halls and 'opera' houses, attracted the masses to the numerous 'openings,' pacified the romantic ideals of the 'naturalists' with their out-door concerts, stirred the emotional senses of 'nationalism' at the parades and political rallies, entertained at the picnics, concerts, fairs, and balls and in general became one of the main attractions of the numerous social events which enabled the pioneer to engage in his much needed 'social intercourse.'"[46] The general history of Civil War military bands has been well documented, but research on the activities of specific bands and musicians is continuing, as is the investigation into the influence these bands had on postwar musical taste.[47]

45. Quoted in Harry Hall, *A Johnny Reb Band from Salem, the Pride of Tarheelia* (Raleigh: North Carolina Confederate Centennial Commission, 1963), 104.

46. Clayton Howard Tiede, "The Development of Minnesota Community Bands during the Nineteenth Century" (Ph.D. diss., University of Minnesota, 1970), 208.

47. Cf. Maureen Manjerovic and Michael J. Budds, "More Than a Drummer Boy's War: A Historical View of Musicians in the American Civil War," *College Music Symposium* 42 (2002): 118–30, who claim, "The participation and activities of thousands of military musicians, representing both the Union and the Confederacy, have gone under-appreciated and under-reported. Their many contributions to the war

INNOVATIONS

The decade of the 1860s was a period of technological and pedagogical innovation. Armies needed to train field musicians and form bands, sometimes from scratch. The growth of the middle class meant an increase in the pedagogical needs of amateur musicians, and instrument designers were making significant technical changes to their instruments and winning awards for their innovations. Steinway and Sons, for example, won a gold medal at the 1862 London World's Fair for technological advances in piano manufacture. The *Preliminary Report on the Eighth Census, 1860,* contained a report by one government official who claimed, "Our advancement and refinement is attested to by the rapid increase in the manufacture of pianofortes and other Musical Instruments." Instrument manufacture was no small business. The *American Musical Directory* of 1861 stated, "the capital invested in the manufacture of pianofortes alone in the United States is fully equal to that employed in the manufacture of cotton goods."[48] This may be an overstatement, but in 1860, twenty-one thousand pianos were manufactured, and sales nationwide averaged thirty pianos every working day.[49]

The rapid development of new technologies and pedagogies during the mid-1800s has stimulated a varied body of research. Philip Gura and James Bollman's *America's Instrument: The Banjo in the Nineteenth Century,* for example, discusses the production, distribution, and marketing of the banjo, chronicles the transition from artisan production to factory production, and documents the dramatic change

effort between 1861 and 1865 are often marginalized or overlooked entirely in both historical and musicological literature" (118). Their point is well taken; however, *comparatively* speaking, the role of military bands has received more scholarly attention than many areas of research in Civil War music.

48. Nancy Groce, *Musical Instrument Makers of New York: A Directory of Eighteenth- and Nineteenth-Century Urban Craftsmen,* Annotated Reference Tools in Music 4 (Stuyvesant, N.Y.: Pendragon Press, 1991), xiii; Joseph C. G. Kennedy, *Preliminary Report on the Eighth Census, 1860,* (Washington, D.C.: Government Printing Office, 1862), 69, quoted in Groce, *Musical Instrument Makers,* xiv; *American Musical Directory* (New York: Thomas Hutchinson, 1861), quoted in Groce, *Musical Instrument Makers,* xiv.

49. Mueller, "Concepts," 4.

in banjo design and manufacture during the war era.[50] Not all of the research, however, has recognized the effects of the war on the development and manufacture of instruments. Nancy Groce's *Musical Instrument Makers of New York: A Directory of Eighteenth- and Nineteenth-Century Urban Craftsmen,* quoted above, makes no mention of how the war may (or may not) have affected instrument manufacturing in New York. It would seem probable, however, that conscription, the draft riots, the increasing demand for military instruments, and the small but significant reduction of the Southern consumer base must have had some consequences for New York instrument makers.

The increase in musical amateurs and the need to train musical novices for military roles led to the development of several pedagogical resources. Geary Larrick's article "Drumming and Fifing of the Civil War" closely examines *The Drummer's and Fifer's Guide* by George Bruce and Daniel Emmett, which was published in 1865. He contends that "The Civil War marked a high point for the rudimental style of drumming in the United States. The Civil War was a mobile war: whole armies covered much ground on the march, fought their battles, and often retired in quick retreat. Musically, it was really a drummer boy's war, for it was he who called the great formations to battle, tapped the camps to sleep, and together with the fifes, set the cadence for those long and weary marches." Beginners' aids were also produced for other instruments as well. Septimus Winner's *New Primer for the Banjo* was published in New York by W. A. Pond in 1864 and is investigated briefly in Robert Winans and Elias Kaufman's "Minstrel and Classic Banjo: American and English Connections." Sheryl Mueller's "Concepts of Nineteenth-Century Piano Pedagogy in the United States" examines several piano primers from the war period, including *Hunten's Celebrated Instructions,* which was published in Richmond in 1864.[51]

50. Philip Gura and James F. Bollman, *America's Instrument: The Banjo in the Nineteenth Century* (Chapel Hill: University of North Carolina Press, 1999), see especially pp. 75–136.

51. Geary Larrick, "Drumming and Fifing of the Civil War," *NACWPI Journal* 37, no. 1 (fall 1988): 9; George Bruce and Daniel Emmett, *The Drummer's and Fifer's Guide* (New York: Pond, 1865); Robert B. Winans and Elias J. Kaufman, "Minstrel and Classic Banjo: American and English Connections," *American Music* 12, no. 1 (spring 1994): 1–30; Mueller, "Concepts."

It is difficult to ascertain the depth of research in this particular field. Many of the generalized histories of military bands listed in the previous section contain some discussion on technical innovations in instrument design and manufacture and describe common military pedagogical practices. Few resources, however, have documented the war's specific impact on instrument manufacture and innovation.

MUSIC PUBLISHING

The American music-publishing industry experienced sustained expansion prior to the war, corresponding to a rise in the number of consumers with a taste for popular sheet music and the means to purchase it. Northern and Southern publishers prospered during the initial stages of the conflict, but as the war progressed Confederate presses had to cope with paper shortages, transportation difficulties, and property destruction. Publishers often felt that they were an integral part of the war effort. A. J. Bloch of Mobile, Alabama, advocated in his sheet-music series *Southern Flowers* that "The South must not only fight her own battles but sing her own songs and dance to music composed by her own children."[52]

Richard Wetzel examined the Cincinnati publishing firm of W. C. Peters and Son, contending that this company was the earliest and most prominent publisher of liturgical music in the Midwest from 1845 to 1865, based on two catalogs of sacred music that were issued by the firm in 1856 and 1862. Dena Epstein described the history of the Chicago music-publishing industry, focusing on the firm of Root and Cady. This firm was perhaps the most prolific publisher during the Civil War, employing writers such as George Root and Henry Clay Work. Chicago had a strong publishing industry that peaked during the Civil War, but the fire of 1871 wiped out much of the inventory and machinery for many of the firms and effectively eliminated Chicago as a center of music publishing.[53]

52. Quoted in *The New Grove Dictionary of American Music* (1986 ed.), s.v. "Confederates and Music," by Frank Hoogerwerf.

53. Richard D. Wetzel, "Catholic Church Music in the Midwest before the Civil War: The Firm of W. C. Peters and Sons," in *American Musical Life in Context and Practice to 1865,* ed. James R. Heintze (New York: Garland, 1994), 203–230; Dena

While Northern presses were relatively well poised to take on the needs of "Union" composers, the war caused a boom in publishing in the Confederate States. Frank Hoogerwerf's *Confederate Sheet-Music Imprints* provides a brief history of Southern publishing and an extensive bibliography (almost seven hundred different titles) of sheet-music imprints published in the Confederate States of America. Richard Harwell's *Confederate Music* provides a complete list of sheet music printed in the Confederate states, as well as lists of Confederate publishers and sheet-music dealers.[54]

The effects of the Civil War on the music-publishing industry are uncertain, and many questions have yet to be explored. What was the economic cost of the war (positive or negative) for various publishers? How did presses in the South overcome trials of shortage and relocation? How did specific publishing firms fare during the war? Research in this area has much yet to accomplish.

COLLECTION AND DESCRIPTION

There are a large number of public and private collections of Civil War music. The contents of these collections and the history of their creation have generated a small but important number of articles and dissertations. Paul Leclair cataloged the Francis Scala collection in his dissertation "The Francis Scala Collection: Music in Washington, D.C., at the Time of the Civil War." This collection of band music (all in manuscript) was compiled between 1855 and 1871 through the efforts of the Marine Band director, Francis Scala. It is an extensive source of information about the Civil War–era band most central to the political and social activities of the White House. Oral Coad analyzed and classified the Rutgers University collection of American song sheets according to categories such as "tender songs of young love," "motherhood," and "religion." Other authors have similarly classified the musical collections of the Maryland Historical Society

Epstein, *Music Publishing in Chicago before 1871: The Firm of Root and Cady, 1858–1871,* Detroit Studies in Music Bibliography 14 (Detroit: Information Coordinators, 1969).

54. Frank Hoogerwerf, *Confederate Sheet-Music Imprints,* ISAM Monographs 21 (Brooklyn: Institute for Studies in American Music, 1984); Harwell, *Confederate Music.*

(William Filby), the Robert W. Woodruff Library of Emory University (Frank Hoogerwerf), and the Buffalo and Erie County Library (Charlotte Kolczynski).[55]

Norm Cohen compiled a bibliography of pocket songsters, including many from the Civil War era, and described the role of songsters and their usefulness in cultural research. J. Heywood Alexander's "Brainard's (Western) Musical World" describes the history of one of the most prominent musical journals published in the nineteenth-century United States. *Brainard's Musical World* originated in Cleveland in 1864. Alexander's article lists the journal's editors, the names of American musicians who were featured in each issue, and describes some of the new music printed within the journal.[56]

Preparing bibliographies and cataloging the holdings of collections is an important, if unsung, facet of research on music of this era. The single most important resource that is needed is a comprehensive listing of all public and private collections in the United States that contain Civil War music, indexed to specific Civil War events and persons. *Resources of American Music History: A Directory of Source Materials from Colonial Times to World War II* is the closest such resource that is currently available and is of great value to the potential researcher.[57]

55. Leclair, "Francis Scala Collection"; Oral S. Coad, "Songs America Used to Sing," *Journal of the Rutgers University Library* 31, no. 2 (June 1968): 33–45; P. William Filby, "Music in the Maryland Historical Society," *Notes: Quarterly Journal of the Music Library Association* 32, no. 3 (March 1976): 503–17; Frank Hoogerwerf, "Confederate Sheet Music at the Robert W. Woodruff Library, Emory University," *Notes: Quarterly Journal of the Music Library Association* 34, no. 1 (September 1977): 7–26; Charlotte A. Kolczynski, "American Nineteenth-Century Broadsides at the Buffalo and Erie County Library: A Catalogue and Index" (master's thesis, State University of New York at Buffalo, 1987).

56. Norm Cohen, "Report on a Proposed Bibliography of American Pocket Songsters of the Nineteenth Century," *Sonneck Society for American Music Bulletin* 23, no. 3 (fall 1997): 65–70; J. Heywood Alexander, "Brainard's (Western) Musical World," *Notes: Quarterly Journal of the Music Library Association* 36, no. 3 (March 1980): 601–14.

57. D. W. Krummel et al., *Resources of American Music History: A Directory of Source Materials from Colonial Times to World War II,* Music in American Life Series (Urbana: University of Illinois Press, 1981). At the time this chapter was written, two Web sites contained exceptional collections of Civil War–era music: the American Memory Web site of the Library of Congress (http://memory.loc.gov/ammem/amhome.html) and the Lester Levy Collection at Johns Hopkins University (http://levysheetmusic.mse.jhu.edu/).

NEW BEGINNINGS

On October 13, 1861, after attending a black church service, Mary Boykin Chestnut wrote in her diary, "Suddenly, as I sat wondering what next, they broke out into one of the soul-stirring Negro camp-meeting hymns. To me this is the saddest of all earthly music, weird and depressing beyond my powers to describe." Over thirty years later, on May 25, 1893, the *New York Herald* would print the celebrated European composer Antonín Dvořák's praise for the folk music of African Americans: "These beautiful and varied themes are the product of the soil. They are American. They are the folksongs of America, and your composers must turn to them. In the Negro melodies of America I discover all that is needed for a great and noble school of music."[58] The Civil War created tremendous social upheaval as soldiers and civilians alike traveled away from the familiar boundaries of home. It has been difficult to pinpoint exactly how the intermingling of various cultures affected the growth of American music, but a number of authors have traced the development of ragtime, blues, and jazz to the juxtaposition of musical cultures that occurred during the war.

Paul Oliver argued that blues originated during or just prior to the war in his article "That certain feeling: Blues and Jazz... In 1890?" He traced the blues as an outgrowth of the change in farming practices that occurred when slavery ended, from the cotton field hollers to the alternating line and choruses found in popular ballads.[59] Patrick O'Connor's "Discovering the Rich Differences in the Blues: The Rural and Urban Genres" contends that the roots of the blues can be traced to just after the Civil War. He argues that

> The blues were not sung in bondage. The master and overseers did not welcome exhibitions of grief. The music of the slaves was as controlled as any other aspect of their lives. Drums were forbidden on plantations for fear they could communicate plans of uprisings or

58. Chesnut, *Diary from Dixie,* 149; *New York Herald,* May 25, 1893, quoted in Tim Brooks, "'Might Take One Disc of This Trash as a Novelty': Early Recordings by the Fisk Jubilee Singers and the Popularization of 'Negro Folk Music,'" *American Music* 18, no. 3 (fall 2000): 278–316.

59. Paul Oliver, "That Certain Feeling: Blues and Jazz... in 1890?" *Popular Music* 10, no. 1 (January 1991): 11–20.

> escapes. Spiritual music was allowed, as well as work songs which seemed to help the blacks abide the merciless rigors of field work. Field hollers, sung a capella, come the closest to the disturbing messages of the later blues.... When the Afro-Americans discovered that after the initial jubilation of emancipation, and particularly with the end of Reconstruction in 1877, their plight was little changed (the major difference being the ability to move from place to place), the blues became a natural repository for feelings of woe.[60]

Samuel Floyd and Marsha Reisser surveyed dance pieces from the middle of the late antebellum period through the turn of the century to discover links between the social dance music of African American composers and the development of ragtime. They concluded that there existed an "unbroken line of development from the music of the early black composers of social dance music . . . to the beginnings of notated ragtime." Karl Koenig's "Louisiana Brass Bands and History in Relation to Jazz History" evaluated the influence of Federal brass bands in and around New Orleans on the development of jazz. He claimed that the heritage of these Civil War–era bands formed an important foundation for the formulation of jazz.[61]

If the Civil War played a pivotal role in the development of music of the nineteenth century, it could also be said to be the genesis of much of the popular music of the twentieth century. Ragtime, blues, jazz, and all their progeny trace their beginnings to the cultural interchanges made possible because of the war.

FINALE

So what have we to learn from studying the music, the musicians, and the musical culture of the Civil War? Shall old times there be truly forgotten? Music has always been an integral part of American life, and the Civil War profoundly influenced the future of American

60. Patrick Joseph O'Connor, "Discovering the Rich Differences in the Blues: The Rural and Urban Genres," *Midwest Quarterly* 33, no. 4 (fall 1991): 28–42.

61. Samuel A. Floyd and Marsha J. Reisser, "Social Dance Music of Black Composers in the Nineteenth Century and the Emergence of Classical Ragtime," *The Black Perspective in Music* 8, no. 2 (fall 1980): 161–93; Karl Koenig, "Louisiana Brass Bands and History in Relation to Jazz History," *Second Line* 35 (summer 1983): 7–15.

music and musicians. Research has begun to investigate the war's effect on music, but there is no single source currently in print that is dedicated to understanding the pivotal interaction of music with the wider military, political, social, and technological changes occurring during this era. As Allan Peskin has stated, "the Civil War is the great laboratory of American history. Just as physicists can learn more about matter by observing it under conditions of extreme stress, so historians can learn from the stress engendered by America's greatest trauma. The coming of the war reveals the weaknesses in the American national compact; the healing process of the postwar years reveals something of the enduring strength of that compact."[62] The essays in this book each contribute partially to an understanding of music of the Civil War era. This anthology is in no sense the final word on music of the war, but it hopefully presents an interdisciplinary model that may be repeated many times over. We have yet to explore fully how this "great laboratory of American history" affected musical life of the Civil War era, or indeed, of our own time.

62. Allan Peskin, "The Civil War: Crucible of Change," *Timeline: A Publication of the Ohio Historical Society* 3, no. 3 (1986): 12–27.

Music and Community in the Civil War Era

DEANE L. ROOT

The Civil War, the nation's most consuming conflict, was also the period of its first outpouring of enduringly popular songs. Was the connection between war and music a coincidence? Or did the songs take some special hold of the public imagination across subsequent generations because of their association with battles and so had the ability to evoke the feelings of wartime? Or was there perhaps a deeper reason for their popularity, perhaps stemming from some fundamental aspect of human behavior? Much of the literature on music of the Civil War era develops the second of these questions. This paper makes a case for the third one, examining ways that individuals and groups used music to create notions of communities with shared interests.

The historians and performers brought together by the National Conference on Music of the Civil War Era focused on a wide array of topics, but much of the music they described could also be identified with distinct groups or communities of people. Although the presenters employed several different methods of humanistic inquiry and discussed different formats of materials (for example, songsters, archives, and instruments), they also drew attention to practices employing those materials that built a sense of community among even far-flung practitioners of the music.

Understanding history through communities is a hallmark of Civil War studies, as it underlies much of the humanities. Many of the historians who attended the conference relate to their topics through their own connections or fascinations with historical communities. But the orientation to communities is not only a trait of scholarship, it was also a part of life during the Civil War era. Thus to view the music of the era in terms of a nation, a city, a regiment, an ethnic group, or a trade—to mention just five types of communities that were subjects of presentations—mirrors the ways in which those musicians and audiences lived their own lives and viewed their activities as taking place within their multiple communities.

Any single instance of musical performance may have multiple functions. One of the most important functions of music during the Civil War era was to enhance shared ideas among groups of people, in order to strengthen bonds of affinity. Music is potent because it can strengthen the ties among people even while it serves other functions. As musical anthropologist John E. Kaemmer puts it, "Through enhancing communication, music is often a way of building and maintaining group identity."[1] The papers and performances at the conference explained and demonstrated a number of musical functions, including (1) music serving as entertainment and amelioration of life's difficulties, (2) music's role in a sustaining trade, (3) music as a source of income, (4) music as a regulating device for men in uniform, and (5) music giving voice to communal emotions—as a rallying call to arms, an expression of pride, and a solace in grief. These functions were not incidental to the practice of music or to the lives of the participants; the practitioners intended them and employed music purposefully and even systematically to create these effects. Groups employed the multiple functions of music as a way of indicating boundaries between themselves and other groups, or to strengthen their own solidarity, or to express belief, kinship, or custom. Civil War–era American society, viewed from an anthropological perspective, had a highly developed musical strategy for creating community.

Music's role in strengthening group identify depends on it being perceived as conveying social ideas. Musical performance styles, instruments, melodies, and song forms are not devoid of social meaning. Quite apart from the more evident meanings of song lyrics themselves, these musical elements can take on extramusical connotations symbolizing or suggesting class, race, region, and even nationality.

1. John E. Kaemmer, *Music in Human Life: Anthropological Perspectives on Music* (Austin: University of Texas Press, 1993), 157; Kaemmer's chapter 6, "Uses and Functions of Music," offers a useful explanation of musical functions in society.

Certain musical instruments, meters, or dance forms may be seen as representing ethnic identity; likewise a social class can share aesthetics of affect, formal structure, and harmony. More complex groups of people comprising multiple ethnic or class distinctions employ these and other musical elements more subtly to create the sense of community across the more apparent boundaries. Where the community has major internal differences—such as strong language or dialect variants, wide geographic spread, or conflicting social and political theories—music can "provide a degree of unity" across those internal lines.[2]

The community-building strategies in the Civil War era used popular song as a primary musical medium. No group of pieces more clearly demonstrates those practices than the songs of Stephen Collins Foster. His songs were the most popular of the antebellum period, and many of them were used and adapted for community-building strategies before and during the war. Moreover, they have been viewed—not only by historians but also by the general public—as representative of groups during that period.

Foster was a twenty-two-year-old bookkeeper for his brother's steamship company in Cincinnati when his first hit song, "Oh! Susanna," was taken up by minstrel performers; it quickly entered the oral repertoire (some might say it became "folk music") of all classes, races, and regions of Americans and became the unofficial marching song of the forty-niners.[3] This and other early Foster melodies and lyrics were our first repertory of published, popular songs that afforded a degree of unity to the nation across immense distances, ethnic differences, and political philosophies. According to the musicologist Charles Hamm, with Foster's songs, "Never

2. Ibid., 158.

3. Ken Emerson, *Doo Dah! Stephen Foster and the Rise of American Popular Culture* (New York: Simon and Schuster, 1997), 127. Ken Emerson calls September 11, 1847, the date of the song's first public performance, "a firm date for the birth of pop music as we still recognize it today. No popular song is more deeply rooted in American consciousness than 'Oh! Susanna'" (127). Other principal writings on Foster's life and music are John Tasker Howard, *Stephen Foster: America's Troubadour* (New York: Thomas Y. Crowell, 1934; 2d ed., 1953); and Evelyn Foster Morneweck, *Chronicles of Stephen Foster's Family* (Pittsburgh: University of Pittsburgh Press, 1944), 2 vols. The principal repository of Foster manuscripts, scores, books, artifacts, and other materials is the Foster Hall Collection in the Center for American Music, University of Pittsburgh.

Stephen Collins Foster was born July 4, 1826, in a white cottage high on the hillside above the Allegheny River in Lawrenceville, east of Pittsburgh. *Foster Hall Collection, Center for American Music, University of Pittsburgh.*

before, and rarely since, did any music come so close to being a shared experience for so many Americans."[4]

"Susanna's" unprecedented success emboldened Foster to write a contract with the New York music publisher Firth, Pond and Co., move back to his hometown of Pittsburgh, set up shop as the United States' first professional songwriter, and start churning out minstrel tunes and parlor ballads to satisfy the demand for music in the nation's theaters and on its piano racks. His were the first songs to sell in the hundreds of thousands of copies, enriching publishers and emboldening other musicians—such as George Frederick Root (who would later pen "Tramp! Tramp! Tramp!" and "Battle Cry of Freedom")—to take up the business of songwriting.[5]

"SUSANNA" AND SOCIAL IDEALS

Historians' standard summary of Foster's songs, reflecting America's temperament a century and a half later, is that they evoked nostalgia and sentiment. What is not so widely understood is that, for the audiences of his time, Foster's songs strongly conveyed a social philosophy concerning ideas and policies of public life and affairs.

A powerful case in point is his first hit song. For at least the past century we have been accustomed to thinking of "Oh! Susanna" as a children's tune. But Americans of the Gold Rush era thought of it as a way to pass the time and a means to express their feelings during their trek across the prairies or their journey across the Isthmus of Panama. They adapted its words and invented new verses of their own, creating countless versions, most of which were never written down. One of the most widely known adaptations, sung alike on

4. Charles Hamm, *Music in the New World* (New York: Norton, 1983), 231.

5. Root recalled, "I saw that mine must be the 'people's song,' still, I am ashamed to say, I shared the feeling that was around me in regard to that grade of music. When Stephen C. Foster's wonderful melodies (as I now see them) began to appear... I 'took a hand in' and wrote a few.... It is easy to write *correctly* a simple song, but so to use the material of which such a song must be made that it will be received and live in the hearts of the people is quite another matter.... It was much easier to write when the resources were greater." George Frederick Root, *The Story of a Musical Life* (Cincinnati: John Church, 1891), 83, 96–97, quoted in Hamm, *Music in the New World,* 232.

prairie schooners and on clipper ships by travelers to the California goldfields, ran thus:

I come from New York City
With my wash bowl on my knee,
I'm going to California
The gold dust for to see.
I'll scrape the mountains clean, old girl,
I'll drain the rivers dry,
I'm off for California,
Susanna, don't you cry!

Oh, Susanna,
Don't you cry for me,
I'm off for California
With my wash bowl on my knee![6]

This version of the song expressed an ambition acted on by tens of thousands and dreamt of by countless more; its repeated performance helped to fire the imagination and to forge a bond among fellow travelers. The words are full of bravado about individual ambition, but no singer failed to understand that the results foretold in these lyrics would entail a joining of forces, the combined efforts of legions of fortune-seekers like themselves.

Whether viewed in the twenty-first century as a children's ditty or in the 1850s as the theme song of America's westward expansion, Foster's original song was probably written sometime before 1847, well before the discovery of gold at Sutter's Mill, and it had a different meaning altogether. His own lyrics contain the kernel of a social philosophy that would come to dominate his minstrel songs, which gave popular voice to a growing segment of northerners uncomfortable with slavery.

I come from Alabama with my banjo on my knee
I'se gwine to Lou'siana My true lub for to see.
It rain'd all night de day I left, De wedder it was dry;
The sun so hot I froze to def—Susanna, don't you cry.

6. Meade Minnigerode, *Oh, Susanna! Romance of the Old American Merchant Marine* (New York: G. P. Putnam's Sons, 1922), 252.

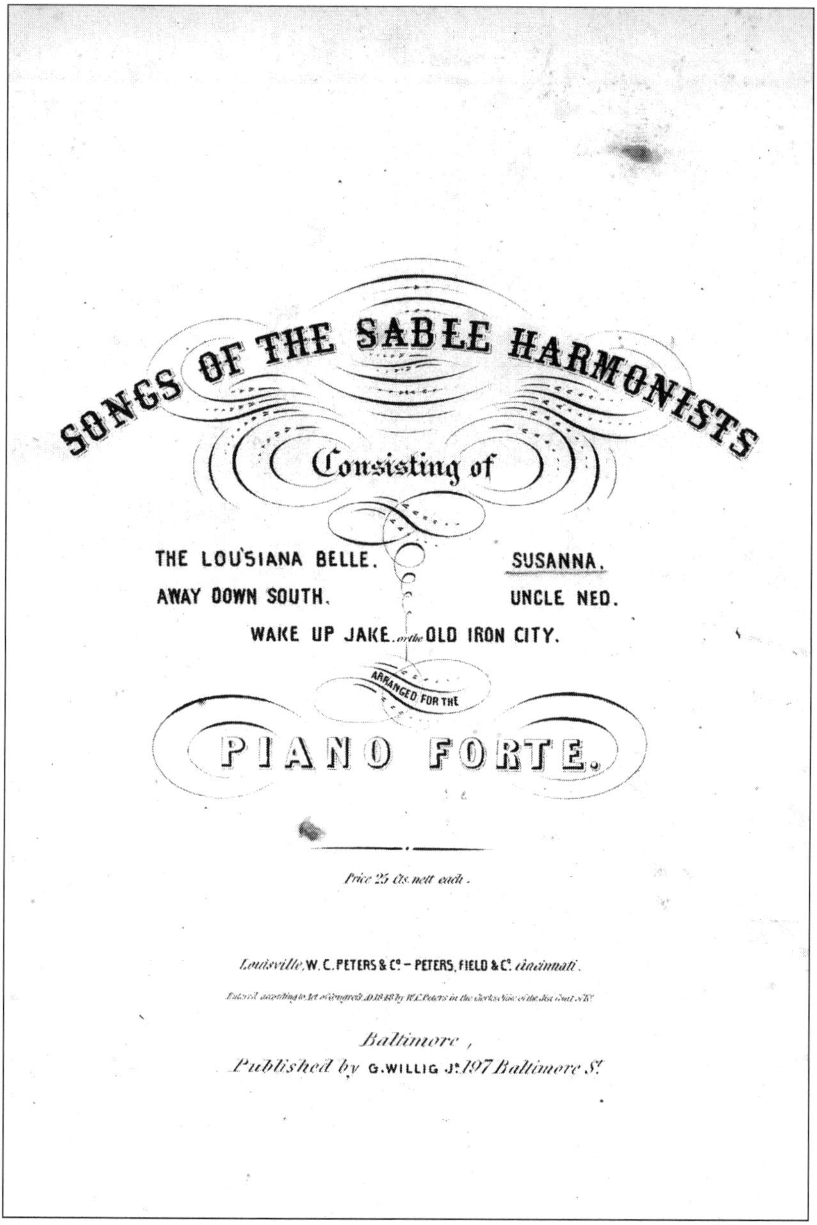

Foster's "Susanna" is identified with other songs that contain subtle social messages that gave voice to the growing antislavery movement.

Oh! Susanna, do not cry for me;
I come from Alabama, Wid my Banjo on my knee.[7]

Clues to the identity of the singer are the geographical placement (the South), the dialect (African American), and the musical instrument (an African one, associated with slaves). Audiences understood that this song was supposedly being sung by a slave (or a performer portraying a slave), but the actions are not those of a slave. Foster knew that slaveholders' practices and local and state laws would not allow a black man to travel freely from one state to another for personal interest; indeed, in most slave states, slaves were not allowed to travel freely at all.

In addition to pointing out slaves' inability to travel freely, the song has a social philosophy with even more powerful implications. Foster's lyrics proclaim "true love" between the singer and Susanna; to assert that they might truly love one another flew in the face of the actual practices of the slave trade, which forcibly separated families and denied slaves real marriage bonds. The standard slave image in popular culture was overwhelmingly derisive. That Foster's songs portrayed slaves as more fully human caused some listeners to understand that he was criticizing slavery; a few contemporaries even assumed that slaves themselves had created Foster's songs.[8]

And what about the terrible irony of a "sun so hot I froze to death"? What does Foster mean by these horrific contrasts of nature, and their implications for human beings? The second verse, which has been repressed in most editions of the song, extends the contrast:

I jump'd aboard the telegraph and trabbled down de ribber,
De lectrick fluid magnified, and kill'd five hundred Nigga.
De bulgine bust and de hoss ran off, I really thought I'd die;
I shut my eyes to hold my bref—Susanna don't you cry.

7. "Susanna" (Louisville, Ky.: W. C. Peters, 1848), verse 1.

8. For example, a Scandinavian visitor to the South in 1850 wrote, "Another young negro . . . sang with his banjo several of the negro songs universally known and sung in the South by the negro people, whose product they are, and in the Northern States by persons of all classes, because they are extremely popular. . . . Many of the songs remind me of Haydn's and Mozart's simple, artless melodies; for example, . . . 'Oh, Susannah,' 'Uncle Ned.'" Frederick Bremer, quoted in Dena J. Epstein, *Sinful Tunes and Spirituals: Black Folk Music to the Civil War,* Music in American Life series (Urbana: University of Illinois Press, 1977), 241.

In this verse, so repulsive to us today, the danger is not natural but man-made—electricity, steam-powered ships, and railroads. These epitomize society's greatest technical achievements in harnessing nature's energy, but at the same time they introduce new sources of fatal disaster on a massive scale. The lyric is rich in metaphor and double meanings. Foster is not only commenting on the social paradox of progress and peril inherent in what would later be called the Industrial Revolution, he is also reminding his listeners that, in this society, it is African Americans (slave or free) who are the most vulnerable. The comic veneer makes the song appealing, but it is a sugar coating on a bitter pill. The underlying message is serious: the powerful imperils the powerless; modern transportation and technology imperil the individual who trusts them with his or her life; society's progress bears a great cost. No wonder the verse was suppressed after the Civil War and all through the twentieth century, when Americans wanted to see Foster as a sentimentalizer of antebellum society and particularly the South—not as a critic.[9]

The year Foster turned twenty-three and signed his first publishing contract, 1849, he wrote "Nelly Was a Lady," the first American popular song that insists, in every chorus, that a slave woman was a *lady,* a term hitherto reserved for genteel white women. More clearly than in "Oh! Susanna," the song depicts the slave man and woman as devoted husband and wife, torn apart when the man (the singer) was sold down the Mississippi, and his wife is dying of a broken heart back in Virginia. The prevailing depiction of slaves in the literature, music, and theater of the time was of infidelity, carelessness, and ignorance of even such basic human needs as love and family. With this song and a string of about a dozen more—including "The Old Folks at Home" (1851), "My Old Kentucky Home" (1853), "Angelina Baker" (1850), and even the rollicking "Ring, Ring de Banjo" (1851)—Foster created a genre and attracted a large audience to a popular song literature that for the first time in American history suggested a

9. The notion that Foster voiced a sentimental view of the South was reflected even in the foremost scholarly reference works. For example, *Grove's Dictionary of Music and Musicians: American Supplement,* ed. Waldo Selden Pratt (New York: Macmillan, 1944), 117, said, "By descent and temperament he was a Southerner, and this explains his keen sympathy with the sentiment and form of the songs and music of the plantation."

humane intelligence and a measure of dignity in place of the prevailing cartoonish ridicule in minstrel portrayals of African Americans.

Foster's role in helping articulate the values of this social movement has not been widely recognized because he did not go so far as to publicly espouse abolition (for a host of reasons having largely to do with his family's prominence in the Democratic party in Western Pennsylvania). But in addition to using his songwriting as a source of income, Foster, through his songs for minstrel performance, tried to create a large audience among the "refined" middle and upper classes for his social philosophy. At the height of his career he wrote to the minstrel leader E. P. Christy:

> As I once intimated to you, I had the intention of omitting my name on my Ethiopian [minstrel] songs, owing to the prejudice against them by some, which might injure my reputation as a writer of another style of music [for the parlor], but I find that by my efforts I have done a great deal to build up a taste for the Ethiopian songs among refined people by making the words suitable to their taste, instead of the trashy and really offensive words which belong to some songs of that order. Therefore I have concluded to reinstate my name on my songs and to pursue the Ethiopian business without fear or shame and lend all my energies to making the business live, at the same time that I will wish to establish my name as the best Ethiopian song-writer.[10]

Thus his stated goal was to raise the quality of minstrel songs in order to make them palatable among a higher class of society, moving the minstrel business away from its "trashy and really offensive words." Not only was he trying to strengthen the group of listeners "among refined people," but also he was trying to reform the community of minstrel writers and performers. And to a great measure he was successful in his goal, though the minstrel troupes never abandoned their "trashy" songs. Several of his melodies were so well received that they became the most widely published music of the era, and at the same time they evinced so much compassion for slaves that they were sung by slaves themselves, while white audiences understood them as expressing antislavery sentiments, and abolitionists

10. Stephen C. Foster letter to E. P. Christy, May 25, 1852; original in the Library of Congress.

adapted their melodies and words to advocate their cause. Foster's songs—even in their original form—had a powerful effect in creating a sea change in the North's opinion of slavery, that is, in helping forge a large community of citizens who viewed slaves as human beings rather than as chattel. The abolitionist orator Frederick Douglass, himself a former slave, remarked on Foster's songs: "It would seem almost absurd to say it, considering the use that has been made of them, that we have allies in the Ethiopian songs. . . . 'Old Kentucky Home,' and 'Uncle Ned,' can make the heart sad as well as merry, and can call forth a tear as well as a smile. They awaken the sympathies for the slave, in which anti-slavery principles take root and flourish."[11]

SONGS AND POLITICS

It has long been recognized that members of Foster's family were "intensely interested in politics. The careers of his father, his brothers, and his sisters were closely associated with the political activities of the day, in their native city of Pittsburgh, and in Pennsylvania."[12] The issues that motivated his father and brothers to campaign for public office were not slavery and abolition—the causes that endure for us today—but banking laws, federalism, and restraint of commerce. The Fosters were against them all and had suffered repeatedly, they felt, because of federal barriers to free enterprise. They were Jacksonian Democrats.

Stephen Foster, as a writer whose income depended on the public's good favor in buying his song sheets, was savvy enough not to put into print anything that might offend the politics of a large segment of his audience. He nevertheless privately supported his family's political interests by writing and performing songs for their campaign

11. Frederick Douglass, "The Anti-Slavery Movement: Lecture Delivered before the Rochester [New York] Ladies' Anti-Slavery Society, January 1855," *The Life and Writings of Frederick Douglass,* ed. Philip S. Foner, vol. 2, *Pre–Civil War Decade, 1850–1860* (New York: International Publishers, 1950), 356–57.

12. Fletcher Hodges Jr., "Stephen Foster, Democrat," *The Lincoln Herald* (Harrogate, Tenn.: Lincoln Memorial University, June 1945; reprint, Pittsburgh: University of Pittsburgh Press, 1946), 4.

rallies, using music overtly as a tactic for attracting and encouraging political supporters. One example stems from the autumn of 1851, when the Democratic candidates for governor of Pennsylvania and California were the brothers William and John Bigler: "For the Pennsylvania campaign, Stephen wrote a set of lyrics to be sung to the air of his own famous 'Camptown Races.'"[13] The verses survive only in Foster's manuscript sketchbook, with references to the incumbent Pennsylvania governor of the Whig party (William F. Johnston) and the U.S. president whose coattails he had ridden into office (Zachary Taylor). Here are the first and fifth verses:

> They say that Johnston's up once more,
>   Hurrah! Hurrah!
> But things ain't now as they were before,
>   Hurrah for the Bigler boys!
> Then he run his face in a Taylor shop,
>   Hurrah! Hurrah!
> But the Taylor's gone and he has no prop.
>   Hurrah for the Bigler boys!
>
>   [Chorus]
>   Going to run again?
>   Johnston, you're insane!
>   I'll bet my money on the Bigler boys
>   For the Whigs have had their reign!
>
> We've let the Whigs elect an ass,
>   Hurrah! Hurrah!
> But now we'll turn him out to grass,
>   Hurrah for the Bigler boys!
> For when the tug of war is over,
>   Hurrah! Hurrah!
> The Democrats will live in the clover.
>   Hurrah for the Bigler boys!

For the presidential campaign of 1856, the Foster family had even more to cheer about. Stephen's sister, Ann Eliza, was the wife of the brother of James Buchanan, the Democratic candidate, and Stephen wrote this song—words and music—for the campaign in western Pennsylvania:

13. Ibid., 6.

The White House Chair
Let all our hearts for Union be,
For the North and South are one;
They've worked together manfully,
And together they will still work on.

[Chorus]
Then come ye men from every State,
Our creed is broad and fair;
Buchanan is our candidate,
And we'll put him in the White House chair.

We'll have no dark, designing band,
To rule with secret sway;
We'll give to all a helping hand,
And be open as the light of day.

[Chorus]
We'll not outlaw the land that holds
The bones of Washington,
Where Jackson fought and Marion bled,
And the battles of the brave were won.[14]

Campaign songs were all about communicating the party's platform, trumpeting the noble traits of the standard-bearers, and crying down the opponent. Within public gatherings, they were among the most effective form of communication in forming the identity of the political group and at the same time building a sense of solidarity among its supporters who were geographically widely dispersed.

Even though Stephen Foster never offered any overtly political songs for publication before the war, other writers used several of his familiar songs for political purposes—Democrats, Whigs, and Republicans alike. Here's how the Republicans used the familiar tune of "Old Uncle Ned" (which had been published in 1848 at the same time as "Oh! Susanna"), parodying its lyrics in order to poke fun at Stephen Douglas, who vied with Lincoln in the 1860 campaign:

There was a little man, and his name was Stevy Doug,
To the White House he longed for to go;

14. *The Music of Stephen C. Foster: A Critical Edition,* ed. Steven Saunders and Deane L. Root (Washington, D.C.: Smithsonian Institution Press, 1990), 2:11.

But he hadn't any votes in the whole of the South,
In the place where his votes ought to grow.
His legs they were short, but his speeches they were long,
And nothing but himself he could see,
His principles were weak, but his spirits they were strong,
For a thirsty little soul was he![15]

In the same campaign, *The Wide-Awake Vocalist, or Rail Splitters' Song Book* carried the following verses under the title "Hi, Rally! Ho, Rally!" sung to the tune of Foster's "Nelly Bly":

Hail with joy
The Farmer's boy—
Shout! Oh, shout with glee!
For LINCOLN, true,
And HAMLIN, too,
The Champions of the Free!
East and West,
Do your best,
Now, with heart and voice,
For LINCOLN, true,
And HAMLIN, too,
They are the people's choice.

Hi, rally! Ho, rally!
Round the polls with me,
For LINCOLN, true,
And HAMLIN, too,
The Champions of the Free!

In 1864, supporters of both Lincoln and McClellan borrowed Stephen Foster's songs to get their messages across and build groups of supporters. Lincoln's is more evocative, borrowing on "Old Dog Tray":

To friends of Freedom all,
Upon you we now call,
To help us sustain a noble, honest man,
Who is acting for the right,

15. These and the following lyrics may be found in ibid., 2:189–92.

To conquer traitors' might,
And crush out treason's lofty plan.

[Chorus]
Then up with the stripes and the stars,
Down with the cross and the bars,
For Lincoln we will cheer,
McClellan we'll not fear,
Nor all the Union's Northern foes.

It is interesting to note that most of these parodies and borrowings would not be possible under our modern copyright laws (which, ironically, are intended to encourage creativity rather than suppress it). But under the laws of Foster's era, they were more than simply possible—they were the grist for the creative mill of the songwriter. Foster and every other songwriter relied on and used the familiarity of another's lyric or melody. The currency of songs made them ripe for parody or adaptation, and nearly every new song evoked connotations of some other well-known piece of music.

Not until after the Civil War had begun did Stephen Foster write lyrics for publication that were openly political, and by then his songs were firmly in support of Lincoln and the Union. Aside from his musical settings of other poets' lines, such as James Sloane Gibbons's "We Are Coming, Father Abraham, 300,000 More" (1862), Foster's own politically tinged lyrics included only six songs, "I'm Nothing but a Plain Old Soldier" (1863), "Better Times Are Coming" (1862), "We've a Million in the Field" (1862), "I'll Be a Soldier" (1861), "Was My Brother in the Battle?" (1862), and "That's What's the Matter" (1862). The most forceful of these is the last:

We live in hard and stirring times,
Too sad for mirth, too rough for rhymes,
For songs of mirth have lost their charms,
  And that's what's the matter.

[Chorus]
  That's what's the matter
  The rebels have to scatter,
  We'll make them flee by land and sea,
  And that's what's the matter.

Foster's song then cites a number of issues (untrustworthy "Neighbors" of the South, maintenance of "Law and Rights," undivided loyalty to the Union) and celebrates victories and soldiers (the *Merrimac* and *Monitor,* Captain Ericsson, defeat of "Gen'ral" Beauregard) before ending:

> So what's the use to fret and pout,
> We soon will hear the people shout,
> Secession dodge is *all* play'd out!
> And that's what's the matter!

CONCLUSION

In the end, Foster's overtly political songs had less influence on the course of the nation—they had less of a role in creating communities of like-minded citizens—than did his "Ethiopian" melodies. For it was his songs written for the theater that worked their way into all segments of the American public, north and south, east and west, rich and poor, slave and free, native-born and newly immigrated. The ubiquitous familiarity of these songs allowed them to create vastly shared sympathies and massive if not easily identified communities of people who responded to the songs' social philosophy.

Did Foster's songs incite any members of those communities to act on their sympathies? Undoubtedly, although we have no way to measure that response. Who is to say that families did not decide to join a wagon train because they were infected by the spirit of the "land of glittering dreams" sung to the tune of "Oh! Susanna," or that men in Foster's hometown of Pittsburgh did not vote for Buchanan because the credo of "The White House Chair" was running through their minds? It is reasonable to think that the economic and political ramifications of abolition were made more palatable by repeated hearings of "Nelly Was a Lady" and "My Old Kentucky Home." Would the North have gone to war to preserve the Union, and would emancipation have succeeded, without communities of supporters forged, at least in part, by the songs they sang?

One cannot answer such questions with complete certainty, but we do know that Foster's songs—and their parodies—were accepted into homes and parlors, at a time when political tracts, sermons, and other forms of persuasion were considered intrusive. In a nation with insurmountable internal differences across immense geographic spread, music provided an essential "degree of unity" for communities of citizens.

As these few examples illustrate, the music of the Civil War era had a powerful role in expressing shared experiences, dreams, ideals, and beliefs among communities of people. Especially in times of severe conflict, songs can be heard strategically, as part of the complex negotiations over political ideologies and expressions of social philosophies. One reason why the music of the Civil War era was so powerful a force in American history, and why it still has such a strong attraction to us nearly a century and a half later, is that it had a major role in the community-building strategies for the great social and political issues of our country's most devastating conflict.

They Weren't All Like Lorena

Musical Portraits of Women in the Civil War Era

Lenora Cuccia

Women of the Civil War era were dedicated to their cause, inspirational to their men, and highly patriotic—according to the lyrics of Civil War songs. It takes little imagination to envision a group of soldiers sitting around the campfire on the eve of battle singing the lyrics to "Just before the Battle Mother," or lovesick warriors writing by candlelight to their wives or sweethearts while humming the melody of "Lorena." Likewise, our mind's eye can take us back to the summer of 1864 when ill-clad Confederate soldiers went marching through Tennessee or Virginia while they sang "The Yellow Rose of Texas." This study considers about sixty songs that were popular during the Civil War era, including songs that were written before the war—such as "Lorena"—but continued in popularity during the conflict. The songs can be divided into four categories: "Mother" songs, "Sweetheart" songs, "Wife and Family" songs, and "Other Gutsy Girls." Analysis of these songs suggests that Civil War soldiers marched and fought for their wives and sweethearts, dreamed of their mothers (especially as the soldier's life is ebbing away), and died for their country's honor.

"Mother," in the imagery of Civil War songs, shone like a light in the soldier's memory during his dark and lonely hours. The soldier, according to the lyricists, thought of his mother before the battle, after the battle, while in prison, when going to sleep, and while lying on his deathbed. Songs usually were written in the form of a conversation of the soldier with others, in an imagined conversation with "Mother," or in a letter written to her. Most of the "Mother" songs focus on the soldier's relationship with his mother, whom he longed to see. An example of this genre is illustrated by "Just before the Battle, Mother," words and music by George F. Root:

1. Just before the battle, Mother,
I am thinking most of you,
While upon the field we're watching,
With the enemy in view.
Comrades brave are 'round me lying,
Filled with thought of home and God;
For well they know that on the morrow,
Some will sleep beneath the sod.

Farewell, Mother, you may never
Press me to your breast again;
But, Oh, you'll not forget me, Mother,
If I'm numbered with the slain.

2. Oh, I long to see you, Mother,
And the loving ones at home,
But I'll never leave our banner,
Till in honor I can come.
Tell the traitors all around you
That their cruel words we know,
In every battle kill our soldiers
By the help they give the foe.

3. Hark! I hear the bugles sounding,
'Tis the signal for the fight,
Now, may God protect us, Mother,
As he ever does the right.
Hear the "Battle Cry of Freedom,"
How it swells upon the air,
Oh, yes, we'll rally 'round the standard,
Or we'll perish nobly there.[1]

The soldier's mental image of his mother comforts and strengthens him for the battle ahead. He knows that he will be remembered, even

1. George F. Root, "Just before the Battle, Mother," in Irwin Silber, ed., *Songs of the Civil War* (1960; reprint, Mineola, N.Y.: Dover, 1995), 151–53.

if he dies. In the sequel to this song, "Just after the Battle," the thought of his mother and home gives the wounded soldier the will to live and persevere: "Mother, dear, your boy is wounded, / And the night is drear with pain, / But still I feel that I shall see you, / And the dear old home again."[2]

Even when he made it through a battle unscathed, the weary, hungry soldier wistfully longed for the happier days of his youth, when his mother's loving care was always near. "Rock Me to Sleep, Mother" seems hopelessly saccharine from a twenty-first century perspective, but it enjoyed wide popularity when Elizabeth Allen first published it as a poem in the *Saturday Evening Post* in 1860, and it was sung by Confederate soldiers after being set to music by John Hill Hewitt:

> 1. Backward, turn backward. O! Time in your flight.
> Make me a child again, just for tonight,
> Mother, come back from the echoless shore,
> Take me again to your heart as of yore,
> Kiss from my forehead the furrows of care,
> Smooth the few silver threads out of my hair.
> Over my slumbers your loving watch keep,
>
> Rock me to sleep, Mother, rock me to sleep.
> Rock me, rock me, rock me to sleep.
> Rock me, rock me, Rock me to sleep.[3]

Many songs enjoyed equal popularity among Union and Confederate troops, sometimes with very slight alterations to the lyrics, and "Mother" songs were no exception. One example is "Tramp! Tramp! Tramp!" which was originally a Union song by George F. Root but was later adapted by the Confederates, who added a "little sister" in the fifth verse.

> 1. In the prison cell I sit,
> Thinking, mother, dear, of you,
> And our bright and happy home so far away,

2. George F. Root, "Just after the Battle," in Silber, *Songs,* 154–56.
3. Elizabeth Ann Allen, "Rock Me to Sleep, Mother," in Henry S. Humphreys, ed., *Songs of the Confederacy* (Cincinnati: Willis Music, 1961), 98–100.

And the tears they fill my eyes
'Spite of all that I can do,
Tho' I try to cheer my comrades and be gay.

Tramp, tramp, tramp, the boys are marching,
Cheer up comrades they will come,
And beneath the starry flag
We shall breathe the air again
Of the free land in our own beloved home.

[Southern Version, words anonymous, verse 5]
5. When I close my eyes in sleep,
All the dear ones 'round me come,
At night my little sister to me calls;
And mocking visions bring all the warm delights of home,
While we freeze and starve in Northern prison walls.[4]

A few songs were written from "Mother's" perspective, and in them she missed her soldier son as much as he missed her. The Union song "The Faded Coat of Blue," by J. H. McNaughton, depicts a mother's sorrow at the thought of her son's lonely death and his unmarked grave. The first verse, chorus, and last verse illustrate this point of view:

1. My brave lad he sleeps in his faded coat of blue,
In a lonely grave unknown lies the heart that beat so true;
He sank faint and hungry among the famished brave,
And they laid him sad and lonely within his nameless grave.

No more the bugle calls the weary one,
Rest noble spirit, in thy grave unknown!
I'll find you and know you among the good and true,
When a robe of white is giv'n for the faded coat of blue.

5. No sweet voice was there, breathing soft a mother's prayer,
But there's One who takes the brave and the true in tender care.
No stone marks the sod o'er my lad so brave and true,
In his lonely grave he sleeps in his faded coat of blue.[5]

4. George F. Root, "Tramp! Tramp! Tramp! (The Prisoner's Hope)," in Silber, *Songs,* 35–37. Southern version anonymous, words given in Silber, *Songs,* 37.
5. J. H. McNaughton, "The Faded Coat of Blue," in Silber, *Songs,* 161–63.

The middle verses of "The Faded Coat of Blue" include the last words of the dying boy—that he will meet his mother and sister again someday in Heaven. Of all the songs in which women are mentioned, "Mother" songs tended to be the most religious in nature. Many of these compositions make frequent mention of God and flow naturally into a prayer for a verse or two. In Charles C. Sawyer's "Who Will Care for Mother Now?" the soldier expected to be "marching with angels" soon, and his only regret at his death was the sorrow he knew his mother would feel:

> 2. Who will comfort her in sorrow?
> Who will dry the falling tear?
> Gently smooth her wrinkled forehead?
> Who will whisper words of cheer?
> Even now I think I see her
> Kneeling, praying for me!
> How Can I leave her in anguish?
> Who will care for mother now?[6]

In "For the Dear Old Flag I Die," a wounded drummer boy, whose mother apparently has made it to his dying side, hears "the angel band calling from their starry shore" and assures his mother that "Though 'tis hard" to part with her, he "would not wish to stay." In another death scene, that of "Somebody's Darling," with words by Marie Ravenal de la Coste and music by John Hill Hewitt, the narrator describes a beautiful, young, dead boy and wonders plaintively, "Who'll tell his mother where her boy died?" This song closes with a charge to those who will bury the unknown boy: "Carve on the wooden slab over his head, 'Somebody's darling is slumbering here.'"[7] This sort of picturesque poignancy was typical of the "Mother" songs.

Based on popular images illustrated by these songs, every soldier's mother was unfailingly dear, sweet, loving, comforting, patient, faithful, holy, prayerful, inspiring, unselfish, and sorely missed. The mothers in these songs could have been interchangeable; they all had the same attributes. Perhaps this is an indication of an age in which indi-

6. Charles C. Sawyer, "Who Will Care for Mother Now?" in Silber, *Songs,* 157–59.

7. George Cooper, "For the Dear Old Flag I Die," in Silber, *Songs,* 27–29; Marie Ravenal de la Coste, "Somebody's Darling," in Humphreys, *Songs,* 101–3.

vidualism was not valued as highly as universally respected virtues, and the virtues a mother was expected to have were all rolled together into the perfect image presented in the "Mother" songs.[8] There was such a proliferation of "Mother" songs that Eugene T. Johnston wrote a song making fun of them, called "The Mother of All Songs," in which he strung together numerous well-known titles and phrases from "Mother" songs, suggesting that "Mother on the brain" was a curious modern malady afflicting young soldiers.

The "Sweetheart" songs divide nicely into two main groups: those bearing directly on the war, and those that do not. The former are patriotic and inspirational, and the latter are either lighthearted or sentimental. All these songs highlight various aspects of love and courtship, from joyous hope to bitter parting.

The war-related sweetheart songs include numerous good-bye songs in which the parting is difficult but rendered possible by the strong patriotism of the male and the resigned devotion of the female. The same themes appear regardless of Union or Confederate affiliation: sadness, a sense of duty to one's country and flag, conviction of being in the right, and the desire to be remembered. In "The South Shall Rise Up Free" by John Hill Hewitt, the soldier admonishes his sweetheart,

> 1. The bugle sounds upon the plain,
> Our men are gath'ring fast;
> You would not have your friend remain,
> And be among the last.
> Cheer up, cheer up, my southern flow'r,
> There's joy for you and me;
> While Right is strong and God has pow'r,
> The South shall rise up free!
> While Right is strong and God has pow'r,
> The South shall rise up free![9]

In a similar vein, Harry Macarthy's "The Volunteer" consoles his sweetheart, his "pet":

8. This song sheet, published by H. De Marsan (undated) may be viewed at the Library of Congress web site (http://memory.loc.gov) under "America Singing: Nineteenth-Century Song Sheets." Its digital ID number is sb30304b.

9. John Hill Hewitt, "The South Shall Rise Up Free," in Humphreys, *Songs,* 34–36.

Then weep not, dearest, weep not,
If in her cause I fall,
O, weep not, dearest, weep not,
It is my country's call.

3. I knew you'd let me go, pet,
I saw it in that tear.
To join the gallant men, pet.
Who never yet knew fear.
With God and Right upon our side,
We'll win the day or die,
The foemen's hosts will shrink dismay'd
Before our battle cry.[10]

In John Hill Hewitt's "The Young Volunteer," the same themes emerge:

1. Our flag is unfurled and our arms flash bright,
As the sun wakes up the sky;
But ere I join the doubtful fight,
Lovely maid, I would say, "Good-bye."
I'm a young volunteer, and my heart is true
To our flag that woos the wind;
Then three cheers for that flag and our country too,
And the girls we leave behind.

Then adieu, then adieu, 'tis the last bugle's strain,
That is falling on the ear;
Should it so be decreed that we ne'er meet again,
Oh, remember the Young Volunteer.[11]

All three of the previous examples of sweetheart good-bye songs were Confederate songs in a moderately slow tempo, which complemented the touching quality of the texts. The next two examples are Union songs, and both were sung at a lively tempo. The first, the well-known "Girl I Left behind Me," was already an old Irish song at the time of the Civil War but was readily adapted to the present situation by troops leaving their sweethearts. The lighthearted joy of the melody does not seem to match the melancholy of the words:

10. Harry Macarthy, "The Volunteer," in Humphreys, *Songs,* 48–50.
11. John Hill Hewitt, "The Young Volunteer," in Humphreys, *Songs,* 69–72.

1. The hour was sad I left the maid,
A ling'ring farewell taking;
Her sighs and tears my steps delayed,
I thought her heart was breaking;
In hurried words her name I blessed,
I breath'd the vows that bind me,
And to my heart in anguish pressed
The girl I left behind me.[12]

The quick tempo, major harmony, duple meter (like a march), and cheery melody make this song sound happy, not anguished. Despite the sad imagery of the lyrics, it was a fine song for marching and lifted the spirits of many men who had certainly experienced a degree of anguish in their good-byes. Perhaps "optimistic" would be a good adjective for this "good-bye" song, for while the Confederate "good-byes" sometimes had hopeful, optimistic words, they were much less likely to make a departing soldier whistle as he marched.

Another Union soldiers' song, "I'll Be a Sergeant," was also light-hearted; its rousing final chorus looked forward to many happy reunions when the war was over:

For, dear girls, we soldiers adore you;
Make us brave through your love, we implore you!
Then happy shall we be
To bend the suppliant knee,
When we come marching home.
Marching home, marching home, marching home,
Marching home to the roll of the drum.
Then, freed from war's alarms,
To you we'll yield our arms,
When the drum taps, "Marching home!"[13]

Other "sweetheart" songs were purportedly written from a woman's perspective, although two of the following three examples were written by men and the third's author is anonymous. "You Are Going to the Wars, Willie Boy!" is by John Hill Hewitt and is quite similar to

12. Anonymous Irish version in Joe Chapple, ed., *Heart Songs* (Boston: Chapple, 1909; reprint, New York: Da Capo Press, 1983), 66–67; anonymous Union version (adapted from Samuel Lover) in Silber, *Songs,* 327.

13. Anonymous, "I'll Be a Sergeant," in Silber, *Songs,* 204–6.

the other Confederate "good-bye" songs, except that it presents the girl's perspective. In addition to rights, laws, the flag, and remembrance, this young lady wants to make it quite clear to her "Willie" that although he may meet other pretty girls in his travels, there won't be any others as true as she is.

1. You are going to the wars, Willie boy, Willie boy,
You are going to the wars far away,
To protect our rights and laws Willie boy, Willie boy,
And the banner in the sun's golden ray;
With your uniform all new,
And your shining buttons too,
You'll win the hearts of pretty girls,
But none like me so true.
Oh! Won't you think of me, Willie boy, Willie boy;
Oh won't you think of me when far away?
I'll often think of ye, Willie boy, Willie boy,
And ever for your life and glory pray.

2. You'll be fighting for the right, Willie boy, Willie boy,
You'll be fighting for the right and your home;
And you'll strike the blow with might, Willie boy, Willie boy,
'Mid the thundering of cannon and of drum;
With an arm as true as steel,
You'll make the foe-men feel
The vengeance of a Southerner,
Too proud to cringe or kneel.
Oh! Should you fall in strife, Willie boy, Willie boy;
Oh should you fall in strife on the plain,
I'll pine away my life, Willie boy, Willie boy,
And never, never wear a smile again.[14]

The next two songs, one Union and one Confederate, both describe the arrival in town of volunteer troops and a young lady's happy experience with them. In both cases, the young lady falls in love and, by the end of the song, is waiting hopefully for the end of the war and the return of her beloved. "Johnny Is My Darling" featured lyrics by Father Reed and was meant to be sung to the tune of "Charlie Is My Darling."

14. John Hill Hewitt, "You Are Going to the Wars, Willie Boy!" in Humphreys, *Songs,* 65–68.

Johnny is my darling, my darling, my darling,
Johnny is my darling, the Union Volunteer.

1. 'Twas on a sunny morning,
The brightest of the year,
When Johnny came to my town,
A Union Volunteer.

2. As he came marching up the street,
The bands played loud and clear;
And everyone came out to greet
The Union Volunteer.

3. With proudly waving starry flags
And hearts that knew no fear;
He came to fight for Freedom's rights,
A Union Volunteer.

4. But though he's gone to glory win,
And I left lonely here,
He'll soon return to me again
As *Cupid's Volunteer.*[15]

The similar theme of the Southern song "The Captain with His Whiskers" is highlighted with a sunny major key, in contrast with the minor mode of the previous song. The author is unknown.

1. As they marched through the town, with their banners so gay,
I ran to the window just to hear the band play.
I peeped through the blinds very cautiously then,
Lest the neighbors should say I was looking at the men.
Oh, I heard the drums beat, and the music was sweet,
But my eyes at the time caught a much greater treat.
The troops were the finest I ever did see,
And the Captain with his whiskers took a sly glance at me.

2. When we met at the ball, I of course thought 'twas right
To pretend that we had never met before that night,
But he knew me at once, I perceived by his glance
And I hung down my head when he asked me to dance.

15. Father Reed, "Johnny Is My Darling," in Silber, *Songs,* 209–10 (emphasis added).

Oh, he sat by my side at the end of the set,
And the sweet words he spoke I shall never forget.
For my heart was enlisted and could not get free
As the Captain with his whiskers took a sly glance at me.[16]

The lyrics of the next two songs—after sharing the excitement and hopefulness of the sweethearts as their volunteers marched off to war—remind us of the many anxious days these sweethearts had ahead of them. In "Weeping, Sad, and Lonely," by Charles C. Sawyer and Henry Tucker, and "The Southern Soldier Boy," by Captain G. W. Alexander (sung to the tune of "The Boy with Auburn Hair"), both sweethearts worry that their beloved soldier might be slain in battle, but both console themselves that it would be for their country's glorious cause:

Weeping sad and lonely,
Hopes and fears how vain!
(Yet praying,) when this cruel war is over,
Praying that we meet again![17]

3. Oh! If in battle he was slain,
I am sure that I should die;
But I am sure he'll come again
And cheer my weeping eye;
But should he fall in this our glorious cause,
He still would be my joy,
For many a sweetheart mourns the loss
Of a Southern Soldier Boy.[18]

Song lyrics also indicate that for some of the brave soldiers who returned from the war, courtship proved more difficult than expected. For example, the song "The Johnson Boys," which refers to "that

16. Anonymous, "The Captain with His Whiskers," as sung by Bobby Horton, *Homespun Songs of the C.S.A.,* vol. 3 (audiocassette recording, Birmingham, Ala., 1987). An early published version of this song, "as sung by Mrs. W. J. Florence," may be viewed on the Library of Congress Web site (http://memory.loc.gov) under "America Singing: Nineteenth-Century Song Sheets," digital ID sb10059b.

17. Charles C. Sawyer, "Weeping, Sad, and Lonely," in Silber, *Songs,* 124–26.

18. G. W. Alexander, "The Southern Soldier Boy," in Silber, *Songs,* 148–50.

awful Civil War" in the third verse, describes a scene where, despite the "skill and courage" the Johnson boys displayed as scouts in the Rebel army, their courtship skills were dismally lacking. The last verse concludes:

> Johnson boys went a courtin',
> Coon Creek girls, pretty and sweet,
> They couldn't make no conversation,
> Didn't know where to put their feet.
> Hop up.

The following chorus seems to reinforce the idea that the Johnson boys were a bit grizzled and formidable, since it directs the pretty girls not to be afraid.[19]

"The Yellow Rose of Texas," "Rose of Alabama," and "Cindy" are all lighthearted sweetheart songs that Southern soldiers sang. The last two are quite humorous, with Rose's suitor's banjo floating away in the river, and Cindy's mouth being so sweet that honeybees swarm around it. "Wait for the Wagon," a lively courtship song, was so popular that both the North and the South had parodies of it that promoted their causes. But the original, attributed to R. Bishop Buckley, was just a sweet love story:

> 1. Will you come with me, my Phillis dear,
> To yon blue mountain free?
> Where the blossoms smell the sweetest,
> Come rove along with me.
> It's ev'ry Sunday morning,
> When I am by your side,
> We'll jump into the wagon
> And all take a ride.
>
> Wait for the wagon,
> Wait for the wagon,
> Wait for the wagon,
> And we'll all take a ride.[20]

19. Anonymous, "The Johnson Boys," on Wayne Erbsen, *Southern Soldier Boy* (audiocassette recording, Asheville, N.C.: Native Ground, 1992).
20. R. Bishop Buckley, "Wait for the Wagon," in Silber, *Songs,* 193–95.

The next four "sweetheart" songs do not bear directly on the war; these, for instance, relate stories about unattainable love. In "Evelina," the narrator is too poor to marry Evelina, but he still swears he will love her "forever and ever." Poor "Katy Wells" died before her fiancé could marry her. "Aura Lee" is all written in the past tense, leaving the listener to wonder what happened to her. And "Lorena," despite being one of the most wildly popular of all sweetheart songs, is about a woman who broke up with her beloved and left him grieving for over a hundred months.[21]

The overall picture that emerges from the war-related sweetheart songs is that sweethearts were sad but proud to see their suitors marching off to war and that they had confidence both in their men's abilities to fight and their own strength to endure separation. The typical sweetheart in these songs also had confidence that God would allow her to see her beloved again, if not in this life, then in Heaven.

We can make a category for "Wife and Family" songs, for even though wives were not popular subjects for Civil War songs, they often got one line in a song that was primarily about something else. In "Morgan's War Song," a line says, "Cheer, boys, cheer for our sweethearts and our wives." In "Goober Peas," we hear "I wish this war was over, / When free from rags and fleas, / We'd kiss our wives and sweethearts, / And gobble goober peas!" In "Marching Along," one verse is a little prayer: "Our wives and our children we leave in your care, / We feel you will help them with sorrow to bear; / 'Tis hard thus to part, but we hope 'twon't be long, / We'll keep up our heart as we're marching along." In "Stonewall Jackson's Prayer," the General prays, "In ev'ry danger, ev'ry woe, / O, God, protect my wife and child." In "Stonewall Jackson's Way," all manner of women are encouraged:

> Ah, maiden, wait, and watch, and yearn
> For news of Stonewall's band!
> Ah, widow, read, with eyes that burn,
> That ring upon thy hand!

21. The story behind "Lorena" is told in E. Lawrence Abel, *Singing the New Nation: How Music Shaped the Confederacy, 1861–1865* (Mechanicsburg, Pa.: Stackpole Books, 2000), 213–15.

Ah, wife, sew on, pray on, hope on!
Thy life shall not be all forlorn.
The foe had better ne'er been born
That gets in Stonewall's way.[22]

No picture of the wife's personality or characteristics really develops. The picture of the wife's personality and role within the family is subtly, if stereotypically, cast through these descriptions. She sews (providing material support for the family), prays (providing spiritual support), and hopes (providing emotional support). The wife is an important, if sometimes understated, character in songs of this era.

It is interesting to note that one of the most poignant portraits of married love in a Civil War song, "All Quiet along the Potomac Tonight," was authored by a woman, Ethel Lynn Eliot Beers. Numerous composers set her poem to music. The second and third verses describe the sentry's thoughts of his wife, children, and home:

2. There's only the sound of the lone sentry's tread,
As he tramps from the rock to the fountain,
And thinks of the two on the low trundle bed,
Far away in the cot on the mountain.
His musket falls slack, his face, dark and grim
Grows gentle with memories tender,
As he mutters a prayer for the children asleep,
And their mother "May heaven defend her."
"All quiet along the Potomac tonight."

3. Hark! Was it the night wind that rustles the leaves?
Was it the moonlight so wond'rously flashing?
It look'd like a rifle! "Ha! Mary, good-bye!"
And his life-blood is ebbing and splashing.
"All quiet along the Potomac tonight,"
No sound, save the rush of the river;
While soft falls the dew on the face of the dead.
"The Picket's" off duty forever.
"All quiet along the Potomac tonight."[23]

22. J. W. Palmer, "Stonewall Jackson's Way," in Humphreys, *Songs,* 90–91; L. Rieves, "Stonewall Jackson's Prayer," in Humphreys, *Songs,* 92–94.

23. Ethel Lynn Eliot Beers, "All Quiet along the Potomac Tonight," in Humphreys, *Songs,* 95–97.

The sadness of the sentry's death is magnified because of the details we learn about him in the previous verses. We have pictured his cottage home on a mountainside, where his two little children and his wife are sleeping, and in our mind's eye we have seen his moonlit face soften at the thought of them. By the end, when he chokes, "Mary, good-bye!" we nearly feel as if we have met him. It is no wonder that after this song was published, the general outcry against sniping at pickets increased to the point that the practice was banned by both armies as "barbaric."

The last category, "Other Gutsy Girls," includes songs that do not fit under the other categories. These songs depict women—often without being specific to marital status or age—who are filled with patriotism and are compelled to take action to further the war effort.

In the anonymous ditty "The Why and the Wherefore," a conversation between a questioner and a volunteer gives the listener an understanding of why the boys volunteered:

> "Who, who, who, and who,
> And who goes with you to the war?"
> "Ten thousand brave lads, and if they should stay here,
> The girls would cry shame, and *they'd* volunteer.
> They speak their mind quite freely—Now reely."[24]

Another anonymous song, "John Harrolson," recounts the patriotic actions of the ladies of Selma, Alabama, in response to a request from John Harrolson regarding his gunpowder plant. He sent barrels around town to collect a liquid "ingredient" that could be made into nitre, a component of saltpeter, which is necessary for gunpowder.

> John Harrolson, John Harrolson, You are a funny creature,
> You've given to this cruel war a new and curious feature.
> You'd have us think while every man is bound to be a fighter,
> The women blest, the pretty dears, should be put to making nitre.
>
> John Harrolson, John Harrolson, how could you get the notion,
> To send your barrels round the town to gather up the "lotion."
> We think the girls do work enough in giving love and kissing,
> But you'll now put the pretty dears to patriotic ________.

24. Anonymous, "The Why and the Wherefore," in Silber, *Songs,* 41–42.

John Harrolson, John Harrolson, could you not invent a neater,
Or some less immodest mode of making your saltpeter.
The thing it is queer you know, gunpowder like the cranky,
That when a lady lifts her shift, she shoots another Yankee.[25]

Two other "gutsy girl" songs are both by Carrie Bell Sinclair. The first, put to music by E. Clarke Isley, is "The Soldier's Suit of Grey." In it, the female narrator assures her audience that even though the officers look more dashing, she prefers to honor the soldier lads.

1. I've seen some handsome uniforms deck'd off with buttons bright.
And some that are so very gay, they almost blind the sight;
But of these handsome uniforms I will not sing today.
My song is to each soldier lad, who wears a suit of grey!

Hurrah! Hurrah! Hurrah! Hurrah! For Southern boys we say,
And God bless ev'ry soldier lad who wears a suit of grey.[26]

"The Homespun Dress," set to the tune of "The Irish Jaunting Car" (which was also used by Harry Macarthy for "The Bonnie Blue Flag") typifies the "gutsy girl" response to the war. She is going to do whatever she can to further the war effort, regardless of the personal cost to her. Of course she likes to look pretty, but if the economy of a homespun dress and a palmetto hat are going to help her cause, she will make them and wear them. Perhaps her true character shows most clearly in the final verse, in which she offers advice to a nameless young man:

And now, young man, a word to you;
If you would win the fair,
Go to the field where honor calls,
And win your lady there.
Remember that our brightest smiles
Are for the true and brave,
And that our tears are all for those
Who fill a soldier's grave.[27]

25. "John Harrolson," on Bobby Horton, *Homespun Songs of the C.S.A.,* vol. 5 (audiocassette recording, Birmingham, Ala., 1993).
26. Carrie Bell Sinclair, "The Soldier's Suit of Grey," in Humphreys, *Songs,* 51–53.
27. "The Homespun Dress," attributed to Carrie Bell Sinclair, in Silber, *Songs,* 68.

If the songs we have examined are any indication, women played a significant, if often behind-the-scenes, role in the Civil War. Lyrics abound regarding their strengths. Yet perhaps the most important role played by women in furthering the war effort on both sides was inspirational. Mothers, wives, sisters, daughters—and their images, as conveyed by songs that emphasized them—were enormously successful in rallying the troops. Their influence in the minds of fighting men was substantial. But regarding their own feelings on war, perhaps the women's perspective could be best summed up by these lines from "The Southern Soldier Boy": "I hope for the best, and so do all whose hopes are in the field."

"An Inspiration to All"

New Hampshire's Third Regiment and Hilton Head Post Bands in Civil War South Carolina

Richard C. Spicer

Dispersed among libraries in New Hampshire and Washington, D.C., are three sets of small manuscript books, worn and undistinguished in appearance, that nevertheless constitute a rare musical treasure. Likely compiled from 1863 to 1864 and put to use at Hilton Head Post, an unlikely South Carolina Sea Island outpost, by a Union army band from New Hampshire, they form one of very few remaining complete sets of Civil War band books from either side of the conflict. The music they contain represents some of the best band music of the day, mostly arranged or written by Claudio Grafulla (1812–1880), a Minorcan immigrant who, by the outbreak of war, had achieved a national reputation as a band composer and conductor in New York. The first set, of twenty-two books (containing tunes 1–50), is at the Music Division of the Library of Congress; the second set, of twenty-one books (containing tunes 51–100), is at the New Hampshire Historical Society, Concord; and the third set, of seventeen books (containing tunes 101–33), is at the New Hampshire Antiquarian Society, Hopkinton. Among the other known sets of Union army band books are those of the Twenty-fifth Massachusetts Regiment and of the Wisconsin's Brodhead Brass Band (which became the brigade band for the First Brigade, Third Division, Fifteenth Army Corps); the only

This essay was published previously in *Historical New Hampshire,* vol. 54, nos. 1 and 2 (spring and summer 1999). The editors express their sincere appreciation for permission to reproduce it, and for assistance with illustrations, to the New Hampshire Historical Society.

Confederate army band books are those of the Twenty-sixth North Carolina Regiment of Salem. All contained Grafulla's music and are today used frequently for concerts and recordings.[1]

A century later, the Hilton Head band books were discovered with delight by those eager to revive the period-instrument performance of Civil War band music, a movement that began with Frederick Fennell's pioneering recording project in 1960 and 1962 with the Eastman Wind Ensemble, *The Civil War: Its Music and Its Sounds*.[2] More than forty years later, this and subsequent recordings continue to bring into our homes music long forgotten.

What neither band book nor recent recordings reveal, however, is the unusual and colorful history behind the books and the band, which is as interesting as the music itself. The band to which these books belonged was no ordinary organization. Stationed at the huge army base on Hilton Head Island in South Carolina, the Hilton Head Post Band was a superior musical outfit that earned a lasting reputation during its short existence from February 1863 to July 1865. It also enjoyed an unusually stable and luxurious life for an army band, by virtue of its affiliation with the stationary Department of the South and the support of its commanding officers.[3]

1. The books of the Twenty-fifth Massachusetts Regiment (at the American Antiquarian Society) are described in William Alfred Bufkin, "Union Bands of the Civil War (1862–1865): Instrumentation and Score Analysis" (Ph.D. diss., Louisiana State University, 1973); the books of Wisconsin's Brodhead Brass Band (at the Gorr Collection, University of Wisconsin Library) are described in Lavern John Wagner, "Volunteering Twice: The Brodhead, Wisconsin, Brass Band in the Civil War," *Journal of Band Research* 25, no. 2 (spring 1990): 22–37; the band books of the Twenty-sixth North Carolina Regiment of Salem are at the Moravian Music Foundation. For more on Grafulla's skill as a bandmaster and arranger, see Kenneth E. Olson, *Music and Musket: Bands and Bandsmen of the American Civil War* (Westport, Conn.: Greenwood Press, 1981), 228.

2. The project resulted in a set of LP records by Mercury Living Presence, rereleased in 1990 on CD (Mercury 432 59102). See also Frederick Fennell, "The Civil War: Its Music and Its Sounds," pts. 1–4, *Journal of Band Research* 4, no. 2 (spring 1968): 36–44; 5, no. 1 (fall 1968): 8–14; 5, no. 2 (spring 1969): 4–10; 6, no. 1 (fall 1969): 46–58.

3. The best general histories of the department's activities at Hilton Head include Robert Carse, *Department of the South: Hilton Head Island in the Civil War* (Hilton Head Island, S.C.: Impressions Printing, 1987); and Charles C. McCracken and Faith M. McCracken, eds., *The Forgotten History: A Photographic Essay on Civil War Hilton Head Island* (Hilton Head Island, S.C.: Time Again Publications, 1993).

Francis Harvey "Saxie" Pike, drum major of the Hilton Head Post Band, 1863–1865. "In the whole Army of the Potomac there was never such a Drum Major as Pike. . . . No one in a similar position seemed to have so adequate a conception of the dignity of the office." A member of Manchester's respected cornet band before the war, Saxie objected to the diminutive baton the state supplied him to lead its first troops to the front in 1861. As a result, he "was provided with a regular sky-scraper of a hat, and a baton, with a silver globe upon it" (*New Hampshire Statesman,* November 13, 1863). The inscribed baton is today in the Manchester (N.H.) Historic Association collections. *Manchester (N.H.) Historic Association.*

Early in the war, an impressive joint army-navy invasion had secured Hilton Head Island and adjacent Port Royal Sound as a base of operations for a blockade of the Confederate coastline. Easy victory ended there, however, for the obsessive attempt to capture Fort Sumter where the war began, and, in turn, the very "Cradle of Secession" it protected, nearby Charleston, ended in relative futility. Blockade runners carrying supplies for the city repeatedly evaded the Union navy, while on shore a costly campaign of progressive bombardment from hard-won island beachheads failed to force the surrender of Sumter; the Confederate garrison withdrew only when needed to oppose Sherman's approaching forces in February 1865.[4]

Meanwhile at Hilton Head, Union army commanders built up an impressive military outpost and supply base that, to the frustration of many, was to offer little gain for "Lincoln and Liberty," except perhaps as the site of an unexpected experiment in handling the many refugee slaves seeking the protection of Union forces. Regardless, some officers were able to enjoy the comforts of Sea Island life for the war's duration, and Hilton Head band members benefited directly from the easy life that resulted, even if not so much for the regular soldier. Almost anywhere else, musicians labored hard to assist exhausted surgeons in gruesome work during battle after battle; between engagements they tromped around in Virginia mud or were sent hurriedly west in cattle cars to malarial swamps surrounding Vicksburg.[5] Battle, sickness, and death were by no means strangers to the Sea Islands, but much of the time Hilton Head bandsmen would find themselves lazing in their tents or collecting seashells on a breezy beach to relieve the boredom of isolation and inactivity.

Through cheering concert and sweet serenade, the Post Band nevertheless provided, for troops and officers alike, an important morale-boosting service during this most musical of wars. Reactions to the

4. Two recent general histories include E. Milby Burton, *The Siege of Charleston, 1861–1865* (Columbia: University of South Carolina Press, 1970); and Stephen R. Wise, *Gate of Hell: Campaign for Charleston Harbor, 1863* (Columbia: University of South Carolina Press, 1994). The classic early history from the Confederate side is John Johnson, *The Defense of Charleston Harbor* (Charleston, S.C.: Walker, Evans, Cogswell, 1890).

5. See, for example, the manuscript memoirs of New Hampshire bandsmen Charles Watson Washburn of Hancock (American Antiquarian Society) and John Bachelder Bailey of Nashua (New Hampshire Historical Society).

band's activities clearly document the emotional power of music during wartime. It is interesting to learn, too, how the bandsmen themselves viewed their role, and in particular, how they justified to themselves this work that spared them the likely fate of an early grave far from home, even while other soldiers in their own regiments inevitably became battle casualties.

The Hilton Head Post Band was typical, too, as a product of earlier community music making. It was a nearly all-brass group that drew its membership from similarly composed town bands and performed comparable literature.[6] It is unusual, however, how many of its members moved into positions of musical leadership in their hometowns after the war. Not only did the band's leader, Gustavus Ingalls (1824–1903), choose his musicians well, but it would appear also that he provided them with a valuable musical experience that continued making a lasting contribution after the war's conclusion.

THE ORIGINS OF THE HILTON HEAD POST BAND

Formed in the midst of war in February 1863, the Hilton Head Post Band was actually a brigade band, technically the Second Brigade Band, Tenth Army Corps, New Hampshire Volunteers. At full strength, four regiments of a thousand men each typically composed a brigade, although regiments were rarely even close to full strength. The War Department had authorized the establishment of bands at the regimental level in May 1861, and Congress set their size at twenty-four members in August. The regimental bands lasted little more than a year, however, as an army steadily increasing in size yet lacking in military success found them too costly and unjustifiable an expense. By July 1862, Congress mandated the mustering out of regimental

6. Most late-eighteenth-century town bands were patterned as much as possible after European military models of "Harmoniemusik," or octets of paired oboes, clarinets, horns, and bassoons. The development of keyed and then valved brass instruments and improvements in their manufacture caused a musical revolution that rapidly swept through Europe and the United States alike. The first all-brass bands appeared in this country in the mid-1830s in New York. For an overview of these developments, see *The New Grove Dictionary of American Music* (1980 ed.), s.v. "Bands," by Raoul Camus; and Jon Newsom, "The American Brass Band Movement," *Quarterly Journal of the Library of Congress* 36, no. 2 (spring 1979): 114–39.

bands and authorized sixteen-member brigade bands, like the Post Band, as their only official replacement. This action reduced the number of military musicians by more than three-quarters and, indeed, represented tremendous savings.[7]

In the case of the Hilton Head Post Band, its name also reflected the payment of certain band members, in whole or in part, from the Hilton Head Post Fund, used at the discretion of the post commander. This supplementary support the brigade band enjoyed beyond prescribed army funds allowed it gradually to expand from the official sixteen-member size to involve another twenty-two musicians.[8]

A relationship of close continuity existed between the Post Band and the Third Regiment Band that preceded it, as indeed, between the latter and the town bands from which it had derived. Seven members of the Post Band, including its energetic, thirty-seven-year-old leader, Gustavus Ingalls of Concord, had served previously in the regimental band. Members of the Third Regiment Band came from several towns in the central part of the state, and Ingalls already boasted a distinguished career directing Concord bands. Seven members of the regimental band, in turn, had belonged to a cornet band in Fisherville, a manufacturing community just north of the state capital.[9] These seven, it seems, had formed an important core of the regimental band.

The Fisherville Cornet Band was founded in 1858 and, like a number of other antebellum bands throughout the state, benefited from the tutorship of itinerant bandmaster Alonzo Bond, a native of Hampstead, New Hampshire. Though based in Massachusetts during the two decades before the war, Bond's work took him to a remarkable number of New Hampshire towns, where he exerted singular influence on the development of the state's bands and upon many boys and men who would serve as Civil War musicians. Lorenzo Currier, the leader of the Fisherville Cornet Band, furnished his fine musicianship to the group, too, as he would later with the Hilton

7. Daniel Eldredge, *The Third New Hampshire and All about It* (Boston: E. B. Stillings, 1893), 995, 1002–3.

8. Band member Benjamin C. Stevens mentioned that when he arrived in May 1863 the fund from which his salary was paid amounted to $19,000. Benjamin C. Stevens to Father and Mother, Hilton Head, May 10, 1863, Benjamin C. Stevens Papers, 1861–1879, Perkins Library, Duke University, Durham, North Carolina.

9. Fisherville, a mill village partly in Concord and partly in Boscawen, was renamed Penacook in 1883.

The Third New Hampshire Band, photographed by Henry P. Moore, 1862. "Whatever New Hampshire does in the way of sending men, it is certain that she sends the best bands, and in all the regiments I have seen—and I have seen a few—I have never seen such instruments as the New Hampshire bands have, or heard such music" (John W. Odlin, December 1861). At far right is Billy Seabrook, or "William Butler, Boss," as he called himself; he was one of many refugee slaves who remained on the Seabrook plantation after its owners fled the island. "He is a bright, intelligent Negro, and has already learned to spell and read many words correctly. He has been provided with a uniform and carries the bass drum." *New Hampshire Historical Society.*

Head Post Band. But it was mainly because of Bond's involvement that the band developed a reputation that placed it "among the best . . . in the state." As one member recalled, "The old band, before the war, left many pleasant reminiscences. . . . Then the village was often enlivened by the promenade concerts given in their bandroom, notably so when Alonzo Bond was the teacher."[10]

10. John C. Linehan, "The Fisherville Cornet Band," in David Arthur Brown, *The History of Penacook, N.H., from Its First Settlement in 1734 up to 1900* (Concord,

Though greater challenges awaited those band members destined to serve at Hilton Head, already the Fisherville Cornet Band was no stranger to adventure. A visit to Portsmouth in 1859 found the band becalmed on a schooner headed for the Isles of Shoals, losing overboard much of what they had sampled earlier at Frank Jones's newly established brewery.[11] A more sobering adventure just after the outbreak of war provided unsettling moments as well, when the band learned to play on horseback to accompany the brilliantly uniformed Governor's Horse Guards. Formed in November 1859, this group had as its primary function the privilege of escorting the governor to his inauguration. For the first such procession in June 1860, the Guards had hired Hall's Band of Boston, under Lyme native and keyed-bugle soloist D. C. Hall. In 1861, however, the Guards opted for the local Fisherville band, and member John C. Linehan (who later served in the regimental band at Hilton Head) reported the uncertain results: "Not half a dozen members had ever mounted a horse, and now, men grown, to be expected to ride and play too, it was too much." Nevertheless, "horses [were] procured, and the band went into training. It was a moving spectacle. The moving, however, for a time was from the horses to the ground . . . but [the bandsmen] persevered and succeeded"—all except for one unfortunate musician who had to be taken to the hospital later that day.[12]

Not long after, Gustavus Ingalls received authorization from the governor to recruit musicians for the Third Regiment's band. By August 1861, the troops were ready for transport to the front and, in early September, a "Home Guard and Serenade Band" that would remain in Concord escorted the Third Regiment with its newly formed

---

N.H.: Rumford Press, 1902), 247–50. Sources found so far indicate that, between 1835 (possibly) and the Civil War, Alonzo Bond led bands in New Hampshire communities as widely separated as Littleton (1835?), New London (1839–1842), Milford (1840s), Portsmouth (1856), and Fisherville (1858). His music was also known and performed in Manchester; he performed in dance bands with bandmaster and keyed bugle soloist D. C. Hall of Lyme; and he was a friend of Samuel Graves of Winchester, the first American manufacturer of brass and woodwind instruments to seriously challenge the European market.

11. Ibid., 251.

12. James O. Lyford, "The Governor's Horse Guards," in James O. Lyford, ed., *History of Concord, New Hampshire* (Concord, N.H.: Rumford Press, 1903), vol. 1, Appendix, iii–iv, quoting John C. Linehan.

military band to the depot. While awaiting the train's departure, the two bands played back and forth to one another strains of "Auld Lang Syne" and "Home, Sweet Home."[13] The troops traveled by train and boat through New England to Long Island, and from there to Baltimore, Washington, and Annapolis, where they departed under sealed orders in late October for their Sea Island destination.

All along the way, cheering crowds and performing bands buoyed the spirits of the troops, and local citizenry offered generous hospitality. On Long Island, the New Hampshire band "serenaded the fair donors" to thank local residents who had "attended to our wants with as much eagerness as if we were their own kin."[14] In Baltimore, where a mob not long before had attacked Massachusetts troops and killed a few soldiers, the band played "our favorite 'Camp Quickstep,'" as the regiment began its march through the city.[15] One band member recalled a memorable moment in the nation's capital, when "at dress parade . . . one evening President Lincoln visited us. At no time during our term of service was 'Hail to the Chief' played with more feeling and spirit than at this visit from our commander in chief." Finally, in Annapolis, as six large steamers lay in the river ready to transport the Third Regiment and others southward, the band's expert clarinetist, Karl Krebs, "played the Mockingbird at dress parade."[16]

Eleven months after setting out from Concord, the band's tour of duty in South Carolina ended abruptly following the order of July 1862 eliminating regimental bands. As early as December, bandsmen were concerned about rumors that this might happen, but when the time came for a decision, interestingly enough, not one member of the Third Regiment Band voted for the option of reorganizing as a brigade band.[17] All went home in early September. While the band's

13. Henry S. Hamilton, *Reminiscences of a Veteran* (Concord, N.H.: Republican Press Association, 1897), 131.

14. Ruthven W. Houghton, "Transcription of the Civil War Journals of Ruthven W. Houghton, 3rd New Hampshire Volunteers," Marjorie Ladd, comp., New Hampshire Historical Society, 1997–029, September 4, 1861, 7.

15. Hamilton, *Reminiscences,* 133, 134.

16. Anonymous War Diary, 1861–1862, Third New Hampshire Volunteers, MS 34–588, South Carolina Historical Society, Charleston, South Carolina.

17. Odlin to friends, December 26 and December 30, 1861, in *Concord Independent Democrat,* January 9, 1862.

mustering-out on August 27 was an emotional experience for all, "most . . . were glad to return to their homes and friends in the old Granite State."[18] The local garrison newspaper, too, lamented the loss, but noted laconically the substantial savings that resulted from the elimination of the regimental bands:

> Congress towards the close of its last session set itself briskly to playing tunes on the economies, and turning the key of retrenchment, wherever there was opportunity for staving off army expenditures. Among other methods of barring the public money chest and stopping the holes through which it was becoming empty, a ban was placed upon regimental bands. Without casting any slur upon the usefulness of musicians, we cannot but endorse the action of our M.C.'s. The minimum estimate of the sum devoted to payment of regimental bands last year exceeded $4,000,000, and in view of the vast increase of the army, had the old system continued in force, the money expended would swell that sum to an extent altogether disproportionate to the benefit which music confers. Thus it will be seen that it was not simply a crotchet of Congress to take note of this matter.[19]

Immediately following its return to Concord, the Third Regiment Band gave a "Promenade Concert" in front of the statehouse and, so far as is known, this was that band's last official function.[20] Ingalls, however, was determined to continue on at Hilton Head. By early December, he had obtained authorization to recruit a brigade band, and on January 15, 1863, the following notice appeared in Concord's *Independent Democrat:*

> BRIGADE BAND. We learn that G. W. Ingalls, Band Master of the 3d Reg't Band, is organizing a Band for General Terry, the present Commandant of the Po[s]t, at Hilton Head S.C. The popularity of the 3d Reg't Band has secured to him the privilege of furnishing this Band. He is arranging to furnish both Brass and String Bands for the purpose of giving concerts, &c. A few more are wanted. Musicians who play a variety of instruments can obtain good situations. We have no doubts of his success, and continue to sustain the reputation of furnishing the best band in the Department.

18. Eldredge, *Third New Hampshire,* 994; Hamilton, *Reminiscences,* 171.
19. *Port Royal New South,* August 30, 1862.
20. *Concord Independent Democrat,* September 11, 1862.

By February 1863, the new band was organized, and when they left Concord on the twentieth of that month, they were the "first brigade band sent out as such from the 'Old Granite State.' "[21] Within another month, Ingalls had permission to hire ten additional musicians and to purchase instruments from William Hall and Son of New York. Eight of the new musicians arrived at Hilton Head by steamer in mid-April. In September, Ingalls obtained authorization to hire yet another ten musicians and to purchase horns for them, as well as to have instruments repaired that already were in use.[22]

Even with all the new personnel, Ingalls's brigade band showed strong continuity with his earlier regimental band. In fact, the regimental band already had acted officially for the brigade during its service. This was probably because the Third Regiment's colonel, Enoch Q. Fellows, became commander of the post after arrival at Hilton Head but remained partial to the band of his regiment. One musician in the Third Regiment Band specified the expansive scope of its duties in a letter to his brother: "I think that there are more bands than there is any need of. We have 4 in our brigade and ours is the only one of them which has anything to do. We do the brigade duty." Another Third Regiment musician described the brigade band, a composite of four regimental bands plus the drum corps of a fifth regiment in this brigade, as consisting of "ninety-one in all, and under the direction of Mr. Ingalls, our leader." He then opined: "Our band is, of course, the nucleus, being the best in the brigade and as our Colonel says, 'the very best in the whole division.' "[23]

21. Ibid., February 26, 1863.

22. Eldredge, *Third New Hampshire,* 260, 996–97. Receipts show that twenty instruments originally used by the Third Regiment Band were shipped back to Hilton Head in June 1863 (New Hampshire Division of Records Management and Archives). What band then used them is not clear, for this postdates by three months Ingalls's trip to New York to procure new instruments from William Hall and Son. For information about these makers, see Nancy Groce, *Musical Instrument Makers of New York: A Directory of Eighteenth- and Nineteenth-Century Urban Craftsmen,* Annotated Reference Tools in Music 4 (Stuyvesant, N.Y.: Pendragon Press, 1991), 70. The only instrument now remaining that verifiably was used either by the Third Regiment or the Post Band is a drum played by Nathan M. Gove.

23. Letter from the Third N.H. Regiment, Hilton Head, March 13, 1862, *Concord Independent Democrat,* March 27, 1862; Eldredge, *Third New Hampshire,* 87, 728–29, 994; Lewis Henry Stark to Brother Hen, Hilton Head, February 5, [1862], Goffstown Historical Society, Goffstown New Hampshire; Odlin to friends, December 29, 1861, in *Concord Independent Democrat,* January 9, 1862. Throughout

The Hilton Head Post Band, probably photographed by bandsman Jacob R. Foster not long after its arrival in South Carolina in 1863. The regimental band and this brigade band that succeeded it shared a leader and seven musicians in common. The new band served four regiments and enjoyed the favor of the post's commander. Saxie Pike, sporting his legendary hat and baton, proudly leads the musicians wearing their own new brigade hats. *New Hampshire Historical Society.*

In any case, whether by virtue of continuity in function or in personnel, the Post Band remained closely associated with the earlier Third New Hampshire Regiment Band and was considered by the soldiers virtually its direct lineal descendant. Men of the Third were "overjoyed" whenever the Post Band was stationed near the regiment, as during the Morris Island campaign in the summer of 1863. "We yet called it 'our band,'" commented the regimental historian. "These music dispensers filled a place none others could."[24]

---

this essay, idiosyncracies of spelling and punctuation are presented as in the original letters; any changes made for clarity are indicated with brackets.

24. Eldredge, *Third New Hampshire,* 997.

The daily experiences of bandsmen in both regimental and brigade bands in the Sea Islands were remarkably similar. Among the contemporary sources that permit us to piece together the history of the two bands, most useful, of course, are the words of the bandsmen themselves—the musicians who shouldered the fashionable "back-firing" horns and fingered the books that remain their documentary legacy. Three band members wrote letters home to relatives in New Hampshire that provide contrasting personal accounts of their wartime experiences: John W. Odlin of Concord, Lewis Henry Stark of Goffstown, and Benjamin C. Stevens of Franklin.[25] Nineteen-year-old Odlin served as second principal musician—the second ranking member—in the regimental band from October 1861 to April 1862, when ill health forced him to return to New Hampshire before the band's discharge. The letters he sent home to family and friends provide the only contemporary account of the band's journey southward. Concord's *Independent Democrat* published these in a regular column titled "Letters from Port Royal." Twenty-year-old Stark first played E-flat cornet in the regimental band (1861–1862) and returned to join the Post Band in September 1864 when Ingalls recruited a second time. Twenty-four-year-old Stevens was a mechanic who joined the Post Band in 1863 as a hired member from the initial recruitment, but after becoming bored and dissatisfied with life at Hilton Head, he arranged to leave that fall; even though his letters, therefore, span only a four-month period, they offer a unique perspective at a time not covered by the accounts of other musicians.

Contemporary sources also include several wartime newspapers the invading army produced (notably, the *New South* and the *Palmetto Herald* of Port Royal and the *Free South* of Beaufort), valuable in providing official local commentary. Finally, the now-famous photographs

25. Over-the-shoulder, or "back-firing" horns, with bells projecting behind the player, had become popular in the 1840s and 1850s among military-style bands that paraded frequently, so that those marching behind could still hear and keep in time to the music. A good collection of illustrations is found in Robert Garofalo and Mark Elrod, *A Pictorial History of Civil War Era Musical Instruments and Military Bands* (Charleston, W.Va.: Pictorial Histories, 1985). Letters by John W. Odlin were published in the *Concord Independent Democrat,* November 21, 1861, to March 27, 1862; Civil War letters of Lewis Henry Stark and William Frank Stark are in the Goffstown Historical Society; Benjamin C. Stevens Papers, 1861–1879, are in Perkins Library, Duke University, Durham, North Carolina.

taken during several sojourns to the Sea Islands by Concord photographer Henry P. Moore provide a complementary visual perspective. Post Band member Jacob R. Foster, who after the war would become a professional photographer in Concord, also captured a few images with the "apparatus" he sent home to obtain.[26]

Later in life, several bandsmen recorded their recollections. B-flat cornet player Henry S. Hamilton (an English immigrant who later married into the Stark family of Goffstown) and B-flat bass player John C. Linehan served only in the regimental band. Although their accounts were written more than three decades later, they nevertheless provide interesting anecdotes not recorded elsewhere. Mechanic David Arthur Brown, an E-flat cornet player from Fisherville, was second leader of the regimental band and a hired member of the Post Band throughout its duration; his later history of Penacook is the source for comprehensive information on bands in that community. Finally, Third New Hampshire regimental historian Daniel Eldredge compiled important personnel and organizational documentation outlining the development of both bands.[27]

ARRIVAL IN SOUTH CAROLINA

Travel to Hilton Head necessarily involved a sea voyage of several days even from Annapolis, where the regimental band embarked as part of the fleet of fifty vessels forming the Port Royal expedition. Not long after the fleet's departure in late October 1861, a sudden gale off Cape Hatteras struck with fury, scattering the ships for days and sinking four vessels and nearly a fifth. Bandsmen aboard the

26. See W. Jeffrey Bolster and Hilary Anderson, *Soldiers, Sailors, Slaves, and Ships: The Civil War Photographs of Henry P. Moore* (Concord: New Hampshire Historical Society, 1999). On Foster, see Benjamin C. Stevens to Father and Mother, May 24, 1863, and July 12, 1863, and Concord City Directory, 1872. The author thanks Hilary Anderson for sharing information about Foster and his work.

27. Hamilton, *Reminiscences;* John C. Linehan, "War Pictures," published in seven parts in the *Granite Monthly,* vols. 18–19 (June–December 1895) (before the war, Hamilton served in the U.S. Army with a first cousin of Lewis Henry Stark, who persuaded him to move to Goffstown); Brown, *History of Penacook,* and *The Staccato,* Fisherville, New Hampshire, March 2, 1876, and May 2, 1878; Eldredge, *Third New Hampshire.*

steamer *Atlantic* weathered the storm without serious incident, bunking in her hold near the vessel's hospital. One night, they listened not only to the whining wind, but also to the pathetic cries of a young lad delirious with a raging fever, calling continuously to his mother until death relieved his suffering just before dawn.[28]

The brilliant capture of Confederate batteries surrounding the entrance to Port Royal Sound in but a few hours with little loss of life is recounted in many sources. Not so well known, perhaps, is that the Third Regiment Band in multiple concert with bands aboard other ships heralded the hoisting of the U.S. flag ashore at Hilton Head's Fort Walker. As recorded by one soldier on the *Atlantic:* "1861 Nov 8th 2:½ P.M. The battery has surrendered and the glorious old Stars and Stripes are floating once more in South Carolina Gov Pickens boast to the contrary notwithstanding. Bands playing S[tar] S[pangled] Banner."[29]

Whether bandsmen arrived with the Port Royal expedition or came by later steamship, the exotic landscape and inhabitants of South Carolina's Sea Islands were a source of immediate curiosity for these impressionable New Hampshire farmboys. Some, it would appear, had never even seen a saltwater beach, much less black slaves in the sultry South. Bandsmen quickly conveyed impressions of their new surroundings to wondering relatives at home. After confinement aboard ship for nearly three weeks, Stark probably spoke for all as he rejoiced simply to be ashore:

> We are safely encamped on the "Sacred Soil" of South Carolina and I think they can't drive us off easily. There were only 1400 Rebels here when we came and they have all gone and have left all of thier stores behind. They didn't even have time to spike thier guns. There were only 20 killed and wounded on our side[.] Don't know the loss of the enemy. Our Regt didn't land for two days after the fight. So we didn't have an opportunity to see much[.] I saw one poor fellow's head that was all smashed in pieces by a shell. This island is what would be called beautiful by some, but I haven't seen any place yet that comes up to New England in my estimation. Maybe it's because my home is there.[30]

28. Hamilton, *Reminiscences,* 139.
29. Anonymous War Diary, 1861–1862, South Carolina Historical Society.
30. Stark to Sister, Hilton Head, November 11, 1861.

Henry Hamilton waxed eloquently about the flora, but was less enthusiastic about the island's fauna: "Some of its products, which yielded most abundantly, could willingly have been dispensed with, such as alligators, wood-ticks, fleas, and mosquitoes."[31]

As the band settled in to do its work, the unaccustomed weather became a subject of comment as well. Summer's heat arrived as early as April, only adding to the discomfort:

> At night one could not sleep, as the heat was so oppressive and the fleas so numerous. In order, if possible, to get a little rest, many of the men made bags from their blankets, and crawled into them, drawing the string around their necks. Immense mosquitoes kept humming and stinging until one was glad when daylight appeared, only to be again tortured by myriads of midgets [midges] crawling into the eyes, nose, and mouth, and causing intense pain.[32]

During the hottest weather, bandsmen discovered that it helped to set small evergreen trees around their tents and to confine themselves to the shade within. When winter brought the onset of the rainy season, feelings of confinement and boredom prevailed. During his last January at Hilton Head, with "nothing to do, but to eat our bread and rice," Stark found plenty of time to write his sister: "Very exciting life isn't it?"[33]

CAMP LIFE

Such extreme weather was only occasional, however, and spring and fall on the Sea Islands were more reminiscent of summer in New Hampshire. For the most part, bandsmen had it well off—and they knew it—with "very good" floored tents, wooden bedsteads, chairs and tables, sinks for washing, and quarters near the shore refreshed daily with a good afternoon sea breeze that chased away the midday heat. "We live first rate for soldiers and have excellent quarters," noted

31. Hamilton, *Reminiscences,* 141.
32. Ibid., 151.
33. Stark to Sister May, Hilton Head, January 17, 1865.

Stark in the fall of 1864.[34] Stevens had developed perspective on this matter already by the time he settled in with the Post Band in the spring of 1863, having experienced a year of war in a Massachusetts regimental band that moved around with the Army of the Potomac in Maryland and Virginia:

> We have got just as good a location as Gen Hunter or Gen Terry. Our quarters are only about eight or ten rods from the seashore and a finer beach you never saw. We get as good air as comes across the sea. It hasn't seemed as though I was in the army since I have been here and I can't make it. I am inclined to think that the farther any one gets from Washington the better he is off. At any rate I have no desire to exchange my place with any Army of the Potomac man at present.[35]

Proximity to the beach provided additional recreational possibilities. Stevens went bathing two or three times a week, generally in the morning when it was cool: "It is nice fun to go into the water here it is so warm." He also found the beach near their tents "a nice place . . . to get shelles and stones" and enjoyed collecting seaside treasures to send home. Twice, he took time to explain such foreign phenomena as the formation of coral and appearance of starfish to land-locked family members, who must never before have seen such oddities: "I have just been sealing up a small box of shells to send home by mail which I hope you will have the good luck to get. I put in a Star-fish with the shells. You will have to be careful and not break it as it is quite brittle. I suppose you will think it don't look much like a fish or any kind of a living creature. . . . I have got two more drying on the side of my tent which I got the other day."[36]

For other pleasures, there was always good eating, and plenty of it, too, at a post where the first commanding officer was well known for his interest in the garrison bakery. A cook assigned to the Post Band, in fact, was lauded as an "ornament to his profession." Stevens

34. Stark to Mother, Hilton Head, November 3, 1864; Stevens to Father and Mother, Hilton Head, April 23, 1863; Stark to Sister, Hilton Head, October 11 and 25, 1864.

35. Stevens to Father and Mother, Hilton Head, May 24, 1863.

36. Stevens to Mother, Hilton Head, May 31, 1863; Stevens to Sister, Hilton Head, June 16, 1863; Stevens to Father and Mother, Hilton Head, July 19, 1863.

elaborated in letters to concerned relatives at home about the meals served in camp:

> I guess it is pretty near dinner time now as I hear the dishes rattle out in the cook house. I wish you could be down here and see how we live. Our living is as good as anyone need ask for. Potatoes and beef, nice soft bread and butter and pickles for breakfast—Potatoes and beefsteak &c for dinner. Boiled rice or hominy for supper with bread and butter &c. We have tea or coffee (just which we choose) at every meal. I do not use any coffee at all. We have got a good brick oven, and we have baked beens every Sunday morning. We have a table which reaches the whole length of the cook house and will seat the whole band. Each man has a knife and fork an earthen plate a cup and saucer. So you see we have everything here pretty much our own way.[37]

Bandsmen could pay three dollars per month for extra items like buttermilk, which the government did not furnish; additional fresh produce, like watermelons, green corn, and blackberries, was procured locally "from the colored people, either by purchase or otherwise." Sometimes, band members in their spare time went fishing. Hamilton appears to have had greater appreciation for certain local delicacies than did native New Englanders more used to the taste and texture of an old-fashioned boiled dinner: "In the creeks we found the periwinkle, a delicious shell-fish, which in the English market is the choicest and most high-priced of mollusks, but only one of the band indulged in eating 'snails,' as they were termed by the rest."[38]

Stevens at first enjoyed the easy life: "The longer I stay and the more I see the better I like." There was another side to life at Hilton Head, however. Beyond musical duties, the band members had very little to do, and their reports of boredom and inactivity were recurrent. Within two weeks, Stevens amended his initial enthusiasm, reporting that the island was "about the dullest place that I ever got into in my life—in the army I mean—There is nothing to be seen here except the vessels in the harbor and a few niggers strolling around camp." By the next month, Stevens had taken the initiative to fix up his tent

37. Stevens to Sister, Hilton Head, June 16, 1863.

38. Stark to Mother, Hilton Head, November 3, 1864; Hamilton, *Reminiscences,* 168; Stevens to Mother, Hilton Head, May 31, 1863; Hamilton, *Reminiscences,* 153–54.

Field music cookery and quarters, 1862. Henry P. Moore, a photographer visiting from Concord, captured in his views of camp life the fifers and drummers of the Third Regiment near their "cook tent" awaiting dinner. Food was often the topic of letters home to family and friends, and meals were eagerly anticipated as an antidote to boredom. *New Hampshire Historical Society.*

with a drafting board and began work, when off duty, on detailed drawings for a "machine"—probably a knitting machine related to his previous work at the shop of Walter Aiken, an inventor and textile entrepreneur back home in Franklin. "I have got a good place to work and all the time I want, which is at least nine hours a day and if I don't make something that will work, it will be [only] because I don't know what I am doing."[39]

39. Stevens to Friends at Home, Hilton Head, April 25, 1863; Stevens to Sister, Hilton Head, May 9, 1863; Stevens to Father and Mother, Hilton Head, June 10 and July 12, 1863; Stevens to Father and Mother, Hilton Head, July 12, 1863. After the war in 1873, Stevens filed a patent for an "improvement in knitting machines" (U.S. Patent No. 148,388, dated March 10, 1874; application filed September 5, 1873). In 1881, the Franklin Directory listed him as a machinist and mechanical engineer, making "power knitting machines, some of his own designs." "Franklin and Franklin Falls: A Brief Historical Sketch, with a Glance at Its Business Industries," p. 7, in

By the bandsmen's own descriptions, theirs was a lazy lifestyle not generally conducive to application of the New England work ethic. In the first winter of war, Josiah Dadmun confessed to his sweetheart that "I am having fine times here, plenty to eat, and but little work to do. This is just the kind of life to suit me, and exactly agrees with my lazy disposition!" Two years later as a member the Post Band, Stevens experienced the same: "My bed makes a nice lounge to lye on daytimes when it is so hot—I generally have a nap right after dinner, or after rehearsal." Boredom plagued non-bandsmen, too. One soldier actually confided in his journal: "I would rather a leaden ball would terminate my existence, than the monotony and contagion of camp life."[40]

After five months in the Sea Islands, Stark was pleased to report home, as a sign of good health, that he had gained ten pounds. Somehow, Stevens had managed to avoid growing fat; he even lost ten pounds during his four-month sojourn. By summer's end, however, he was eager to return home: "By George if I ever get back into New Hampshire to stay where I can get all the milk and potatoes I want, I shall expect to live to be a hundred years old. I haven't seen any place that I would swap for old New Hampshire."[41]

Unwelcome disruptions to camp routine did occur from time to time, as when the Post Band was ordered successively to Morris and Folly islands in the summer of 1863 to accompany the officers waging war on coastal Confederate batteries. Other excursions band members undertook more resembled pleasure outings. Odlin described the friendly reception he and other musicians received while exploring one of Hilton Head's many forts. "The guard was kindly disposed and said, 'Seein' you are Band fellers I'll let you in.'" On another occasion one of the band members—it was most likely Odlin, one of the most versatile and ablest musicians in the regimental band—

1881 *Franklin Directory;* personal communication, Richard Candee, May 1999; see also Richard M. Candee, "The 'Shaker Sock': A New Hampshire Contribution to Nineteenth-Century Machine Knitting," *Historical New Hampshire* 52, nos. 3 and 4 (fall/winter 1997): 61–78.

40. Josiah Dadmun to Susie, Hilton Head, December 14, 1861, New Hampshire Historical Society, 1997–013; Stevens to Sister, Hilton Head, June 16, 1863; Houghton, "Transcription of Journals," 41 (February 12, 1862).

41. Stark to Sister, Hilton Head, February 2, 1865; Stevens to Sister, Morris Island, August 11, 1863.

played the organ in a mock service at a church he found while exploring local plantations.[42] Towards the war's end, band members enjoyed accompanying their officers on tours of the coastline to Fort Pulaski, near Savannah. Such exceptions to the tedium of life on the Sea Islands were few.

MUSICAL DUTIES

This is not to say that the bandsmen did not perform important functions at Hilton Head. To the contrary, both the Third Regiment and Post bands achieved solid musical reputations that were widely recognized and appreciated. The earlier band's performance "drew tears or cheers. 'Twas an *inspiration to all* who stepped to its music, whether at dress-parade, review, or on the march. The weariness of a march was largely diminished by its cheering notes."[43] In December 1861, soldiers constructing fortifications, for example, enjoyed the accompaniment of the band as they returned to camp at noon and night.[44] The band proved its worth again when the regiment reconnoitered St. John's Island in June 1862: "We were weary, nigh unto death, as we then thought—in fact, had not more than got half rested from our terrible march of the 2d; but the music of the band as it struck upon our ears in that dismal, dreary, God-forsaken place, lifted us at once out of our weariness and cheered us along in the aforesaid review, which we all thought was sheer nonsense and worse than useless."[45]

By the late spring of 1863, the reorganized brigade band was at Hilton Head ready to play at the behest of the post's officers, who clearly appreciated the band's performances. Stark observed in 1864 that the officers thought so much of the new band that they "will do almost anything for us that we ask them to which is quite an item in the army." Perhaps the best indication of the Post Band's importance and popularity was the commandant's decision to augment the band

42. Odlin to Friends, January 19, 1862, in *Concord Independent Democrat,* January 30, 1862; Hamilton, *Reminiscences,* 154.
43. Eldredge, *Third New Hampshire,* 993 (emphasis added).
44. *Concord Independent Democrat,* December 26, 1861.
45. Eldredge, *Third New Hampshire,* 994.

beyond the officially authorized sixteen members, "to increase the number and effectiveness." Stevens commented repeatedly in letters home that the band was playing well, tackling difficult music, and continuing to improve, calling it "just such a band as I shouldn't be ashamed of anywhere." In short, "Every body here considers the Post band a little ahead of any thing that has been in this *show* down here since it first started."[46]

The official functions of the Hilton Head bands included regular parade duty for guard mounting at eight o'clock in the morning and other drills, dress parades, and troop reviews; serenading the officers and serving, at their frequent request, at private gatherings; weekly concerts at the hospital and at the end of the pier; and providing solemn accompaniment for funerals and an occasional execution. Members of the regimental band were known to have formed smaller ensembles as well, including a quadrille band that accompanied singers and, perhaps, as the name would suggest, an occasional dance. By 1863, members of the Post Band had a "good large building to rehearse in," which they did twice a day. There were many times, however, when bandsmen had the day to themselves after morning guard mounting.[47]

A band's principal responsibility was always to the officers, and fortunately the musicians at Hilton Head had supportive superiors. The Third Regiment Band enjoyed the favor of the regimental (and later brigade) commander, Enoch Fellows. The Post Band was affiliated with General Alfred Howe Terry's brigade in Hunter's Division. The band played three times a week for an hour near General Terry's

46. Stark to Sister, Port Royal, October 25, 1864. Stevens to Friends at Home, Hilton Head, April 25, 1863; to Father and Mother, Hilton Head, June 19, 1863; and to Father and Mother, June 25, 1863; Stevens to Father and Mother, June 25, 1863 (emphasis in original). General Terry, on March 10, 1863, authorized the enlistment of five additional musicians and the hiring of five others (including Benjamin C. Stevens); and the Post Council of Administration at Hilton Head, on September 8 of that year, recommended, and the post commandant approved, the hiring of ten additional musicians (including Lewis Henry Stark). In addition, at various times, soldiers were detailed from other regiments to further augment its ranks. Eldredge, *Third New Hampshire,* 1002.

47. Hamilton, *Reminiscences,* 149; Stevens to Friends at Home, Hilton Head, April 25, 1863; Stevens to Sister, Hilton Head, June 16, 1863. Note also that in Concord in 1863, Ingalls was recruiting for a string band as well as a brass band. *Concord Independent Democrat,* January 15, 1863.

quarters and accompanied him on excursions away from the base as well.[48] Stevens noted with respect that Terry was "a fine musician himself and know[s] what good music is and that is the reason why he goes in for the extra's in getting up a band."[49]

When the band traveled to Morris Island in August 1863, it went with General Quincy A. Gillmore, newly appointed commander of the entire Department of the South, and played at his headquarters every evening as its main duty.[50] As the troops worked their way up the coast toward Sumter that summer, war was becoming serious business, giving even the bandsmen pause for thought. En route to Morris Island, Stevens clearly understood the advantages of his position as a musician: "There are quite a number of officers on board the boat here now and they all look rather 'blue' for I suppose they know that they will be sure to have some fighting to do soon. Our band played them a few peices of music this morning. I have been thinking that I wouldn't give four Brass Buttons for a commission [during] these times." Two weeks later, he continued to be thankful for his musical abilities. "I'm for the Union and the *constitution* but I don't mean to get my head shot off if somebody's else will do just as well."[51]

Playing for officers had a practical side, too. Performances earned income for the band: a colonel of the Corps of Engineers once paid thirty dollars for three-quarters of an hour's work during which the band performed five tunes. Bandsmen also knew that it was important "to keep on the right side" of the officers. A close relationship sometimes resulted, especially when, after a serenade, an officer entertained the band within his private quarters. As fighting on Morris Island intensified in the middle of July 1863, Stevens learned with sorrow that Brigadier General George Strong had been wounded, for, as Stevens reported to his parents, he had recently enjoyed the "honer of shaking hands, and taking a glass of wine with [the general] a short time ago."[52] It worked the other way, too, as bandsmen lifted

48. Stark to Sister, Port Royal, October 25, 1864.

49. Stevens to Father and Mother, Hilton Head, April 23, 1863.

50. Stevens to Father and Mother, Morris Island, August 3 and 21, 1863.

51. Stevens to Father and Mother, Steamer Delaware, July 30, 1863; Stevens to Father and Mother, Morris Island, August 11, 1863.

52. Stevens to Father and Mother, Hilton Head, May 24, 1863; Stark to Sister, Port Royal, October 25, 1864; Stevens to Father and Mother, Hilton Head, July 19, 1863.

the spirits of the officers during their times of loss: "On Thursday night of last week the Post Band serenaded Colonel Peter Dunbar, at his quarters in Merchants' Row. . . . He thanked them most heartily for the flattering compliment they had paid, and for the relief afforded by their sweet strains from the sadness occasioned by letters he had just received, announcing the death of friends in the Virginia armies."[53]

Officers sometimes vied for the services of a particular band. During the war's first year, a famous rivalry existed between officers of New Hampshire's Third and Fourth Regiments, both with excellent bands stationed at Hilton Head. The band of the Fourth was under the baton of bandmaster Walter Dignam, director of the famed Manchester Cornet Band, a crack musical outfit that blossomed under his leadership during the decade before the war.[54] One member of the Third Regiment Band recalled that whenever the two bands came together for a contest, "we reserved for our last piece 'The Mocking Bird,' with trills and warbles by the inimitable Carl [Karl] Krebs on the clarinet, which always settled, for the time being, the disputed question."[55]

By the spring of 1863, camp life had settled into a monotonous enough routine that the post commander instructed the brigade band to play at the end of the pier every Wednesday and Saturday evening at six o'clock.[56] The band also played twice a week at the large general hospital, starting about sunset and playing about half an hour, "as long as we can see to read our music."[57] As a result of the Morris Island campaign, the hospital at this time was full of wounded men:

> There is a good many sesesh wounded [at the hospital,] captured in the last battles on Morris Island, so the last time we played there

53. *Port Royal Palmetto Herald,* June 2, 1864.
54. Two sets of band books (1852, 1854) used by the Manchester Cornet Band and a smaller set used by the earlier Manchester Brass Band in the late 1840s are now in the collection of the Manchester Historic Association. They are among those used by period instrument ensembles for performance and recording (e.g., *Homespun America,* VoxBox CDX 5088; and *Our Musical Past,* Library of Congress OMP 101/102).
55. Hamilton, *Reminiscences,* 148–49.
56. *Port Royal New South,* May 30, 1863.
57. Stevens to Father and Mother, Hilton Head, July 21, 1863.

> we gave them a taste of Yankee Doodle and the Star Spangled Banner. One of our boys who is sick in the hospital said that when we were playing Yankee Doodle, one of our soldiers asked a wounded rebel who was lying by the side of him how he liked it. He said it was a good tune, and well played, but it was d[amne]d near played out.[58]

In March 1864, enlisted men from the Forty-eighth New York Regiment (part of the Second Brigade, as was the Third New Hampshire) formed the Barton Dramatic Association and opened the "Union Theater" at Hilton Head. An orchestra under Mr. Henry Murphy began the first evening's program with "Gen. Gilmore's Grand March." For subsequent theatrical performances, ranging from melodrama to popular song, a "Third New Hampshire Band" would furnish the orchestra "in the absence of the Post Band, away on special duty"; exactly what ensemble this meant is not clear.[59] In early April, the Post Band held a benefit concert to reimburse its "considerable outlay in providing suitable music" for this new undertaking. And, during an absence of several members of the dramatic group in June, the band is said to have performed with "the best vocal talent procurable" to continue to provide suitable entertainment for the camp.[60]

Band members received an occasional furlough, and some were lucky enough, when ill, to take a steamer home. As the first winter of war dragged on, a few members, like Stark, took the experience in stride and determined to "*see it out,*" just as well contented as if at home, but most members had had enough and were already eager to leave. One malcontent, in fact, tried thinly disguised theatrics to push the system: "One of our band members has got his discharge and is feeling first rate I tell you. He played his game pretty well. He enlisted with a *good* set of false teeth and as he began to get a little sick of this kind of life his teeth began to *come out (accidentally of course)* and at last he got so many of them out that he *pretended* that he couldn't play and accordingly g[o]t discharged."[61]

58. Stevens to Father and Mother, Hilton Head, July 19, 1863.
59. *Port Royal Palmetto Herald,* March 17, 1864; March 31, 1864.
60. *Port Royal New South,* April 2, 1864; *Port Royal Palmetto Herald,* June 2, 1864.
61. Stark to Brother Hen, Hilton Head, February 5, [1862] (emphasis in original).

BATTLE, SICKNESS, AND DEATH

Actual illness was widespread at Hilton Head, particularly in the form of dysentery and malaria, which affected civilian and soldier alike. Neither band ever lost any members, but most of the musicians were taken with fevers or other sickness at one time or another. By the time of the regimental band's voyage home in September 1862, drummer boy Nathan Gove was dangerously ill with malaria. He managed to recover enough to return south with the Post Band in April 1863; but even after an adult career in the U.S. Navy, chosen in the hope that going to sea would improve his health, he would write to the Pension Office in 1891, "Entering the army at 11 years of age as drummer my service for nearly four years cost me my health and education and changed the whole current of my life. I have never been well since."[62]

At times, the band experienced almost daily the deaths of others, as Stark dispassionately observed during one such period: "For the past fortnight it has been quite sickly in our reg't, have lost a number of men. I came near being sick myself a few days since. . . . Went [on] a walk and got tired out and then played for a funeral in the rain and took a slight cold."[63]

During combat, bandsmen served as stretcher bearers and assisted the surgeons. The Third Regiment Band performed this duty once, during the Battle of Secessionville in June 1862:

> This was a very hard and trying day for the band. . . . The agonizing groans of the wounded thickly strewn around, calling for help, left no time for reflection, but hard, steady work was before us, picking out the wounded from the dead, and, as tenderly as possible, placing them in the ambulances to be carried to the hospital, and administering water to the parched throats of the suffering fallen, torn by shot or shell, or encouraging them as best we could with words of comfort. This work was trying to the nerves of the bravest. For the rest of the day, and far into the night, the band labored at the hospital, attending

62. Garofalo and Elrod, *Pictorial History,* 104–5. Carl Krebs was also seriously ill for a while. Odlin to Father, December 15, 1861, and Odlin to Friends, December 26, 1861, in *Concord Independent Democrat,* December 26, 1861, and January 9, 1862.

63. Stark to Sister May, Hilton Head, February 24, 1865.

Nathan Marcel Gove, probably 1861. Born in Derry, Nathan Gove was only eleven years old when he enlisted as a drummer. During his year in South Carolina with the Third Regiment Band, he contracted malarial poisoning and never fully recovered from the disease. He nevertheless returned to Hilton Head with the Post Band and participated in the final ceremonies at Fort Sumter (William Henry Gove, *The Gove Book: History and Genealogy of the American Family of Gove and Notes of European Goves* [Salem: Sidney Perley, 1922]).

> the wounded. We washed them, changing their clothing, and gave them food and stimulants, and also assisted the surgeons. We obtained but a few hours' sleep, and again the next day, went through the same ordeal.[64]

It was double duty for the band on such occasions: "A battle, even to the victorious side, is depressing, but to the defeated it is heartrending. The men walk about in silence, and a gloom seems to pervade the entire camp. On this evening we were called out and played a few inspiring airs, which for the time being, seemed to dispel the gloom."[65]

The funerals that followed furnished further work for the band on this and other occasions. The sad ceremonial function the regimental band performed after the Battle of Secessionville was recalled by one of the bandsmen: "Four of the wounded died and were buried the next afternoon. It was a solemn scene as they were borne to their graves, on the shoulders of their sorrowing comrades; the band, with slow, noiseless step, with muffled drums, playing the 'Dead March in Saul,' followed by the regiment."[66]

Although the Post Band played regularly for funerals, the group was spared battle duty. Just a few days after the Fifty-fourth Massachusetts (Colored) Infantry Regiment was sacrificed at nearby Fort Wagner in July 1863, Stevens sat in his tent observing passively that "ambulances filled with wounded men have been going past . . . for several hours." On his way to Morris Island ten days later, he warned his parents to "look for some pretty tough news about the fights here before many weeks." At the same time, he learned, however, that "we shall not have any wounded men to take care of. The commanding Gen. told Mr. Ingalls that his band would have nothing of that kind."[67]

The Post Band, however, did have the unfortunate duty of providing music for what was an even more macabre form of death, the carefully staged spectacle of a military execution. In April 1864, two

64. Hamilton, *Reminiscences,* 163–64.

65. Ibid., 166.

66. Ibid., 165–66. The "Dead March" that was frequently used for military funerals was from Handel's oratorio *Saul.*

67. Stevens to Father and Mother, Hilton Head, July 19, 1863; Stevens to Father and Mother, Steamer *Delaware,* July 30, 1863.

"Dead March," arranged or composed by Claudio Grafulla, from a first E-flat cornet book used by the Post Band. In the semi-tropical Sea Islands, many died from disease while awaiting action. "The Dead March was played on every side, and the files of men with reversed arms and slow step, told the observer that another one had fallen." Also used for funerals and executions was a tune with the same name from Handel's oratorio *Saul*. *New Hampshire Historical Society.*

privates from the Sixth Connecticut Infantry were recaptured repeatedly after several attempts to desert. They were given a court martial and sentenced to death. The Post Band joined the band from the Connecticut regiment, and newspaper accounts noted, "Their fine music added greatly to the solemnity of the occasion."[68] One wonders what the bandsmen were thinking as they accompanied the prisoners, who were seated on their own coffins in a wagon as they were paraded to the middle of a huge square formed by the troops. All were ordered to watch as the condemned were executed by firing squad.

CEREMONY AND SORROW

A year later, two dramatically contrasting events capped the Post Band's career at Hilton Head. Upon the Confederate evacuation of Charleston Harbor in February 1865 and the Federal reoccupation of the pile of rubble that was Fort Sumter, orders came from Washington for a grand celebration to re-raise the fort's Union flag. The date chosen, April 14, was symbolic: it was the fourth anniversary of the fort's evacuation by Major Robert Anderson's garrison. This clearly was a day for bands, and many participated. Unfortunately, no printed programs or newspaper accounts specify either the performing groups or tell much about the repertoire. The raising of the flag, "all tattered with shot and shell," prompted several bands to play "their most inspiring music." All then burst into the national song, and the Post Band undoubtedly joined in a stirring performance of "The Star-Spangled Banner." Drummer boy Nathan Gove noted in his part book that the Post Band also played "Red, White, and Blue" that day.[69]

Sunset saw a grand salute from the fleet, and, as darkness grew, a flagship signal gun magically transformed the entire harbor. Brilliant illumination spread instantly for miles around as, in the day's final

68. *Port Royal Palmetto Herald,* April 21, 1864.

69. A full account is given in the *Charleston Courier,* April 15, 1865; a summary of the same is in *Port Royal New South,* April 22, 1865. William Arnold Spicer, *The Flag Replaced on Sumter: A Personal Narrative* (Providence, R.I.: Providence Press, 1885), 47, 48.

demonstration, all ships became suddenly ablaze with lantern lights, and rockets burst into the night sky. Afterwards, those attending a grand reception at the Charleston Hotel were rapt with attention as now-General Anderson offered a concluding toast to "the man who, when elected President of the United States, was compelled to reach the seat of government without an escort, but a man who now could travel *all* over our country with millions of hands and hearts to sustain him."[70]

Little did Anderson realize that, as he spoke, Lincoln lay dying in the nation's capital and, soon enough, indeed would travel around the country—in a coffin. With a single shot, April 14 was forever transformed from triumph to tragedy in the nation's memory. At least one New Hampshire bandsman actually witnessed the horror at Ford's Theater: solo cornet player Amos Rowell of Kensington, who had performed for Lincoln many times as a member of the Marine Band in Washington, was playing in the theater orchestra that night.[71]

It was not until nearly four days later—on Tuesday morning, April 18—that the sad news found its way south. Curious observers returning north aboard the steamer *Oceanus* spied first one and then another vessel with flags drooping at half-mast, and only then did they learn with shocking disbelief what had befallen the nation.[72] Report of the tragedy reached Hilton Head the same day and brought an instant end to any lingering celebration, plunging the outpost instead into the "deepest gloom."[73] Flags across the islands and on the ships in the harbor were immediately lowered to half-mast, and orders were given for suspension of all business the following day. A signal gun fired every half hour from sunrise to sunset, and it was with that solemn punctuation that bandsman Stark penned a letter to his father describing the transformation of mood:

> Today we have rec'd the sadest news of the whole war. What a contrast between the feeling today and that of a week ago. Then every heart was filled with joy and gladness and now the country is draped

70. Spicer, *Flag Replaced,* 57.
71. Roland D. Sawyer, *The History of Kensington, N.H., 1663–1945* (Farmington, Maine: Knowlton and McLeary, 1946), 275.
72. Spicer, *Flag Replaced,* 67–69.
73. *Port Royal New South,* April 22, 1865.

> in mourning. One week ago tomorrow I was present at the raising of the old flag on Fort Sumter and there heard of the surrender of Lee and his entire army and the hearts of all present were filled with joy. Little did that party think that in a few hours, that noble man Abraham Lincoln . . . would be lying dead slain by an assassin.[74]

And so the Post Band had one final, sad ceremony to accompany that evening, playing in the theater to an overflowing crowd of mourners who had come to grieve an incomprehensible loss. Officers arrived dressed with black armbands and sword hilts draped in crepe; after an eloquent speech by the commanding general, all present adopted a set of resolutions in response, and the band intermittently played "music suitable to the occasion." Those who had experienced the earliest days of the regimental band no doubt were thinking about the occasion when they had played "Hail to the Chief" for the president himself at their camp in the capital.[75]

Two and a half months of life at Hilton Head yet awaited the bandsmen. That year, the Fourth of July undoubtedly brought not so much celebration as a welcome end to their wartime sojourn. The band was mustered out on that day, and its members were glad to collect their belongings and mementos and go home at last.

MUSICAL LIVES AFTER THE WAR

Hilton Head musicians returned to a changed musical landscape in the Old Granite State, but by no means one devoid of musical activity. A few town bands left behind, including the Fisherville Cornet Band, had been forced to cease activity during the war because of depleted membership. Many bands, however, did continue and, beyond the basic function of community entertainment, sometimes supported the war effort through rallies and benefit concerts.[76]

It is noteworthy how many Hilton Head band veterans continued with serious musical involvement after the war, especially as leaders

74. Stark to Father, April 19, 1865.
75. Hamilton, *Reminiscences,* 134.
76. See broadside, New Hampshire Antiquarian Society, Hopkinton, New Hampshire.

of community bands. Stark returned to his native Goffstown, where he founded a namesake band in 1874. Stark's Cornet Band enjoyed a fine existence under his direction; it finally disbanded in 1900, failing to survive his death two years before. Manchester's colorful Francis Harvey ("Saxie") Pike, who served as drum major for the Hilton Head Post Band, continued to swing his baton for whatever group would hire him, and by the early 1870s he had become a regular at New Hampshire National Guard events.[77]

In the Concord area, where a number of Civil War bandsmen would resettle, the most direct reincarnation of Hilton Head musical life occurred back in Fisherville, where David Arthur Brown founded his own band in October 1865, within three months of his return. Brown helped lead the Fisherville Cornet Band before the war and afterward became assistant leader of the Third Regiment Band under Ingalls. Now, as leader of Brown's Cornet Band, a group active until 1878, he directed five of the same personnel, including former Fisherville leader Lorenzo Currier. For special occasions, he engaged the ever-popular Saxie Pike as drum major.[78]

In the state capital, the leadership of the newly organized Concord Brigade Band passed from one Hilton Head band veteran to another, including Third Regiment cornetist Henry S. Hamilton, Jonathan C. Lane (who had joined the Post Band along with Stark in September 1864), and John W. Odlin. After his premature return from Hilton Head, Odlin not only directed several bands in Concord at various times, but also was active in Boston, where he played professionally in theater orchestras and other ensembles, notably in the Germania Band and in Patrick Gilmore's band. Perhaps his most interesting and significant musical experience was as Gilmore's private secretary and principal organizer during the Boston peace jubilees in 1869 and 1872. His work for the second festival earned him commendation from visiting conductor Johann Strauss Jr.

77. George Plummer Hadley, *History of the Town of Goffstown, 1733–1920,* 2 vols. (Goffstown, N.H.: By the Town, 1922–1924), 1:454–55, 485. For an early account of the story of Saxie Pike, see *Concord (N.H.) Statesman,* November 13, 1863. See also *The Legend of Saxie Pike, Told by Frank O. Spinney, Director of the Manchester Historic Association over Station WFEA, 7 P.M., November 30, 1948* (Manchester, N.H.: Amoskeag National Bank, 1948).

78. Brown, *History of Penacook,* 254–67.

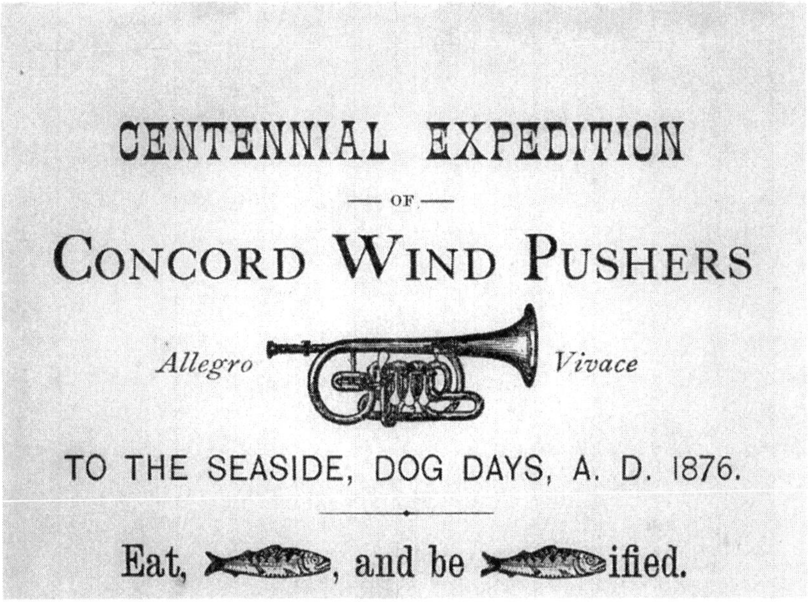

Menu (detail). Brown's Cornet Band of Fisherville provided the music for an earlier seaside gathering, the first reunion of the Third New Hampshire Regiment at Hampton Beach in 1870. *New Hampshire Historical Society.*

By 1871, Odlin had become leader of the Concord Brass Band (active by 1854). In this role, he found himself in conflict with Jonathan Lane, who had returned from Hilton Head to direct the Concord Brigade Band and then founded his own band, the State Capital Band. Lane's conducting style apparently found its local critics, and he, in turn, did not appreciate Odlin's possessiveness of a bandstand in front of the state capitol, the subject of opposing volleys in the local newspapers.[79]

The differences among the bandleaders were not lasting, however. In 1882, veterans of the Third Regiment Band and the Hilton Head Post Band met at the Weirs on Lake Winnipesaukee, where they formed an alumni organization, the First Veteran Band Association of New Hampshire, with Ingalls as president, Brown as secretary,

79. Eventually, the State Capital Band and the Concord Brass Band merged to form Odlin's Band. Longtime Fisherville drummer C. H. Abbott was president, Odlin served as director, and Lane settled for "sub-director." This information comes from a scrapbook owned by Joan Odlin Kalat, a descendant.

and Stark on the executive committee. Fully thirty-three members were present that year (including all whose writings have been quoted in this essay); some twenty took part in afternoon rehearsals of "old army music" under Ingalls and performed four pieces "heartily cheered by the veteran soldiers present." The very formation of the organization itself and the solid participation of so many members of both bands at least fifteen years after the war speaks to the importance of these wartime musical experiences and to the pride these men held for the bands in which they served.[80]

At the same meeting, Odlin was appointed the association's official historian. Unfortunately for the insight and quality of work that would have resulted, it appears he never completed the "full history" of the Third Regiment and Hilton Head Post Bands that was his charge.[81] This essay, offered in its stead more than a century later, attempts to reconstruct the story of the two New Hampshire bands, based upon the documentary, pictorial, and musical sources that remain today.

80. Today, Nevers' Second Regiment Band of Concord claims descent from the bands of Gustavus Ingalls. Nevers' Band evolved more directly from a New Hampshire National Guard band affiliated with the Guard's Third Regiment from its establishment in 1879 and with its Second Regiment after a 1900 reorganization. Hilton Head veteran Henry S. Hamilton served as deputy bandmaster of the Third Regiment Band from 1879 to 1882. This is the only direct connection between Ingalls's band and the National Guard band discovered so far. Claremont cornet soloist Arthur Nevers conducted the band for a remarkable fifty-six years between 1884 and 1940. The author of this article served as the tenth conductor of Nevers' Band, from 1992 to 1996.

81. "Reunion of the First Veteran Band Association of New Hampshire," Stevens Papers, Duke University. This undated flier has recently been determined by Sally Svenson to date from 1882, the only year the veterans' reunion at the Weirs was held in September. The band history Odlin never wrote would undoubtedly have benefited from his professional experience as a journalist, court reporter, and secretary to two U.S. senators.

Confederates at the Keyboard

Southern Piano Music during the Civil War

David B. Thompson

The Civil War touched almost every aspect of life in the South, and music was an important part of that life. Music, often highly emotional, was an integral element in the existence of Southerners, whether they were actively involved in the war effort or not. Representing much of the music performed in private settings among family and friends, the repertoire of Civil War piano music was considerable. Of the approximately one thousand Confederate sheet-music publications cataloged by T. Michael Parrish and Robert M. Willingham Jr., over three hundred are written for solo keyboard, and twenty-five are brass-band arrangements for piano. These numbers do not include compositions written by Southern composers and published elsewhere, or those published in cities under Federal rule (such as New Orleans), or in the border states.[1] Surprisingly, this vast amount of keyboard music has not received much attention by music historians. Only a minute portion of this literature has been republished and is available today, making performances rare.

The piano music composed, published, and performed in the South during the Civil War looks and sounds very much like that of the North. Both sides had their share of songs and band arrangements, dances, descriptive fantasias, and bravura compositions. The amount of piano music published in the North was greater than that of the South because of a larger number of composers, more music publish-

1. T. Michael Parrish and Robert M. Willingham Jr., *Confederate Imprints: A Bibliography of Southern Publications from Secession to Surrender* (Austin, Tex.: Jenkins Publishing, 1987), 560–630.

ers, and a more organized, prosperous society. By contrast, the South experienced much hardship and economic ruin during the war years, touching every aspect of the music business. The lack of metal contributed to a shortage of engraving plates and printing type. Ink had to be made by hand, and paper was rationed. These restrictions led to a decrease in the quality and size of sheet music. In addition, many music merchants had their stores closed because of Union occupation, and some even had their stock and instruments destroyed.[2] Despite these adversities, the amount of piano music actually produced in the South is rather amazing, a credit to the determination of Southern musicians.

Sheet music for piano was one of the main products of some fifty music publishers in the Confederacy. It could be published on short notice and was perfectly suited to the latest wartime event or sentiment. The very first Confederate music sheets, for example, appeared on the streets within days of the South Carolina secession. In order to boost sales of sheet music, publishers often printed lavish covers in color, illustrating the title with minute details. For example, often a catalog of "choice piano music" or "new and beautiful music" was printed on the final page, sometimes including annotations, flowery blurbs, descriptions of a piece, or extravagant boasts of its popularity.[3] Composers often dedicated music to young ladies, and some customers, showing their high esteem for printed music, bound several sheets together into albums with the owner's name printed in gold on the cover. These albums were very popular as gifts.

There can be no doubt that the piano was the most sought-after parlor instrument during the Civil War era, although the harmonium and organ were also used. Square, upright, or grand pianos were affordable for middle-class families, and American-made instruments had come to equal the best foreign ones. Large Northern companies (which advertised heavily in Southern newspapers) manufactured most pianos, and Southern music merchants sold them in large quantities.

2. For a thorough discussion of the Southern music industry during the war years, see E. Lawrence Abel, *Singing the New Nation: How Music Shaped the Confederacy, 1861–1865* (Mechanicsburg, Pa.: Stackpole Books, 2000), 225–75.

3. Margaret Spearly Bauer, "Salon Piano Music in America as Compared to the Piano Works of Louis Moreau Gottschalk during the Years 1853 to 1869" (master's thesis, Indiana University of Pennsylvania, 1975), 18.

There were a few Southern piano manufacturers, with William Knabe of Baltimore being the most successful. By the early 1860s, Knabe and Company Piano Manufacturers controlled the piano trade in the South.[4]

The parlor piano was important in Southern homes for many reasons: as a lovely piece of furniture, a symbol of status, and as an asset in the education of young women. "Ladies of good families" were expected to paint a little, do needlework, speak some French, sing sentimental ballads, and play the piano. Thus the customers for pianos, piano lessons, and sheet music, were mostly women. Civil War diarist Mary Chesnut wrote, "There is a girl in large hoops and a calico frock at every piano between Richmond and the Mississippi, banging on the out-of-tune thing and looking up into a man's face who wears the Confederate uniform." That man usually was her husband, sweetheart, or brother, and he was off to battle.[5]

More than entertainment, music in many homes was an outlet for sorrow and frustration, reliving the problems of the day. Diaries, letters, and memoirs are filled with anecdotes recounting the moving effect of keyboard music in the home, sometimes reaching out to the troops. Josephine C. Habersham, for instance, "felt little like it, but played on the piano for a dozen soldiers, who seated themselves on the green, evidently to hear music!" Henry Graves, a Confederate officer, wrote to his sister Cora: "I want you to give me a list of all the music you have, both songs and instrumental music. If Ma and Pa go to Terrill, you must go to Augusta and spend the winter and take music lessons. I am afraid you are losing precious time. You ought to read a great deal and practice too. I had rather you were accomplished and poor when you are grown than be worth a half-million and be a dunce."[6]

4. Daniel Spillane, *History of the American Pianoforte: Its Technical Development, and the Trade* (New York: Da Capo Press, 1969), 131–33.

5. Diary entry dated September 1863, in C. Vann Woodard, ed., *Mary Chesnut's Civil War* (New Haven: Yale University Press, 1981), 451.

6. "Diary of Josephine C. Habersham," entry dated July 13, 1864, in T. Conn Bryan, *Confederate Georgia* (Athens: University of Georgia Press, 1953), 196; Malvina S. Waring, "A Confederate Girl's Diary," entry dated March 8, 1865, in *South Carolina Women in the Confederacy,* vol. 1, ed. Mrs. Thomas Taylor (Columbia, S.C.: State, 1903), 279.

The war disrupted the genteel traditions, causing some women to express different concerns. As General Sherman was marching through South Carolina, Malvina S. Waring wrote, "I wish I had been taught to cook instead of how to play on the piano. A practical knowledge of the preparation of food products would stand me in better stead at this juncture than any amount of information regarding the scientific principles of music. I adore music, but I can't live without eating—and I'm hungry."[7]

Southerners took great pride in and had much affection for their instruments, so the loss of these important possessions was devastating. Many of the pianos sold nationwide were destroyed during the war. Luluh Vandiver of Columbia, South Carolina, recalled that Sherman's troops came to her homestead and "wreaked vengeance on the property. A large and valuable library vanished in the smoke and ashes under their hands; a brand new piano, which some faithful negroes had taken from the house and tried to hide in a thick orchard, was discovered and hacked into splinters." Ellen Elmore, also from Columbia, remarked that Yankees would destroy a handsome piano because they did that "with such articles that were too heavy to be carried away." A lady in Charleston wrote: "In the parlor the top had been thrown from the piano, some keys broken and wires cut, the music and books lay strewn about the room and yard."[8]

Perhaps the most moving account comes from Shepherdstown, West Virginia, near the Shenandoah Valley region of Virginia. On July 19, 1864, in pursuance of instructions from General David Hunter, Captain William F. Martindale, with a detachment of cavalry, rode up to the home of former U.S. congressman turned Confederate congressman Alexander Boteler. Neither the congressman nor his wife was at home, but his two daughters were—Helen Boteler and the widow Mrs. David Shepherd. Warned of their approach, Mrs.

7. Doris Harrison, "A Survey of Musical Conditions in Montgomery, Louisiana, and the Surrounding Community" (master's thesis, Louisiana State University, 1936), 12.

8. Luluh Ayer Vandiver, "In the Tracks of the Raiders," in *South Carolina Women in the Confederacy,* 1:358; Ellen S. Elmore, "A Southern Household during the Years 1860–1865," in *South Carolina Women in the Confederacy,* 1:202; "'Our Women in the War': The Lives They Lived; The Deaths They Died," *The Weekly News and Courier* (Charleston, S.C.; The News and Courier Book Press, 1885), 367.

Shepherd met the soldiers at the door. Captain Martindale stated that he had come to burn her house and its contents. The daughters protested, but to no avail. Everything would be burned. Helen begged that her piano be saved, but her request was denied. Defiant to the point of recklessness, she went to the parlor and began to play as the flames crackled in the other room and began to sing Charlotte Elliott's hymn:

> My God, my father, while I stray
> Far from my home in life's rough way,
> Oh, teach me from my heart to say,
> "Thy will be done!"

A soldier tried to pull her out of the house, but she eluded him and sang again:

> Through dark my path, and sad my lot.
> Let me be still and murmur not;
> Or breathe the prayer divinely taught,
> "Thy will be done!"

The Union trooper believed that she was crazy, but as the heat and flames approached she closed the lid of the piano, locked it, and left the house to join her sister and the children.[9]

There were fewer composers and visiting pianists in the South, compared to the North, because there were not as many large cosmopolitan areas to support them. Many also left the South because of the war.[10] However, there was a great diversity among Southern composers of keyboard music. Found in every city in the Southern states, these men and women, black and white, nevertheless produced and published similar parlor pieces, accessible to both beginners and advanced pianists. Little is known about the women composers other than their names and the titles of their compositions. African Americans composed many keyboard works, including at least fifty pieces

9. "A Last Song in a Burning Home," in *The Women in the South in War Times,* comp. Matthew Page Andrews (Baltimore: Norman Remington, 1927), 197–99.

10. One example was Louis Moreau Gottschalk, who fled to Cuba prior to the war; see S. Frederick Starr, *Bamboula! The Life and Times of Louis Moreau Gottschalk* (New York: Oxford University Press, 1995).

of published piano music. Most of these composers were English-speaking free people, but some were slaves. Many of the white composers were European immigrants who were engaged in rallying the people during the Civil War. The sense of freedom experienced by many Southerners was their source of inspiration, and they endorsed the idea of seceding from the Union. Thus they composed volumes of politically oriented songs and instrumental music. On the other hand, many of these immigrants were equally successful in writing works not related to the war.

One Virginia composer, Charles (Chaky) de Nordendorf, took his patriotism a bit more seriously and put down his pen to serve in the military. Born in Vienna in 1839, he came to America early in 1863, in the midst of the war. He settled in Danville and began a career as a teacher, composer, and music publisher. During his brief Confederate service, under the leadership of Colonel Robert Enoch Withers, he was assigned to protect the prison camp by digging rifle pits and building redoubts. He later was commended by Colonel A. L. Rivers, chief of the Confederate Engineer Bureau, for his field fortifications along the Richmond and Danville railroad, which helped keep this important supply line open for Robert E. Lee during the Petersburg campaign from June 1864 to April 1865.[11]

Salon music for the piano, written by these and other composers, is above all else elegant, sometimes expressing lofty sentiments. While little musical insight is demanded from the performer, the technical requirements are often considerable. An amateur can easily perform a salon piece that sounds impressive, as the keyboard figurations add a touch of brilliance to the compositions. Although one may not find much intrinsic musical worth in these pieces, the social aspect was the primary reason for their existence. The musical notation was quite simple and formulaic, and it did not incorporate large numbers of black keys so that it would lie well under the hands of the amateur pianist. Emphasis is always placed on the melody, with the right hand dominating, while the left hand usually supplies the necessary accompaniment. The melodies had to be easily remembered, singable, or suitable for dancing.

11. Alvin L. Hall, "Charles 'Chaky' De Nordendorf: Soldier-Songster of the Confederacy," *Virginia Cavalcade* 24 (summer 1974): 43–44.

The parlor repertoire consisted of fantasias, variations on operatic themes, dance music in both functional and stylized forms, marches, and battle pieces. Also included were showpieces inspired by visiting European virtuosos and a great variety of song arrangements. These works were written for pianists on every technical level—beginners to advanced.

A significant portion of the repertoire—marches, quicksteps, schottisches, polkas, and such—could readily assume a respectable Southern viewpoint by title alone. Many were dedicated to significant leaders, military heroes, or stirring events, such as "The Beauregard Charleston Quickstep," "General Morgan's Grand March," or "Our First President's Manassas Quickstep." (The North rarely celebrated its heroes this way, perhaps because Union generals were not as well loved as the Confederate leaders.) The titles that were topical in nature had at least some momentary social meaning, if not a musical one. Geographical names were also popular, and no Southern lady was safe from having her name attached to a polka or waltz.

The popular dance forms—waltzes, quadrilles, galops, polkas, mazurkas, and schottisches—were taught in local dance schools. All had originated in Europe with characteristic rhythms and melodies and remained essentially unchanged when transported to the United States. During the Civil War, there was no significant difference between social dance music written by white or black composers. It was not until after the Civil War that published music took on racial characteristics in titles, texts, or musical content. A distinction was made, however, between ordinary or functional pieces for dancing and those more stylized for performance only.

The social waltzes, those meant for dancing, are generally easy to play, some even indicating fingerings for the beginning pianist. Those waltzes not meant for dancing are obviously of greater musical interest. They are extended in length by the addition of a separate introduction, an elaborate finale, or both. The technical demands of these pieces are often considerably higher. Examples include "General Breckenridge's Grand Waltz," by Charlie L. Ward, published in 1862 and dedicated to the Fifth Kentucky Regiment; and the elegant waltz "Pensiviana," composed in 1863 by William L. Hensler of Baton Rouge, Louisiana.

The mazurka was considered an elaboration of the ordinary waltz and was occasionally called a "fancy dance." It could be performed at several tempos—from moderately slow to quite rapid. Notable ones include "Mathilde Mazurka," composed by Auguste Davis of New Orleans in 1861 and dedicated to his wife; "Crescent Regiment Mazurka," by M. Hoeffner; and the virtuosic "Mississippi Union Mazurka" by C. J. Atwell, written in 1857 in celebration of the joining of the Memphis and Charleston Railroads, during which a barrel of water from the Atlantic Ocean and one from the Mississippi River were poured together at the point where the trains met.

The schottische was a social round dance that became a favorite in American parlors and ballrooms in the 1840s. Nineteenth-century American dance masters believed it to be of German origin and referred to it as the "German polka."[12] Those meant for dancing were easy to play and often two to three pages in length, while the more stylized ones were often technically advanced and generally much longer. Representative works include "Charleston Schottisch," by Cyrus Gill and dedicated to the Ladies of Charleston; "Signal Corps Schottische," by Mason M. Bunow; and "The Clara Schottisch," by J. C. Gleffer, composed and "affectionately inscribed" to his pupil Miss Clara Cato of Brandon Springs, Alabama, published in 1861.

The polka, originating around 1830 in Bohemia, was rather controversial at first. Its quick and jerky movements, requiring the feet to be turned in an "unusual" way, were called "indecent, immodest and scandalous."[13] Nevertheless, people of all social classes danced the polka. The music is essentially no different from that of the schottisch. Examples include "Manassas Polka," by S. Schlesinger, and "The 199 Broad Street Polka," composed in 1864 by Edward O. Eaton. Stylized polkas, perhaps for concert use, are more difficult and are usually between three and six pages in length, as in "Gen'l Beauregard's Grand Polka Militaire!" by J. Ascher.

The galop, performed by couples who "galloped" through the hall to a lively tempo, is related to the polka. It would often end the

12. *The New Grove Dictionary of American Music* (1986 ed.), s.v. "Schottische," by Pauline Norton.

13. Arthur Loesser, *Men, Women, and Pianos: A Social History* (New York: Dover, 1990), 504.

evening leaving the dancers and musicians dizzy, breathless, and overheated. As a dance master remarked, "the only difficulty in the dance is to keep on the feet."[14] "The Alabama Secession Galop," dedicated to Jefferson Davis, by H. Berge, a professor at Wilcox Female Institute in Alabama, was a popular example.

Amateur parlor performers enjoyed Civil War song arrangements in the style of popular dances. Titles include "The Brightest Eyes Galop," arranged by A. Schwartz; "Dixie Polka," by William Herz; "The Bonnie Blue Flag Quickstep," arranged by J. C. Viereck; and "The Volunteer Waltz," by Charles Young. Another large portion of this piano repertoire consists of "music for marching"—music with a strong pulse and short repeated melodies or phrases. Thus many nineteenth-century dances—galops, polkas, and even an occasional waltz—could be called "marches."[15] Dance pieces make up slightly more than half of all music published during this time.

Piano arrangements of brass-band marches were popular, even among female pianists, who seemed to perform them all with "all the gusto and style" that men exhibited in military bands. Their loud percussive playing was compared to "a sort of wood chopping exercise."[16] Three distinct styles of marches emerged in the early nineteenth century: the ordinary "march," the "grand march," and the "quickstep." By midcentury, these styles had become less rigidly defined, but the number of marches that were published quickly increased as the war began.

The grand march is generally slow and ceremonial. The level of difficulty ranges from easy to difficult and the general length is two to five pages. Most are sectional with a contrasting trio that might include the melody of a popular song, as in "Gen. Mercer's Grand March" by Herman Schreiner, which includes the melody "Brightest Eyes" in the trio. Only a few grand marches have introductions, and some, such as "Potomac Artillery Grand March," by Adolphus Brown, has an energetic twenty-four-measure "bugle call" section that precedes

14. Allison Thompson, "Dancing on the Eve of Battle: Some Views about Social Dancing during the American Civil War," *Country Dance and Song* 21 (1991): 20.

15. Pauline Elizabeth Hosack Norton, "March Music in Nineteenth Century America" (Ph.D. diss., University of Michigan, 1983), 17.

16. Ibid., 282.

the introduction. "Gen. Beauregard's Grand March," by Mrs. V. G. Cowdin, published in Augusta, Georgia, and "President Jefferson Davis Grand March," by Mrs. Flora Byrne, published in 1861 in New Orleans, are fine examples of the grand march by female composers. Charles Young's "Stonewall Jackson's Way: Grand March" includes the words of a soldier under Jackson's command, which could be read during the performance, or perhaps just functioned to aid the performer's interpretation of this march:

> Come, stack arms, men! pile on the rails.
> Stir up the camp fire bright;
> Silence! ground arms! kneel all! caps off!
> Old Blue Light's going to pray.
>
> "Lay bare thine arm, stretch forth thy rod, Amen!"
> He's in the saddle now! Fall in! Steady!
> The whole Brigade!
>
> Ah! Maiden, wait, and watch and yearn,
> For news of Stonewall's band!
> Ah! wife, sew on, pray on, hope on!
> Thy life shall not be all forlorn!
> Hill's at the ford cut off: We'll win his
> way out, ball and blade.
>
> Here's Longstreet struggling in the lists
> Hemmed in an ugly gorge.
> The foe had better ne'er been born,
> That gets in Stonewall's way
>
> "Bay'nets and rage!" hear Stonewall roar
> "Charge, Stuart! pay off Ashby's score
> Charge! Charge! Hurrah!"[17]

The ordinary or plain "march" is somewhat simpler in style and texture than the grand march, but with similar introductions that often recall military music. In "Madison Rifles March," by Adolphus Brown, a trumpet-and-drum fanfare is suggested through a brisk

17. Charles Young, "Stonewall Jackson's Way: Grand March" (New Orleans: Blackmar, 1863).

right-hand triadic figure call (marked "trumpet" in the music) while the left hand, simulating a drum roll, plays a continuous half-step trill in a very low range (marked "drum").

A dance as well as a march, the quickstep is characterized by a fast tempo and a lyrical, lilting melody; quicksteps were immensely popular between 1830 and 1869. Most of these pieces are in ternary form with a dance and a trio, and they often include an introduction and closing section. "Maj. General Hampton's Quickstep," by Lizzie C. Orchard, published in Columbia, South Carolina, is one spirited example. Others quicksteps include "The Beauregard Manassas Quickstep," by A. Noir, and "Mason & Slidell Quick Step," by H. N. Hempsted.

The most popular of the march-dance hybrids was the polka-march. The polka flavor is found in characteristic accompaniment patterns and melodic figurations that combine the martial and brilliant with the lyrical and playful. "Parade Polka March" was apparently made popular by the band of the famous Washington Artillery of New Orleans. Louis Grunewald of New Orleans published Theodore von La Hache's arrangement for piano in 1861 and advertised: "Mr. La Hache in one of our most successful teachers of the piano and is one of our best composers. The piece is played by all our brass bands."[18]

The popularity of the "battle piece," a pianistic description of wartime events, began to wane in Europe during midcentury but remained popular in the United States.[19] In these long sectionalized works, patriotic songs and battle sounds are woven into an often technically demanding composition that was amazingly vivid at times, often flooding the audience with emotion. The listener could hear the roar of cannons, the whistling of bullets in the air, the advance of the troops, crushing defeat, and mighty victory. For example, "Battle of Manassas," composed by Thomas Greene Bethune ("Blind Tom"), is an episodic work that requires the performer to make extramusical sounds—tone clusters with the palm in the low register of the piano

18. Warren C. Fields, "The Life and Works of Theodore von La Hache" (Ph.D. diss., University of Iowa, 1973), 150.

19. Elizabeth Ann Wallace, "The Effect of War on the Lives and Work of Piano Composers and the Evolution of Compositional Technique in War-Related Piano Pieces from 1849 through the Second World War" (Ph.D. diss., Texas Tech University, 1990), 32.

to represent cannons, and train sounds ("chu-chu-chu") and whistles actually vocalized by the performer to represent the arrival of troops. His keyboard imitations of fifes, drums, trumpets, and cannons, vividly depicting the Southern victory in this important battle, were so realistic that a performance of this piece could easily elicit protests from Northern audiences. Familiar melodies, including "Dixie," "The Girl I Left Behind Me," "Star Spangled Banner," and "The Marseillaise," are also interwoven in this composition. Although not copyrighted until 1894, the piece was composed and performed in 1866.

Somewhat related to battle pieces, "descriptive fantasies" came with titles bearing a wide range of descriptors, such as "caprice," "souvenir," "echoes," "fantasie-dramatique," "reminiscence," and "illustration." Many of these compositions are potpourris of themes from operas or other stage works. Some are well-constructed works that may vary from the playful or dancelike to the dramatic or martial. "John Morgan's Escape! A Descriptive Fantasia," by A. E. Blackmar, presents the events surrounding Morgan's escape from the State Penitentiary in Columbus, Ohio, in 1863. Jules C. Meinenger's "In Memory of the Confederate Dead: A Requiem," in the style of a funeral march, leads the listener from the news of a hero's death to the lowering of his body into the grave, depicting in the course of the piece the funeral procession to the church with tolling bells and choral lamentations. Such descriptions were often written as performance notes by the composer to aid in the interpretation of the piece.

Other piano works within the genre of descriptive fantasy include such styles as "theme and variations," "improvisation," and the more classically oriented "nocturne," "reverie," and "romance." These lengthy works of up to ten pages are often based on themes borrowed from operatic arias or folk, patriotic, or sentimental songs. Most arrangements or improvisations are nothing more than a set of variations that run together. A "theme and variations" may also feature an introduction, the theme, three or four contrasting variations, and a finale in the form of a waltz or march. Titles include "Improvisation on 'The Bonnie Blue Flag,'" by Theodore von La Hache; "Theme and Variations on 'Home, Sweet Home,'" by Miss Lizzie Tebault; and "When This War Is Over: An Elegant Adaptation for the Piano," by C. Nordendorf. Only a small portion of all the Confederate keyboard music falls into this bravura category, which required a pianist with a solid technique. Many purchasers of sheet music were limited in their facility but nevertheless could satisfactorily perform a wide range of material. A great number of compositions had the added bonus of sounding more difficult than they really were.

Taken as a whole, Civil War–era piano music intended for Southern parlors contains pleasing melodies, creative harmonies, and interesting rhythms, and most of the pieces are enjoyable to perform. Quite a few are musically worthwhile. Although this keyboard music did not stand the "test of time" and has dropped out of the popular repertoire, it is nonetheless socially and culturally important as a part of our nation's musical history. The keyboard music that was played in the homes expressed public sentiments as well as intimate feelings during these years of conflict and hardship. It is unfortunate that most of it is forgotten today. From both musical and historical perspectives, this music warrants rediscovery.

Henry Clay Work

"The Silver Horn" as Civil War Elegy

Walter L. Powell

On Liberty Street in the western New York village of Bath stands a nineteenth-century building once known as the Purdy Opera House—currently the home of Murphy's T.V. and Appliance Store. No sign or plaque stands at the site to inform the passerby that here, on a February evening in 1883, the composer Henry Clay Work reluctantly gave a performance of his celebrated Civil War song "Marching through Georgia" to an enthusiastic crowd of several hundred veterans. Nor would a casual visitor of today have any reason to know that this performance, and the events that followed in the next few weeks, inspired Work to compose one of the finest art songs written in the United States during this period.

The near obscurity of this event parallels the view musicologists generally have had for one of the most prolific composers of the Civil War—a man the music writer Charles Hamm called "the most talented songwriter of the generation after Stephen Foster." A two-part article by the late Richard S. Hill for the Music Library Association's *Notes* fifty years ago remains the most complete source of biographical information, and a Nonesuch recording entitled "Who Shall Rule This American Nation? Songs of the Civil War Era by Henry Clay Work" remains the only major effort to record a substantial portion of his songs.[1]

1. Charles Hamm, *Yesterdays: Popular Song in America* (New York: Norton, 1979), 258; Richard S. Hill, "The Mysterious Chord of Henry Clay Work," pts. 1 and 2, *Notes: Quarterly Journal of the Music Library Association* 10, no. 2 (March 1953): 211–25, and no. 3 (June 1953): 367–90; Camerata Chorus of Washington, *Who Shall Rule This American Nation? Songs of the Civil War Era by Henry Clay*

Henry Clay Work. From *Songs of Henry Clay Work,* comp. Bertram G. Work (New York: J. J. Little and Ives, 1884).

View of the former Purdy's Opera House on Liberty Street in Bath. *Walter L. Powell.*

If Work is a relatively obscure figure today, that was certainly not true during his lifetime. This Connecticut-born composer, who spent much of his youth in Quincy, Illinois, and the Civil War years in Chicago, wrote twenty-nine songs between 1861 and 1865—among them some of the most famous of the Civil War, including "Kingdom Coming" in 1862, "Song of a Thousand Years" and "Babylon Is Fallen" in 1863, "Come Home, Father" in 1864, and "Ring the Bell, Watchman" and "Marching through Georgia" in 1865. In 1884, the year of his death, a book entitled *Our National War Songs* (published by S. Brainard & Sons of Cleveland and Chicago) contained more of his songs than those of any other wartime composer—including those of his famous contemporary George Frederick Root, owner of the

Work (Nonesuch H-71317); Musicologist Benjamin Robert Tubb has recently created an Internet web site called "Public Domain Music" that includes MIDI files of all of Work's songs (http://www.pdmusic.org). He has also compiled and edited *Henry Clay Work: Complete Songs and Choruses* (Philadelphia: Kallisti Music Press, 2002).

largest publishing firm of the era, Root and Cady of Chicago. As the writer of Work's obituary for the *Hartford Courant* observed:

> Our country has produced few songwriters whose works have been more widely sung than Mr. Work. Some few of his productions have not only been on the lips of nearly every man, woman and child in America, but with some variations, in every part of the world. There is scarcely a Grand Army gathering where his songs are not sung, and they are sure to be sung for generations to come.[2]

If Work wrote prolifically during the Civil War, the postwar years were not as productive. A highly successful business relationship with George Frederick Root was strained by personal and philosophical differences and was severed for good after the Great Chicago Fire of 1871. Living at various times over the next decade in Philadelphia, Vineland, New Jersey, and Brooklyn, Work composed only sporadically. When he lost his Chicago real estate in the Great Fire and subsequently lost his savings in a failed fruit farm in Vineland, he did so, according to biographer Samuel Ward Loper, "without a murmur, although discouraged—simply saying 'if he had succeeded in accumulating great riches he might have become a hard man.'"[3] These reverses forced him to find employment wherever he could, usually doing job printing and proofreading—skills he had learned and perfected as an apprentice and journeyman printer in Hartford, Connecticut. His personal life was further marred by the mental illness of his wife, Sarah (who had to be confined to her parents' home in Greenwich, Massachusetts), the death of three of his four children between 1862 and 1871, and the need to care for his surviving daughter, Nellie, as a single parent.[4]

In the fall of 1882, Work turned fifty years old and had become (as Samuel Loper put it) "a sad and somewhat melancholy man, one whose life socially and financially was a continual disappointment." The tremendous popularity and sales of his song "My Grandfather's

2. *Hartford Courant,* June 8, 1884.

3. Samuel Ward Loper, "Biographical Sketch of Henry Clay Work: His Life in Middletown and Hartford," published in the *Hartford Daily Times,* April 1908.

4. Richard S. Hill, "The Mysterious Chord of Henry Clay Work," *Notes: Quarterly Journal of the Music Library Association* 10, no. 2 (1953): 211–25.

Clock" in 1876 had not been matched by more recent compositions, including a "Sequel to Grandfather's Clock" published in 1878. Deciding he needed to leave Brooklyn, he wrote a letter to the editor of the *Corning (N.Y.) Journal* asking where "he could find a still nook in this noisy world where he might engage in literary and musical work, and at the same time find repose for over-strung nerves." The editor suggested the village of Bath, a community of some three thousand people pleasantly situated in the valley of the Conhocton River. On January 12, 1883, the *Steuben Courier* announced: "Mr. Henry Clay Work of Brooklyn, the author of 'Father, Dear Father Come Home With Me Now,' 'Marching Through Georgia,' and 'My Grandfather's Clock' is spending a number of weeks in Bath."[5]

The newspaper announcement of Work's arrival was not something he sought, but he soon adjusted to his renewed celebrity, as he noted in a letter to his friend Susie Mitchell Scupham of San Francisco on March 6, 1883:

> This village life is more of a novelty than I expected to find it. In the heart of N.Y. City I could easily make a hermit of myself when I tried; but here—well, I haven't tried, and shouldn't have succeeded if I had. It is really surprising to find that I have excited so much curiosity and interest, not only among romantic young women—but in all classes. My connection with "Marching Through Georgia" seems to be the cause. A "Soldier's Home" is located here; a soldier's monument has just been erected; and the annual "Camp Fire" of the G.A.R. (local post) took place not long since, on which occasion (to please soldiers and citizens, and thoughtless of the consequences) I sang the song in the Opera House before an audience of several hundred—something I never did in my life. I have been compelled to repeat it at almost every social gathering I have attended. I do not sing the solo well, but I have usually a magnificent chorus, and the auditors seem greatly pleased.[6]

5. Loper, "Biographical Sketch"; *Steuben Courier,* January 12, 1883 (copy at Davenport Library, Bath, New York).

6. Henry Clay Work to Mrs. S. R. Scupham, Bath, New York, February 28–March 6, 1883. This is one of a collection of forty letters (mostly sent to Mrs. Scupham) that she saved until her death in 1921. They now reside in the Music Division of the Library of Congress.

The Grand Army of the Republic (G.A.R.) event to which Work referred was the "Fourth Annual Camp-Fire" of Custer Post 81, held at Purdy's Opera House on February 9, 1883. If "camp-fire" brought to mind intimate moments during the Civil War for soldiers to swap tales, sip coffee, or sing songs, it was also true that by the 1880s the term came to represent a highly ritualized veterans' reunion complete with formal speeches, toasts, singing, and, of course, a good meal. The event sponsored by Custer Post 81 was described in detail in the February 16, 1883, issue of the *Steuben Courier:*

IN BIVOUAC
Fourth Annual Camp-Fire of Post Custer

Scenes of army life were vividly recalled to memory by the fourth annual camp-fire of Post Custer, G.A.R. which took place at Purdy's Opera House on Thursday evening of last week. . . . The Opera House was handsomely decorated with flags, etc. and presented an attractive appearance—greatly in contrast with the old camping grounds—except the stage, which was occupied by a tent, a stack of arms, camp kettle over a mock fire, and the proverbial canteen, without which army life would have been much harder to bear than it was. Upon the chandeliers were placed flags of each army corps—twenty-five in number, and on the walls were flags which had passed through many hard-fought battles. Five tables, extending nearly the entire length of the hall, had been placed in position, and were loaded with hard-tack, pork and beans, cheese, sandwiches, coffee and other delicacies. . . . At half past eight o'clock, Toastmaster Hon. A. C. Brundage called the assembly to order by drumming on an inverted tin cup with his knife; the result was like magic, the familiar sound (to the soldiers) caused them to heed its warning, and they immediately proceeded to stack—or should we say—fold arms and await further developments. . . . Mr. Brundage then delivered a brief but appropriate address, referring pathetically to the War of the Rebellion and the good works of the G.A.R., closing his speech by inviting all present to "get to business" and help themselves. After "rations," pipes and tobacco were passed around, and a majority of those present joined the soldiers in smoking the "pipe of peace."

The Toastmaster then introduced to the audience Mr. H. C. Work of New York City, composer of the famous song "Marching Through Georgia." Mr. Work made a neat little speech, saying that he is not a singer himself, but composed songs for other people to sing; however on this occasion he would endeavor to sing the song mentioned above if all present would join in the chorus; they did so with much enthusiasm.[7]

After Work's performance, the program continued at great length, with more addresses and with songs performed by the Waneta Glee Club. Near the end of the evening, Captain W. S. Burns announced that the long-awaited Soldiers' Monument was "loaded on a railway car and would be here in a few days." Its subsequent arrival and installation in the center of the village a few days later became the proverbial talk of the town and was the subject of a long and congratulatory editorial in the February 23, 1883, issue of the *Steuben Courier:*

IN MEMORIAM

We congratulate the people of Bath upon the fulfillment of a long cherished hope—the completion of the soldier's monument. This merited tribute to departed heroes, this evidence of an appreciative, grateful, and generous people, stands today a more beautiful realization of art than its most sanguine advocate could have anticipated. It is a monument in which Bath may indulge a pride that is pardonable.

After discussing the central location of the monument, the editor concluded by noting:

The monument will stand the bright particular ornament of the village, the admired of all beholders, the beautiful expression of patriotic remembrance, for long, long years after the eyes of today have ceased to admire, and our voices of praise or cavil become silent forever.[8]

On the same day, the *Steuben Courier* had another article that announced that "a few weeks since a half dozen persons met at a private house in Bath, to practice a new piece of music by Henry Clay Work, a song writer, now of Bath . . . these exceedingly pleasant gatherings have continued, and increased in numbers until not many private dwellings can accommodate them, and they occur twice a week."

7. *Steuben Courier,* February 16, 1883. For a compelling discussion of the role of the Grand Army of the Republic in nineteenth-century America, see Stuart McConnell, *Glorious Contentment: The Grand Army of the Republic, 1865–1900* (Chapel Hill: University of North Carolina Press, 1992).

8. *Steuben Courier,* February 23, 1883.

View of the Soldiers' Monument in Bath. *Walter L. Powell.*

Out of these gatherings formed the Bath Social Singing Club, which responded to the news of the Soldiers' Monument with the performance of a song written by member Z. L. Parker, set to the tune of "Marching through Georgia."

In private settings like this, and in many other situations, Work would have constant reminders over the next several weeks of the terrible human sacrifice symbolized by the new monument. On March 2, he visited the Soldiers' Home in Bath, where again he was asked to sing "Marching through Georgia." While this visit was mentioned in the March 7 issue of the *Steuben Courier,* a lengthier and more interesting article appeared in the same newspaper a week later that could not have escaped Work's attention. Titled "As Others See Us," a visiting correspondent for the *Boston Transcript* described Bath and its surroundings, including the Soldiers' Home:

> At each side of a long shaded lane once known as Lover's Lane are the lands of the Soldiers Home Estate, and close behind it rise the great buildings of the Soldiers Home, where over 600 soldiers who served in New York regiments during the Civil War now find a home. The institution was founded by the G.A.R., who raised the money for the erection of the buildings and the purchase of the estate which surrounds them. . . . The three principal buildings are each three stories high and of brick laid in black mortar. On the ground floor of the central and largest building are the dining hall and kitchen. . . . [T]he two upper floors are occupied as dormitories, and each contains 100 beds. Each of the three floors of the two large buildings flanking this one are similarly used.

The author continued at length, noting the presence of a hospital, other outbuildings, and a three-story building housing the general headquarters. But the most poignant part of his narrative comes as he recalls the last part of his visit:

> Our last stopping place was at the pleasant quarters of General Pitcher, at present in charge of the Soldier's Home. From him we learned that the greater number of the soldiers at the Home were over 60 years old, and a few had even passed their 80th year. As a whole, the faces of the soldiers did not inspire one favorably! There were not wanting intelligent faces amongst them, but the majority seemed dull and heavy. . . . Then it came over me that these same men, who seemed so

> dull and uninteresting to my superficial glance, were brothers in arms of those very heroes who so loved Truth that "They died for her / tasting the raptured fleetness / Of her divine completeness." These same men, now seasoning a rather monotonous existence with newspaper and checker-board, had stood shoulder to shoulder with those other men who sleep today in heroes' graves. Had I failed to see the heroes' gleam in the eyes that mine met that day? Yet some of these men were doubtless of the same metal as those to whom a monument is raised, instead of a Home. Mine were the dull eyes, which failed to recognize clearly a hero of the past in these prosaic veterans of the present.[9]

For Henry Clay Work, this editorial was a call to action—a challenge to capture "the heroes' gleam" in music, and to honor all those who had gone before. Throughout his life as a composer, Work was most creative when he could personally identify with places and people about him, and he was deeply moved by his experiences attending the G.A.R. campfire, visiting the Soldiers' Home, and contemplating the upcoming dedication of the Soldiers' Monument on Memorial Day. When he composed "The Silver Horn" is not certain, but it seems likely that it was sometime between March 2 and April 18, 1883, when he left for New York and New England. For as one writer noted, "His gift of song-writing was a peculiar one. A subject would suggest itself to his mind, and oftentimes he would neither eat nor sleep until the song was composed and set to music. He always wrote his own accompaniment."[10] The lyrics of the song express Work's deep feelings upon reflecting on the aging veterans:

THE SILVER HORN

1. Come, rest with me now, my silver horn!
My melodious joy, my silver horn!
These many long years my constant friend,
Together let our toiling end.
Yet fain would I ask (were mine the choice)
For a moment of strength to give thee voice
One silvery peal ere life shall cease;
But not for war—for blessed peace.

9. *Steuben Courier,* March 7 and 14, 1883.
10. *Hartford Courant,* June 9, 1884.

View of the National Cemetery in Bath, adjacent to the Soldiers' Home. *Walter L. Powell.*

Chorus:
Yes once again ring, sweet silver horn
That long ago rang on battle morn—
From vale and glen that summon'd then
To arms! To arms! a thousand men.
For peace ring now! for peace ring high!
Ring a welcoming peal that shall not die
Till mountain and mound, the earth around,
Responsive songs in echo sound.

2. Thy whispers I hear, my silver horn!
My melodious joy, my silver horn!
They comfort me oft with such control,
Methinks thou has a living soul.
Then cherish we both one calm content:
For the land that we love our powers were spent;
And over the turf that greens our grave,
For ages may her banner wave.

3. I kiss thee adieu, my silver horn!
My melodious joy, my silver horn!

Then suddenly loos'd the bugler's clasp;
His kiss was but a dying gasp.
Yet marvels of power can love evoke:
At the touch of his lips the bugle spoke!
And wondrously sweet, and clear, and strong,
From thence outrang a silver song.

The "Silver Horn" of course, is a bugle, and the central figure, an aged dying bugler, seeking "a moment of strength" to give the bugle "voice / One silvery peal ere life shall cease; / But not for war—for blessed peace." There is, perhaps, nothing immediately remarkable in this musical setting, for the themes of death and immortality were conventional ones in the nineteenth-century songs and poems that Work's contemporary Emily Dickinson called the "Flood Subjects." Then, too, the reference to a bugle is a common one—a reminder of the importance this instrument played in camp and combat during the Civil War. Furthermore, Work mixes his metaphors somewhat, for the words used to describe the notes issuing from the bugle's bell remind one of the bell in a church steeple: "For peace ring now! for peace ring high! / Ring a welcoming peal that shall not die."

Despite some of its prosaic qualities, on closer examination one finds that the song is highly evocative. Its beautiful melody echoes several bugle calls, especially "Taps" (written in 1862)—echoes that are reinforced with use of a ¾ time signature, and the frequent use of dotted quarter notes throughout the piece. Here Work seems to evoke the powerful emotions stirred in veterans when hearing the bugle sound—emotions recalled by Delevan S. Miller of the Second New York Artillery, looking back in 1905 at the events of his unit's final dress parade. His description of their bugler "Gracey" is remarkably similar in sentiment to the text of Work's song:

> There never was such another bugler in the whole Army of the Potomac as our little Gracey. Small of stature, gentle by nature, but a marvel with his trumpet.... Gracey was at our last dress parade.... After the parade the guns were stacked for the last time, and then Gracey sounded "Taps" and on this occasion our old bugler seemed to breathe his very soul into his trumpet, for the tears were trickling down his cheeks while strong, bronzed men who had walked into the

cannon's mouth—were not without emotion as they broke ranks for the last time.[11]

More, too, is going on with the text—subtle, but significant. Work was an evangelical Protestant all of his life, and the words of the New Testament and the book of Revelation as written in the King James Bible are evident throughout, as they are in many of his songs. His choice of words was always careful, for as his former publisher George Frederick Root recalled: "Mr. Work was a slow, pains-taking writer, being from one to three weeks upon a song; but when the work was done it was like a fine mosaic, especially in the fitting of words to music."[12] In "The Silver Horn," the central message is the assurance of "blessed peace"—the thousand years of peace promised with the Millennium, Christ's Second Coming. In his fervent desire to hear a note of peace one last time, the dying bugler is not unlike Simeon of Jerusalem in the Gospel of Luke, who is assured by the Holy Ghost "that he shall not see death, before he had seen the Lord's Christ." The Silver Horn will ring Christ's welcoming assurance of his Second Coming in a "peal that shall not die / Till mountain and mound, the earth around, / Responsive songs in echo sound."

Finally, the Silver Horn is a metaphor for Work's own creative powers as a songwriter, for he most certainly projected himself in the role of the dying bugler with the plea "Yet fain would I ask (were mine the choice) / For a moment of strength to give thee voice / One silvery peal ere life shall cease." Like so many of his generation, Work's life had been defined by the Civil War, and he struggled to come to terms with its aftermath. As Richard S. Hill observed, "a song-writer who crowds his most creative period into four short years and then proceeds to outlive that period by twenty years, broken only with the most sporadic and unequal efforts, tempts fate."[13] In a sense, this song is Work's plea for the divine spark of inspiration—a familiar call by artists of all generations.

11. Cited in Kenneth E. Olson, *Music and Musket: Bands and Bandsmen of the American Civil War* (Westport, Conn.: Greenwood Press, 1981), 94.

12. George F. Root, *The Story of a Musical Life* (Cincinnati: John Church, 1891), 138.

13. Hill, "Mysterious Chord," 219.

Just a year later, on June 8, 1884, Work died of a heart attack while visiting his mother in Hartford, Connecticut. He had written just two more songs: "Come, Pretty Schoolgirl; or, The Little White Cottage on Evergreen Square," and "Drop the Pink Curtains." Neither was evident of his greatest talent. "The Silver Horn" became Work's elegy, as it did for many of his generation—and a "marvel of power" evoked by the love of those veterans and friends in Bath with whom he had spent some of his last days.

The Production and Consumption of Confederate Songsters

KIRSTEN M. SCHULTZ

Civil War soldiers have long been identified with song; their reputation has led the historian Bell Irvin Wiley to claim: "The men who wore the blue, and the butternut Rebs who opposed them, more than American fighters of any period, deserve to be called singing soldiers."[1] Although these soldiers heard a great deal of the officially sanctioned music of the field musicians and regimental or brigade bands, many also had opportunities to participate in unofficial music-making, especially singing. Whether in camp, on the march, or even during combat, the men sang and listened to secular and sacred vocal music. Much of that music was transmitted orally, but the rise in literacy rates, an increasingly positive attitude towards public education, and the growth of the book- and music-publishing industries during the antebellum period meant that more Americans could and did turn to written sources when learning and performing songs.

One type of publication associated with the singing of Civil War soldiers is the songster. In essence, a songster is a printed collection of secular song lyrics. Usually compact in size, relatively inexpensive, and not requiring musical literacy of its consumers, the songster could be an ideal accessory for song-loving soldiers who wanted access to the words of songs in a portable form. Both Union and Confederate businesses brought out songsters, but little is known about songsters in the South; an examination of Confederate songsters should lead to a better understanding of popular music during this period in the

1. Bell Irvin Wiley, *The Life of Billy Yank: The Common Soldier of the Union* (1971; reprint, Baton Rouge: Louisiana State University Press, 1988), 157.

South. In particular we seek to answer these questions: Which groups of Southerners were most likely to purchase and use songsters? And how might the actions of compilers, publishers, and consumers have shaped the production of Confederate songsters?

No wartime letters or diaries that contain clear references to the consumption of songsters by pro-Confederate Southerners have yet been located.[2] Therefore, anyone who tries to reconstruct the songsters' audience must rely on other types of evidence. For example, Richard Harwell, while working on a bibliography of Confederate imprints, found in a literary journal one reference that associates songsters with soldiers. By the time he finished *Confederate Music,* Harwell had decided that Confederate soldiers were "well supplied" with songsters and that they experienced "wide circulation at the time they were published." Later researchers, including Charles Hamm, William J. Mahar, and Caroline Moseley have accepted Harwell's conclusion.[3] No one, however, has investigated further to see whether more evidence linking soldiers and songsters exists, or whether other Southerners might have purchased large numbers of songsters.

Before discussing soldiers as songster consumers, two additional groups of pro-Confederate Southerners should be examined. There are indications that compilers, publishers, and retailers believed that

2. James Huffman of the Tenth Virginia Infantry did make a tantalizing statement about songbooks in his memoir: "We kept song books with us and passed much of our leisure time singing. I carried my book even through prison and brought it home with me." James Huffman, *Ups and Downs of a Confederate Soldier* (New York: W. E. Rudge's Sons, 1940), 68. Although songsters were called either "songsters" or "songbooks" during the nineteenth century, the items Huffman mentioned could be manuscripts rather than printed publications. For example, in the Federal prison on Johnson's Island, Ohio, where Huffman was incarcerated, more than one prisoner of war compiled songbooks; see [J. D. Milligan?], Prisoner of War Autograph Book, No. 17, and Walker Peyton Moncure, Prisoner of War Autograph Book, No. 20, Confederate Prisoners of War Collection, Eleanor S. Brockenbrough Library, Museum of the Confederacy.

3. Richard Harwell, *Confederate Belles-Lettres: A Bibliography and a Finding List of the Fiction, Poetry, Drama, Songsters, and Miscellaneous Literature Published in the Confederate States of America* (Hattiesburg, Miss.: Book Farm, 1941), 60–61; Richard Harwell, *Confederate Music* (Chapel Hill: University of North Carolina Press, 1950), 6–7; Charles Hamm, *Yesterdays: Popular Song in America* (New York: Norton, 1979), 231; William J. Mahar, "March to the Music: Twenty Top Hits of the Sixties," *Civil War Times Illustrated* 23, no. 5 (1984): 14; Caroline Moseley, "Irrepressible Conflict: Differences between Northern and Southern Songs of the Civil War," *Journal of Popular Culture* 25, no. 2 (fall 1991): 48.

theater and concert audiences, as well as sheet-music consumers, would buy songsters. Those who made or sold single-performer and performers' songsters, types of songsters devoted to the repertoire of one or more vocalists, would have targeted individuals who attended public theatrical and musical events. These publications promoted singers and the songs they performed, while allowing the public to learn some of those songs. Although many of these songsters, including *The Harmoneons' Casket of Songs and Glees* (1850) and *Tony Pastor's New Irish Comic Songster* (1863), appeared in the United States during the nineteenth century, they never made up a large part of songster production in the Confederacy.[4] Only three songsters, *Original Songs of the Atlanta Amateurs* (1861), *Book of Songs and Duets to Be Sung by the Little Queen Sisters* (1861), and *Harry Macarthy's Personation Concerts* (1862), out of a total output of sixty-three, were single-performer or performers' songsters.[5] Moreover, no songsters of either type were published after 1862, although the performers behind the three songsters were active in the Confederacy at least until 1864. For some reason, these performers turned away from the songster as a promotional tool. Perhaps the costs of production became prohibitive, or the songsters did not sell well enough to warrant further investment.

Songster compilers, publishers, and retailers may have also tried to attract the consumers of sheet music. They were a logical choice as an audience for songsters, because these Southerners already had demonstrated their interest in secular songs and their willingness to turn to the market to acquire copies of them. In addition, the multiple connections between the producers of songsters and sheet music suggest that some compilers and publishers would have had an interest in making songsters appealing to sheet-music consumers. For example,

4. *The Harmoneons' Casket of Songs and Glees as Written and Sung by Them at Their Concerts* (Boston: A. and J. P. Ordway, 1850); *Tony Pastor's New Irish Comic Songster Containing a Superb Collection of Original Irish, Dutch, Patriotic Songs, and Irish Stories* (New York: Dick and Fitzgerald, 1863).

5. References to the publication of sixty-three editions of thirty-seven different songsters were found in Confederate publications. In many of the extant editions the contents were changed; a few lyrics were added or cut by the compiler or compilers. Because of these changes and because a new edition represented another chance for a songster to circulate, each edition is counted as one songster. See the end of this article for a bibliography of the extant and lost Confederate songsters.

two compilers owned a business that sold or published sheet music. Francis D. Allen, a music retailer and proprietor of bookstores in Galveston and Houston, compiled and published the first of a series, *Lone Star Ballads, No. 1* (1863), and almost certainly did the same for the second songster in that series, *Lone Star Ballad Book, No. 2* (1863).[6] In Georgia, John C. Schreiner's son and partner in his music publishing business, Hermann L. Schreiner (1832–1891), put together the *Beauregard Songster* (1864) and the *Gen. Lee Songster* (1865).[7]

The connection between songsters and sheet music is also made evident through advertisements and publication announcements. Many of these advertisements are from firms such as Blackmar of New Orleans and Augusta, Georgia, that were known primarily as music publishers, but sheet-music retailers, like A. Morris of Richmond, also put out some advertisements. In several songsters, such as the *Beauregard Songster,* are advertisements for sheet music, several of which include a catalog of the sheet music available at a specific store.[8] Furthermore, songsters are listed alongside sheet music in advertisements located in periodicals, books, and sheet music. Blackmar made its connection with sheet music doubly clear by placing an advertisement for the company's stock, including sheet music and songsters, on the back of several editions of sheet music.[9]

6. Allen's last name was spelled two different ways during his publishing career. During the Civil War, in his advertisements, as well as in his self-published songster, he is listed as "Allen." By the time he put out the postwar edition of that songster, his name appears as "Allan." Since this essay covers his wartime activities, the wartime spelling is the one used. See the bibliography for the citations of Allen's wartime songsters; see also Francis D. Allan, comp., *Allan's Lone Star Ballads: A Collection of Southern Patriotic Songs, Made during Confederate Times* (Galveston, Tex.: J. D. Sawyer, 1874).

7. Two other compilers may have been associated with Branson and Farrar of Raleigh: Thomas A. Branson, who created the *Jack Morgan Songster* (1864), and Mrs. Marinda Branson Moore, who compiled *Songs of Love and Liberty* (1864). Branson and Farrar published and sold books, such as the songsters Branson and Moore compiled, and the partnership sold sheet music.

8. *Beauregard Songster,* [37].

9. Two examples are "Maryland! My Maryland!" (Augusta, Ga.: Blackmar and Bro.; New Orleans: Blackmar, 1862); and "Origin of the Stars and Bars" (Augusta, Ga.: Blackmar and Bro.; New Orleans: Blackmar, 1862); both are courtesy of the Rare Book, Manuscript, and Special Collections Library, Duke University, *Historic American Sheet Music,* July 13, 2002, http://scriptorium.lib.duke.edu/sheetmusic/. "Maryland! My Maryland!" and "Origin of the Stars and Bars" are numbers 7241 and 7331, respectively, in T. Michael Parrish and Robert M. Willingham Jr., *Confederate*

Notices in some of the songsters informed consumers that they could buy sheet-music editions of one or more of the songs at a local store. One example occurs in *Taylor's Southern Songster, No. 1* (1864): "The Music for all the Songs in this Book can be had on application at Messrs. Welch & Harris."[10] Even more overt is the notice on the front cover of the *Virginia Songster* (1863), which states that "Virginia!" whose lyrics are printed on the cover, is also available as sheet music. The existence of these notices implies that some compilers or publishers thought that owning a songster might lead a consumer to buy the sheet music versions of its contents.

Despite this evidence, the extent to which consumers of sheet music participated in the consumption of songsters is difficult to assess. Almost none of the records of the businesses involved in songster production have survived. Since over a third of the firms that published songsters were also music publishers, dealers, or both, it would have been surprising not to find any connections between the two types of publications (see below). Nevertheless, publishers and retailers might have publicized the links between sheet music and songsters because they hoped rather than knew that the consumers of the one format might be persuaded to purchase items in the other. A musically literate Confederate soldier, for example, might have decided to acquire a songster because it was easier to transport and was less expensive than sheet music. However, an individual who could not read musical notation would be much less likely to buy sheet music.

SONGSTER PUBLISHERS THAT ALSO PUBLISHED OR SOLD SHEET MUSIC

Francis D. Allen
Blackmar and Bro./Blackmar and Co.
Branson and Farrar
H. C. Clarke
A. Morris

Imprints: A Bibliography of Southern Publications from Secession to Surrender (Austin, Tex.: Jenkins Publishing, 1987) (hereinafter referred to as P&W).

10. *Taylor's No. 1,* [3]. Other songsters with similar notices are: *Beauregard Songster,* [3]; *Confederate Flag Song-Book,* 3d ed., [1]; *Confederate Flag Song-Book,* 4th ed., [1]; and *Gen. Lee Songster,* [1].

J. W. Randolph
John C. Schreiner and Son
West and Johnston

Confirming Confederate soldiers' role as major songster consumers is a less daunting challenge, because various references in contemporary publications attest to the association of soldiers with songsters. The most obvious clues are in the titles of songsters. A glance at the bibliography at the end of this essay reveals that many of the titles of Confederate songsters declare their allegiance to the Confederacy through the use of various patriotic symbols. For example, the Confederacy's national flag inspired the title *Southern Flag Song Book* (1861–1863). The title *Cotton Field Melodies* (1863) refers to the preeminent cash crop of the South. More than a third of the songsters, such as the *Army Songster* (1864), were named after a soldier or group of soldiers, but it is not clear whether the words were meant as patriotic symbols, as clues to their audience, or both. Two songsters, however, have titles that plainly identify their audience. The first example, *Camp Songs for Southern Soldiers* (1862) straightforwardly describes the nature of its contents and for whom they were intended. The subtitle of Tentler and Baker's *Southern Songster* (1864) provides the other example, for it assures the consumer that the songster was "Arranged Expressly for Camp." Both songsters' titles imply that their compilers chose material for the songsters with the soldiers' tastes in mind.

The preface of a songster can contain valuable information about the audience for which it was intended. Unfortunately, only five Confederate songsters have a preface, and of them only two communicate anything concrete about their consumers. Yet despite the rarity of the prefaces, the information gleaned from them might apply to other Confederate songsters. The anonymously written preface to the *Southern Soldier's Prize Songster* (1864) expresses no doubts about the identity of the audience for Confederate songsters: "Many Song Books have been issued to supply the great demand for that species of literature"—that is, patriotic lyrics by Southerners—"in our Army." The preface then goes on to claim that most of what these songsters contained was not proper for soldiers; what they really needed were more pro-Confederate lyrics. In contrast, the anonymously written preface of the *Punch Songster* (1864) argues that all a compiler can hope to do at present is to entertain soldiers: the *Punch Songster* "cannot enlarge their patriotic devotion to the best interests of their country—if, however, it tends to lessen the tedium of camp-life, we are more than satisfied."[11] Despite their differences over the true purpose of a songster, both writers do agree that soldiers were buying songsters.

Most of the advertisements that mention songsters do not include information about the intended audience. However, the headings of advertisements by two retailers indicate that they perceived soldiers as songster consumers. A January 1862 issue of the *Richmond Daily Whig* contains an advertisement by J. W. Randolph of Richmond with the title "Army and Navy." Another of Randolph's advertisements, headed by the phrase, "Military Books for Sale," appears on the back cover of the 1863 edition of *Songs of the South.* A year later, T. M. Acton, who described himself as an "Army News Agent, Army of Tennessee," put out an advertisement entitled "New Books for the Army." Alongside the songsters in these advertisements are publications such as drill manuals, cookbooks for the mess, and treatises for surgeons, any of which could have attracted consumers in the military.[12]

Publication notices can be informative because they frequently include one reader's reaction to a songster or point out something remarkable about it. The February 1863 issue of the Richmond journal the *Southern Literary Messenger* contains two examples of notices that connect soldiers and songsters. *Songs of the South* (1863) is described as a practical and inexpensive item "for the boys in camp," whereas *Songs of Humor and Sentiment* (1863) is simply "another book for soldiers." The remaining two examples appear in the *Richmond Whig.* A reviewer in a May 1864 issue of the *Whig* states that the *Army Songster* (1864) is "a new collection of songs for the camp." In the following month, the author of another notice declares that the fourth edition of the *Bold Soldier Boy's Song Book* (1864), has become "a great favorite in the army."[13] The casual tone of these refer-

11. *Southern Soldier's Prize Songster,* [3], 4; *Punch Songster,* [3].

12. *Richmond Daily Whig,* January 1, 1862; *Atlanta Southern Confederacy,* April 2, 1864.

13. *Southern Literary Messenger* 37, no. 2 (February 1863): 128; *Richmond Whig,* May 3 and June 9, 1864.

ences implies that the Richmond press did not find the concept of soldiers as songster consumers extraordinary.

The geographical and chronological distributions of these public notices provide information about where and when the recognition of Confederate soldiers as consumers of songsters developed. The majority of references—eight—are found in Richmond publications, which is not surprising, considering that nearly half of Confederate songsters were produced in Richmond.[14] In addition, there is evidence that some people west of the capital knew that soldiers were buying songsters, for three of the references are from two cities southwest of Richmond: two from Atlanta and one from Mobile. The consumption of periodicals and other publications may have extended knowledge of the existence of songsters and their connection with soldiers beyond the relatively few urban areas in the South. The Confederate postal system, sutlers, and itinerant retailers (like the army news agent Acton) also played an important part in bringing such information, as well as the songsters themselves, to Confederate troops.

The first public notices connecting songsters and soldiers appeared in 1862, but most came out during 1864 (Table 1). This may have occurred because compilers and publishers simply did not expect many soldiers to purchase songsters. Since neither the marketing nor the reception of songsters in nineteenth-century America has been studied extensively, no one has yet determined whether those who produced and sold songsters during the first half of the nineteenth century recognized soldiers as consumers of songsters.[15] If this recognition did not exist before 1861, then it may not have happened in the Confederacy until the latter half of the war.

Like the publication notices, songster production in the Confederacy grew as the war progressed (Table 2). The first year, 1861, when five songsters were published, seems relatively quiet. Over the

14. Kirsten M. Schultz, "Secessia's Song Books: The History of Confederate Songsters," 2 vols. (Ph.D. diss., University of Toronto, 2001), 1:67–68.

15. William Miles and Cheryl Taranto have discussed the production and reception of presidential campaign songsters; in most other studies the emphasis, understandably, has been more on bibliography or on the content of the lyrics. See William Miles, *Songs, Odes, Glees, and Ballads: A Bibliography of American Presidential Campaign Songsters* (New York: Greenwood Press, 1990), xxi–xxxiii; and Cheryl T. Taranto, "Political Songsters for the Presidential Campaign of 1860" (Ph.D. diss., Louisiana State University, 1994), 24–41.

Table 1. Publication Notices

	1861	1862	1863	1864	1865
Notices	0	2	3	6	0

Table 2. Confederate Songster Production[a]

	1861	1862	1863	1864	1865
Extant Songsters	4	4	11	15	4
Lost Songsters[b]	1	3	3	12	0
Total	5	7	14	27	4

a. Songsters without a copyright or publication date are not included in this table.

b. Only songsters that were announced as having been published or were reviewed in a contemporary publication are included here.

next three years the number of songsters increased, especially in 1863 and 1864. During both of these years songsters doubled in number. Despite this promising pattern of growth, songster production abruptly declined in 1865 with the demise of the Confederacy.

A comparison of the number of songsters published with the number of publishers actually involved in songster production further underlines the importance of 1864 for Confederate songsters (Table 3). Whereas the number of songsters increased in every year except 1865, the number of publishers offering songsters remained fairly stable from 1861 to 1863. Then, in 1864, the numbers rose sharply, reflecting the level of activity that took place during that year. However, because of the disintegration of the Confederacy, fewer publishers were active in 1865 than during the first year of the war.

By the time the war ended, a total of twenty-one businesses had published at least one songster for a Confederate audience. However, in 1861, 1862, and 1864, first-time publishers were more numerous than veteran publishers (Table 4). The rate of attrition was high; during each year of the war half or more of the new publishers were unable to bring out a songster in the following year. Furthermore, the majority of publishers produced one songster during the war. Only five firms, or about a quarter of the publishers, were able to bring out three or more songsters. These businesses—H. C. Clarke of

Table 3. Number of Songster Publishers[a]

	1861	1862	1863	1864	1865
Publishers	4	5	5	12	3

a. These figures include unidentified publishers.

Table 4. Number of First-Time Publishers versus Total Number of Active Publishers

	1861	1862	1863	1864	1865
First-Time Publishers	4	5	2	9	1
Total Publishers	4	5	5	12	3

Vicksburg, Mississippi, and later Mobile; J. W. Randolph; Blackmar of New Orleans and Augusta, Georgia; J. W. Randolph, and West and Johnston of Richmond; and Welch and Harris of Charleston—were responsible for the production of most of the Confederate songsters.[16]

Although it might be simpler to ascribe the low survival rate of publishers purely to the failure of the songsters, the varying experiences of the publishers point to different factors as the reasons behind their decision to stop producing songsters. For example, financial problems may have been behind the low output of at least two publishers. According to a notice in the *Galveston Weekly News,* Francis D. Allen's *Lone Star Ballads, No. 1* seemed to have enjoyed a positive reception. Allen then brought out a second songster in the series. Despite this apparent success, Allen sold his Houston bookstore and its stock at the beginning of the next year.[17] His business may have been crippled by the blockade of the Texas coast, which was effective enough to stall trade in Houston and Galveston. He did not publish any more songsters during the conflict, possibly because the weak local economy could not generate enough demand for songsters. The dissolution of the Richmond book and periodical publishers Ayres and Wade at the end of 1864 probably prevented

16. Taylor informed customers that copies of his songster were available for "[W]holesale and Retail" at Welch and Harris's store. *Taylor's No. 1,* [3].

17. *Galveston Weekly News,* September 9, 1863, and January 27, 1864. No information about the reception of *Lone Star Ballads, No. 2* (1863) has been located.

that firm from publishing more than one songster.[18] The partnership may have been suffering financially, unable to keep up with ever-increasing production costs, or unable to sell enough of its products. E. W. Ayres, the partner who retained the rights to the firm's property, decided to continue publishing the *Southern Illustrated News,* the mainstay of the former partnership. However, no other songsters came from the presses of either Ayres or Wade.

Timing may have been the enemy of many songster publishers. John Hopkins of New Orleans definitely brought out one songster in 1861. It is unclear exactly when the firm's other songster came out, but Hopkins could not have openly published pro-Confederate works after April 1862, when New Orleans fell to the Federals. During that same spring, Hutton and Freligh of Memphis published one songster before they had to escape the Union occupation of the city. The partners fled to Mississippi to begin anew, but their business soon fell apart. The newcomers of 1864 and early 1865—Richmond businesses George L. Bidgood, A. Morris, the *Southern Punch,* and Tentler and Baker, as well as an anonymous publisher in Staunton, Virginia, Branson and Farrar, the publisher of *Taylor's Southern Songster, Nos. 1–3* (1864), John C. Schreiner and Son, and W. F. Wisely of Mobile—may have stopped creating songsters when the towns and cities they worked in surrendered. However, other factors, such as financial problems or a negative response to individual songsters, might have caused these publishers to turn away from songsters at some point before Union forces took control.

Despite the trials experienced by many publishers, others still were bringing out songsters. Songster production, the total number of publishers participating in that production, and the number of new songster publishers all reached their zenith in 1864, the same year as when most of the references to soldiers as songster consumers occurred. If compilers, publishers, and journalists did not have this knowledge earlier, then by the end of 1864 many of them certainly understood that the songster was a viable publication that was attractive to soldiers. Why, then, did songster production experience a slow start in the Confederacy, and what might have delayed awareness of the role Confederate soldiers could play in songster consumption? A

18. *Richmond Southern Illustrated News,* December 24, 1864.

Table 5. Songster Production in Several Northern and Southern States, 1821–1860

State	NY	PA	MA	OH	CT	MD	MO	KY	SC	VA	AL
Number of Songsters	167	138	59	48	41	36	15	9	5	5	1

Sources: *WorldCat* and Song Books Catalogue, Center for Popular Music, Middle Tennessee State University.

brief history of songster publication in antebellum America provides a probable answer for both questions.

Although there is no complete bibliographical control over songsters published in the forty years before the Civil War, a survey of two databases—Online Computer Library Center's WorldCat and Middle Tennessee State University's songster catalog—indicates that businesses in the North dominated antebellum songster production (Table 5).[19] Publishers in the border states, such as in Maryland, were relatively active before the Civil War, but in the states that later formed the Confederacy, songsters were rarely published before 1861. Some Southern retailers may have decided that it was more economical to meet local demand by importing songsters either from the North or from one of the more active border states. For example,

19. See *OCLC FirstSearch,* June 2, 2002, http://newfirstsearch.oclc.org; *Song Books,* Center for Popular Music, Middle Tennessee State University, Murfreesboro, June 2, 2002, http://popmusic.mtsu.edu/research.html#songbooks. See also Irving Lowens, *A Bibliography of Songsters Printed in America before 1821* (Worcester, Mass.: American Antiquarian Society, 1976). Only certain types or collections of songsters published after 1820 have appeared in bibliographies, indexes, and checklists; see Frangcon L. Jones, "A Study of American 'Forget-Me-Not' Songsters of the 1840s and 1850s" (Ph.D. diss., Brown University, 1948); Albert Johannsen, *The House of Beadle and Adams and Its Dime and Nickel Novels: The Story of a Vanished Literature* (Norman: University of Oklahoma Press, 1962), 1:380–95; Harry Hertzberg and Leonard V. Farley, *A Bibliography of Nineteenth-Century Clown Songsters of the Harry Hertzberg Circus Collection of the San Antonio Public Library* (n.p.: Carleton Print, 1962); Rachel Young, "American Songsters, Vol. 1: 1800–1860," typescript, 1965–1970, John Hay Library, Brown University, Providence, R.I.; Miles, *Songs, Odes, Glees*; Sion M. Honea, "Nineteenth-Century American Masonic Songbooks: A Preliminary Checklist," *Music Reference Services Quarterly* 3, no. 4 (1995): 17–32; and Kelly M. Wilson, "Singing Clowns and Songsters: An Examination of Nineteenth-Century Popular Music and Circuses in the United States" (master's thesis, University of Wisconsin–Madison, 2001), 88–111.

a commission firm in antebellum Houston received two lots of songsters from Philadelphia (ca. 1836–1845).[20]

When the Civil War broke out, therefore, publishers in the Confederacy were unprepared to take over the niche that Northern publishing houses had previously controlled. Furthermore, secession, the birth of a new nation, and war fever engrossed Confederates during much of 1861, probably keeping demand low. The slow growth of songster production in the Confederacy might have also come about because many compilers and publishers were perhaps uncertain whether any group of literate Southerners would be interested in songsters. If that was what happened, then it took months or years for many of the compilers and publishers to learn that there was a substantial market for songsters.

A few enterprising Southerners brought out songsters in 1861, but it was not until the following year when more than one publisher had definitely produced a songster that performed well enough to cause the firm to risk printing either another edition or a completely new songster. By the end of 1862, four publishers—John Hopkins, H. C. Clarke, Blackmar, and J. W. Randolph—had been able to produce more than one songster.[21] Over the next two years, four more—Francis D. Allen, West and Johnston, the unidentified publisher of Taylor's songsters, and Branson and Farrar—joined the first four in the practice of producing multiple editions, songsters, or both. Of these eight publishers, four—Clarke, Randolph, Blackmar, and West and Johnston—were well-known companies that advertised their songsters in newspapers and journals aimed at local and national audiences.[22] By employing this tactic, a publishing house could publicize its stock over an extensive area.

20. Donald Pugh identifies the *American Songster* and the *Comic Songster* as Philadelphia imprints from two different publishers, Thomas Davis, and Kay and Bros. Donald Wagner Pugh, "Music in Frontier Houston, 1836–1876" (DMA doc., University of Texas at Austin, 1970), 27, 39n129.

21. The undated songster published by Hopkins came out between late May 1861 and April 1862, after the deaths of Union officer Colonel Elmer Ellsworth (1837–1861) and James W. Jackson (d. 1861), a pro-Confederate civilian, over the removal of a Confederate flag in Alexandria, Virginia, and before New Orleans surrendered to Federal forces. The song, "Jackson, of Alexandria, Va." (1861), celebrates Jackson's killing of Ellsworth. *Hopkins* n.d., 12–13.

22. *Richmond Southern Illustrated News,* April 9, 1864; *Richmond Daily Whig,* January 1, 1862; *Richmond Southern Illustrated News,* May 9, 1863.

With such achievements before them, other Confederate publishers evidently began to realize that songsters could be a popular and financial success. Richmond's seven songster publishers, several located within blocks of each other, would have quickly learned of the triumphs and failures of their competitors. Both inside and outside of the capital city publishers could have spread information about songsters and their consumers through advertisements and publication notices, as well as through direct communication with other compilers, publishers, and retailers. For example, when Blackmar issued its third edition of the *Bonnie Blue Flag Song Book* (1863), the publishing house placed an advertisement in the *Southern Illustrated News,* a national newspaper. Almost a week later, the friendly editor of the *Augusta Daily Chronicle and Sentinel* announced that the third edition was available.[23] Blackmar, therefore, received both national and local exposure for its new edition.

Even more impressive to anyone concerned with the sales of songsters was a series of advertisements by West and Johnston and by Clarke during late 1863 and 1864. Appearing in various local and national publications, each advertisement boasts of the thousands of copies of a particular songster the firm sold. These exchanges show that at least two publishers felt that there was enough consumer interest in songsters to make it important to compete actively for market share. The successes of these firms may well have induced other publishers to start bringing out their own songsters.[24]

Confederate compilers and publishers, however, did not have to rely solely on the testimony of fellow Southerners; they could monitor the activities of their counterparts in the Union. The appearance in Confederate songsters of songs recently published in the North,

23. *Richmond Southern Illustrated News,* May 9, 1863; *Augusta Daily Chronicle and Sentinel,* May 15, 1863.

24. For example, West and Johnston declared in 1864 that it had sold "upwards of fifty thousand copies" of the *Stonewall Song Book* (1863–1865). During that same year, Clarke claimed that its customers had bought "over 80,000 copies" of the fourth edition of the *Confederate Flag Song Book.* Southern Literary Messenger 37, no. 12 (December 1863): 751; *Richmond Southern Illustrated News,* January 23, 1864; *Mobile Confederate Spirit and Knapsack of Fun,* July 23, 1864; Dinah Craik, *Mistress and Maid: A Household Story* (Richmond, Va.: West and Johnston, 1864), back cover; *Clarke's Confederate Almanac for the Year of Our Lord 1864.* (Mobile, Ala.: H. C. Clarke, 1864), back cover; *Stonewall Song Book,* 5th ed., 70–71; *Army Songster,* 25.

such as "When This Cruel War Is Over" (1863) and "Who Will Care for Mother Now?" (1863), demonstrates that Confederate publishers did keep abreast of the news from the Northern music industry. Some publishers may have also decided that following the progress of Northern songster publishers was a sound policy. Since the 1860s may have been the most productive decade in the nineteenth century for American songsters, knowledge that a flood of songster publishing was happening in the North might have given more conservative Confederate publishers added confidence in the songster's ability to attract customers.[25]

Whatever the source of a publisher's intelligence, it still took time for new songsters and editions to appear, for the news of their success to travel, and for publishers to act on that information. Awareness of the songster's popularity and of the identity of many of their consumers may have begun sometime in 1862, with the early successes of Hopkins, Clarke, Randolph, and Blackmar. However, more publishers apparently became conscious of the songster's potential and of the soldiers' importance as songster consumers in 1864, when the numbers of songsters, songster publishers, and references linking soldiers and songsters reached their height. Stimulating this growth was consumer demand and some publishers' willingness to support what was for them a seldom-tried format.

The majority of Confederate songsters were commodities, created solely to make a profit. Even the two songsters created for charitable causes, *Book of Songs and Duets to Be Sung by the Little Queen Sisters* and *Original Songs of the Atlanta Amateurs,* had to make money to be considered successful. Compilers, therefore, were not free to randomly collect lyrics or to simply construct an anthology of their favorite works. Instead, the content of songsters depended largely on pragmatic concerns. For example, in order to advertise the performers and the songs they sang, single-performer and performers' songsters were supposed to contain repertoire written or performed by the soloist or group associated with the songster. *Macarthy's Personation Concerts* also serves as a program of his show, so it is clear that

25. According to Cecil Patterson's unscientific survey of six hundred songsters, the largest number of dateable songsters was from the 1860s. Cecil Patterson, "A Different Drum: The Image of the Negro in the Nineteenth Century Popular Song Books" (Ph.D. diss., University of Pennsylvania, 1961), 9–11.

he was somehow involved with every song in his songster.[26] The three Confederate single-performer and performers' songsters also contain works by other authors, frequently antebellum works from Great Britain and the United States. Even Macarthy, who had written the very successful "Bonnie Blue Flag" (1861), included works by others, such as Samuel Lover's (1797–1868) "Widow Machree" (1842).

Compilers, some of whom had connections to a sheet-music publisher or retailer, could choose repertoire from the stock a business had on hand, thus advertising its own products. One might think that a music publisher would insist on a songster dominated by the firm's products, but an examination of the contents of the songsters by the two largest Confederate music publishers—Blackmar and Schreiner—reveals that the compilers of their songsters did not act consistently. Nearly all of the pieces included in the third edition of Blackmar's *Bonnie Blue Flag Song Book* and over three-quarters of the lyrics in Schreiner's *Beauregard Songster* also appear as sheet music produced by the same publisher. However, the majority of lyrics in Blackmar's *Dixie Land Songster* (1863), Blackmar's *Cotton Field Melodies,* and Schreiner's *Gen. Lee Songster* cannot be traced to sheet music produced by the songster's publisher. Apparently, neither Blackmar nor Schreiner considered it necessary to concentrate solely on advertising their own publications in the contents of every songster they published.[27]

The perceived needs of a songster's audience frequently affected what a Confederate compiler decided to include in a songster. For example, presidential-campaign songsters, a staple of American elections from the 1840s to World War I, had a very specific and short-term use: to supply the supporters of a candidate with songs suitable for rallies, parades, and other campaign functions. This type of songster contains primarily new and topical lyrics, because campaign songs needed to discuss the candidates and issues involved in one election. Many of those lyrics were set to well-known melodies such as "Yankee Doodle" (1760s?) or "Old Dan Tucker" (1843), making it easier for consumers to sing the resulting text-and-tune combinations. A

26. *Macarthy's Personation Concerts,* 7–8.
27. Since music and bookstores routinely carried sheet music by more than one publisher, it would also be instructive to discover how much of a songster's content might have been obtained from the sheet music of other firms.

campaign songster that contained mostly nontopical lyrics, or that had lyrics wed to new or unfamiliar tunes, could not meet the expectations of its intended audience and would likely sell poorly.[28]

The contents of songsters can be examined in a variety of ways to ascertain how compilers tried to make them appealing to consumers. Studies of the contents' nationality or genre can yield useful information, but an investigation of the period of the songsters' contents provides the most straightforward demonstration of how compilers' perceptions of consumers' needs influenced the structure of the songsters. To accomplish this, we will divide the lyrics and corresponding, "implied" melodies into two periods, antebellum and wartime, which are broad enough to permit nearly all of the pieces to be placed into a single category.[29] By comparing the numbers of antebellum and wartime pieces, we can see how much of the songster the compiler devoted to each of them. Finally, the results should reveal something of the compilers' actions and the probable motivations behind them.

Before concentrating on the lyrics, the implied melodies need to be included in a brief examination of how the contents of Confederate songsters reflect what many consumers wanted to find in a songster. Confederate compilers, like the compilers of presidential-campaign songsters, depended heavily on lyrics wed to previously published melodies (Table 6). This was a sensible decision, because none of the extant Confederate songsters have any musical notation. If the compiler had included many lyrics set to obscure melodies, or lyrics that had no melodic setting, then the consumer either would have had to spend more time recalling melodies that matched the texts, or would have had to be satisfied with just reading the lyrics more or less as poetry. Therefore, a Confederate songster that implied many familiar antebellum tunes was more accessible than one that primarily

28. Richard Crawford, *The American Musical Landscape* (Berkeley and Los Angeles: University of California Press, 1993), 114–15, 138–40. For more information on presidential campaign songsters, see Miles, *Songs, Odes, Glees;* and Taranto, "Political Songsters."

29. The term *implied melody* is appropriate for the discussion of melodies and text-only sources because the term acknowledges that, although the melodies are usually not provided in musical notation in a songster, many of the lyrics in songsters had been set to one or more melodies, with an accompanying note to that effect. Though a lyric might appear without a melody, a tune still could be present in the mind of the lyricist, compiler, or the person using the songster.

Table 6. Antebellum versus Wartime Melodies in Individual Songsters[a]

Songster Title	Number of Lyrics	Number of Dateable Implied	Percentage of Antebellum Implied Melodies (Out of Dateable Melodies)	Percentage of Wartime Implied Melodies (Out of Dateable Melodies)
Allen's No. 1	48	37	81.08	18.91
Army	80	76	80.26	19.73
Atlanta	15	11	100.00	0
Beauregard	36	33	69.69	30.30
Bold Soldier	76	64	96.87	3.12
Bonnie Blue	27	26	69.23	30.76
Cavalier	41	34	70.58	29.41
Confederate Flag 3d	79	72	75.00	25.00
Confederate Flag 4th	65	59	76.27	23.72
Cotton Field	35	27	96.29	3.70
Dixie Land	27	22	95.45	4.54
Gen. Lee	41	34	64.70	35.29
Hopkins 1861	10	7	100.00	0
Hopkins n.d.	12	6	100.00	0
Humor '63	89	74	98.64	1.35
Humor '64	89	77	98.70	1.29
Jack Morgan	74	68	80.88	19.11
Macarthy	11	7	100.00	0
Prize	62	21	76.19	23.80
Punch	70	36	88.88	11.11
Queen Sisters	18	15	100.00	0
Rebel	58	53	96.22	3.77
Soldier Boy's	70	60	96.66	3.33
Songs of Love	47	44	68.18	31.81
South 1862	57	34	70.58	29.41
South 2d	59	34	70.58	29.41
South 1863	60	35	71.42	28.57
South 1864	63	40	65.00	35.00

Table 6. Antebellum versus Wartime Melodies in Individual Songsters[a] *(continued)*

Songster Title	Number of Lyrics	Number of Dateable Implied	Percentage of Antebellum Implied Melodies (Out of Dateable Melodies)	Percentage of Wartime Implied Melodies (Out of Dateable Melodies)
Southern	26	23	91.30	8.69
Southern Flag 1861	53	36	91.66	8.33
Southern Flag n.d.	50	44	100.00	0
Stonewall 2d	81	73	98.63	1.36
Stonewall 4th	80	71	95.77	4.22
Stonewall 5th	80	71	95.77	4.22
Stonewall 10th	81	73	98.63	1.36
Stonewall 11th	79	71	94.36	5.63
Stonewall 12th	79	71	94.36	5.63
Taylor's No. 1	21	19	68.42	31.57
Virginia	79	60	91.66	8.33

a. The contents of two of the extant songsters, *Southern Monthly Collection* (1862) and *Southern Flag Song Book No. 3* (1863), could not be examined for this article, but these songsters are otherwise included in the discussions about extant and dateable songsters.

implied melodies composed during the war. This explains why tunes that had circulated for decades and had become widely known (like "Annie Laurie" [1838]), were implied much more often in Confederate songsters than were newer ones (like Armand E. Blackmar's [1826–1888] setting of William M. Johnston's "God and Our Rights" [1861]).[30]

30. The melody of "Annie Laurie" is implied in the songsters of eleven publishers, whereas "God and Our Rights" is implied in one. See Schultz, "Secessia's Song Books," 88–112; William Johnston and A. E. Blackmar, "God and Our Rights" (New Orleans: A. E. Blackmar and Bro., 1861), P&W 7061, courtesy of the Rare Book, Manuscript, and Special Collections Library, Duke University, *Historic American Sheet Music,* July 13, 2002, http://scriptorium.lib.duke.edu/sheetmusic/.

Implied melodies were not the only element that could be influenced by consumer demand. Compilers presumably selected many lyrics because their presence in a songster would please consumers. Antebellum lyrics, such as "Oft in the Stilly Night" (1818) and "Bonny Eloise" (1858), outnumber wartime texts in the majority of the Confederate songsters (Table 7), suggesting that compilers and publishers believed that most of their customers wanted or at least accepted large numbers of antebellum lyrics in a songster. Moreover, the success of songsters like the *Stonewall Song Books* (1863–1865), which contain a majority of antebellum lyrics, indicates that consumers did appreciate their presence. Consumers may have valued songsters not only because they could learn new or unfamiliar songs, but also because songsters could remind the user of the words to songs he or she had already encountered.

Both the availability of lyrics and Confederate copyright law reinforced the dominance of antebellum lyrics in Confederate songsters. Since many more antebellum songs existed than wartime ones, compilers obviously had a sizable pool of literature from which to choose suitable material. The large number of available lyrics allowed compilers to concentrate on the ones that had a reputation as popular favorites. In addition, antebellum lyrics were readily accessible in a variety of publications, including periodicals and broadsides. For all of these reasons, compilers should have found it easy to populate a songster with numerous pieces written before 1861.

Confederate copyright law, which the Confederate Congress enacted in 1861, gave compilers the right to use a majority of antebellum lyrics. Following established American copyright law, only pieces created by citizens and residents could be copyrighted; no international copyright law covered the works of foreigners residing outside of the Confederacy. Since many antebellum lyrics were by Northerners and Europeans, their works could not be protected. Consequently, the compilers of songsters were free to use material like "Home, Sweet Home" (1823) and "Let Me Kiss Him for His Mother" (1859).[31]

31. Although the Confederate copyright law was progressive in that it had a provision that permitted the negotiating of international copyright agreements with foreign states, that process was never initiated. Confederate States of America, *Statutes at Large of the Provisional Government of the Confederate States of America, from the Institution of the Government, February 8, 1861, to Its Termination, February 18,*

Table 7. Antebellum versus Wartime Lyrics in Individual Songsters

Songster Title	Number of Lyrics	Number of Dateable Implied	Percentage of Antebellum Implied Melodies (Out of Dateable Melodies)	Percentage of Wartime Implied Melodies (Out of Dateable Melodies)
Allen's No. 1	48	43	4.65	95.34
Army	80	79	79.74	20.25
Atlanta	15	13	15.38	84.61
Beauregard	36	34	55.88	44.11
Bold Soldier	76	64	90.62	9.37
Bonnie Blue	27	27	48.14	51.85
Cavalier	41	39	53.84	46.15
Confederate Flag 3d	79	70	57.14	42.85
Confederate Flag 4th	65	56	64.28	35.71
Cotton Field	35	26	96.15	3.84
Dixie Land	27	25	60.00	40.00
Gen. Lee	41	36	55.55	44.44
Hopkins 1861	10	9	55.55	44.44
Hopkins n.d.	12	6	16.66	83.33
Humor '63	89	74	97.29	2.70
Humor '64	89	76	97.36	2.63
Jack Morgan	74	71	64.78	35.21
Macarthy	11	7	57.14	42.85
Prize	62	62	4.83	95.16
Punch	70	49	48.97	51.02
Queen Sisters	18	13	69.23	30.76
Rebel	58	56	87.50	12.50
Soldier Boy's	70	58	91.37	8.62
Songs of Love	47	46	58.69	41.30
South 1862	57	46	13.04	86.95
South 2d	59	47	10.63	89.36
South 1863	60	49	12.24	87.75
South 1864	63	53	11.32	88.67

Table 7. Antebellum versus Wartime Lyrics in Individual Songsters *(continued)*

Songster Title	Number of Lyrics	Number of Dateable Implied	Percentage of Antebellum Implied Melodies (Out of Dateable Melodies)	Percentage of Wartime Implied Melodies (Out of Dateable Melodies)
Southern	26	23	56.52	43.47
Southern Flag 1861	53	43	51.16	48.83
Southern Flag n.d.	50	47	87.23	12.76
Stonewall 2d	81	76	84.21	15.78
Stonewall 4th	80	73	80.82	19.17
Stonewall 5th	80	78	82.05	17.94
Stonewall 10th	81	77	83.11	16.88
Stonewall 11th	79	72	80.55	19.44
Stonewall 12th	79	72	80.55	19.44
Taylor's No. 1	21	17	58.82	41.17
Virginia	79	61	81.96	18.03

Songs that were deposited for copyright could not legally be published without the copyright holder's consent. Therefore, some wartime lyrics, such as "Bonnie Blue Flag" and John Hill Hewitt's (1801–1890) "The Young Volunteer" (1863), should have appeared only in a songster whose compiler or publisher held the copyright or had obtained permission to copy the piece from the copyright's owner. It would not be surprising, however, to discover that some compilers had violated this law, for the occasional notice protecting individual songs in a songster implies that piracy of lyrics had occurred before.[32]

1862, Inclusive; Arranged in Chronological Order (Richmond, Va.: R. M. Smith, 1864), 157–61. "Home, Sweet Home" appeared in the songsters of six publishers and "Let Me Kiss Him for His Mother" in the songsters of ten. Schultz, "Secessia's Song Books," 2:1–61.

32. For an example from a Confederate songster, see *Songs of the South,* 1863 ed., 35–37. Similar notices appear in antebellum and Union songsters, too; see *The*

Still, this piece of legislation may have discouraged compilers from appropriating certain Confederate lyrics, forcing them to turn to another Confederate text or to an antebellum one.

Southerners' patriotism, unlike the copyright law, actually encouraged the use of wartime lyrics. Through a variety of media, including songs, Southerners could assert their loyalty to the Confederacy. Although compilers did make use of some antebellum lyrics, such as "Listen to the Mocking Bird" (1855), that are set in the South, only a few pieces, like William Gaston's "The Old North State" (1844), are overtly patriotic. Responding to the need for patriotic texts, Southern poets, largely amateurs, flooded publishers with lyrics. Most compilers took advantage of this flood by selecting at least a few wartime pieces that praise the South and its people or demonstrate or discuss what actions were needed from Southerners to defend their country. For instance, a lyricist might remind the reader that the South was a region worth the loyalty and love of its inhabitants (see "The Southern Union" [ca. 1861–1862], and "My Native Land" [ca. 1861–1862]), or he might demonstrate to men and women how to act in a way that would best aid the Confederacy (see "The Old Rifleman. Southern Army" [ca. 1861–1862], and "Ladies, to the Hospital!" [ca. 1861–1863]).[33]

Some wartime lyrics may have been included with the hope that they might become the next sensation. One example is the prize-winning "Southland" (1864), chosen by a committee as the best possible candidate for a Confederate national anthem. Other lyrics, like those of "The Virginian's Song of Home" (1855) and "Way Down in Ole Virginia," may have been put in songsters to flatter the people of a particular state or locale. Such texts are especially common in the

Dime Song Book No. 2: A Collection of New and Popular Comic and Sentimental Songs (New York: Irwin P. Beadle, 1860; reprint, Bedford, Mass.: Applewood Books, n.d.), 11, 13; and *Billy Birch's Ethiopian Melodist: Being a Collection of the Most Popular and Laughable Negro Songs, the Newest and Most Fashionable Sentimental Songs Interspersed with Favorite Comic Songs*... (New York: Dick and Fitzgerald, 1862), 5.

33. *Songs of Love,* 5–6; *Dixie Land Songster,* 17–18; *Southern Songster,* 15–16; *Songs of the South,* 1862 ed., 24–26; *Songs of Humor,* 1863 ed., 35–36; *Songs of the South,* 1863 ed., 20–22; *Lone Star Ballads, No. 1,* 23–26. Additional information on Southern content in antebellum and wartime lyrics is given in Schultz, "Secessia's Song Books," 1:161–72.

songster from Texas, *Lone Star Ballads, No. 1.* One suspects that Allen, the songster's compiler and publisher, exploited his fellow Texans' passionate love for their state by adding a number of lyrics about Texas and Texans to his songster.[34]

Despite the pro-Confederate content of the majority of wartime lyrics, these songs experienced varying levels of success. Many probably never became well known anywhere in the South. Others, such as various lyrics in the *Lone Star Ballads, No. 1,* may have circulated within a limited area. The blockade off the coast of Texas and the occupation of the Mississippi River by Union forces may have hindered the transmission of songs from the Southwest after the summer of 1863. A number of lyrics, such as "Lincoln Going to Canaan/ Send Them to de Happy Land of Canaan" (1861), may have been popular for just a short time. Only a few, such as "My Maryland" (1861), remained in the repertoires of Southerners for decades.[35]

A closer analysis of the composition of the songsters reveals that each songster has one of three structures (Table 8). The first two types, "antebellum-emphasis" songsters (such as *Rebel Songster* [1864]) and "wartime-emphasis" songsters (such as *Hopkins' New-Orleans Five Cent Song-Book* [n.d.]), contain an overwhelming majority of either antebellum or wartime lyrics. "Mixed-period" songsters (such as *Cavalier Songster* [1865]), the third type, have 40 percent or more of both antebellum and wartime lyrics. Of the thirty-nine extant songsters examined, eighteen are antebellum-emphasis, thirteen are mixed-period, and eight are wartime-emphasis. These figures reflect the large number of antebellum lyrics present in most Confederate songsters,

34. *Southern Soldier's Prize Songster,* 7–9; *Virginia Songster,* 7–8, 50–51; Schultz, "Secessia's Song Books," 2:1–2.

35. "Lincoln Going to Canaan/Send Them to de Happy Land of Canaan" appears a total of four times in the songsters of two publishers. Three of its four appearances are in songsters from 1861; the fourth is in the undated edition of the *Southern Flag Song Book,* 1–61. "My Maryland" was included in postwar anthologies of poetry and songs, such as Allen's postwar songster, which contains much of the repertoire in *Lone Star Ballads, No. 1,* plus many new pieces, possibly from *Lone Star Ballads, No. 2.* Francis D. Allan, comp., *Allan's Lone Star Ballads,* 24–26. See also Emily Mason, ed., *Southern Poems of the War,* 5th rev. and enl. ed. (Baltimore: John Murphy, 1878), 67–69. "My Maryland" was chosen for *Heart Songs,* a collection of songs "Dear to the American People"; see Joe Chapple, ed., *Heart Songs* (Boston: Chapple, 1909; reprint, New York: Da Capo Press, 1983), 456. In 1939, this piece became the state song of Maryland.

Table 8. Structure of Confederate Songsters

Antebellum-Emphasis	Wartime-Emphasis	Mixed-Period
Army	*Allen's No. 1*	*Beauregard*
Bold Soldier	*Atlanta*	*Bonnie Blue*
Confederate Flag 4th	*Hopkins n.d.*	*Cavalier*
Cotton Field	*Prize*	*Confederate Flag 3d*
Humor 1863	*South 1862*	*Dixie Land*
Humor 1864	*South 2d*	*Gen. Lee*
Jack Morgan	*South 1863*	*Hopkins 1861*
Queen Sisters	*South 1864*	*Macarthy*
Rebel		*Punch*
Soldier Boy'		*Songs of Love*
Southern Flag n.d.		*Southern*
Stonewall 2d		*Southern Flag 1861*
Stonewall 4th		*Taylor's No. 1*
Stonewall 5th		
Stonewall 10th		
Stonewall 11th		
Stonewall 12th		
Virginia		

but they also prove that wartime lyrics were a substantial part of over half of the songsters.

Arranging the extant songsters by their structure and the year they were published shows that the production of songsters changed dramatically in the middle of the war (Table 9). During the first two years, compilers primarily created wartime-emphasis and mixed-period songsters (such as *Original Songs of the Atlanta Amateurs* and *Macarthy's Personation Concerts,* respectively). Antebellum-emphasis songsters (such as *Virginia Songster*) were rare until 1863, when they became the most common type of songster. During 1864, songster production altered again; mixed-period songsters tripled in number, an increase large enough to make them nearly as common as the antebellum-emphasis songsters. Unsurprisingly, in 1865 all of the songster types decreased dramatically.

Table 9. Songster Types Arranged Chronologically[a]

	1861	1862	1863	1864	1865
Antebellum-Emphasis	1	0	6	7	2
Mixed-Period	2	1	2	6	2
Wartime-Emphasis	1	2	2	2	0

a. Songsters that have no publication or copyright date are not included in this table.

Since the economy of the Confederacy continued to decline as the war progressed, it is doubtful that the financial situations of many publishers abruptly improved, freeing them to experiment with songsters. Consumer demand seems a better candidate for the primary motivation behind the changes in songster production, influencing not only the number of songsters made, but also the types of songsters compilers constructed. The rise in the number of antebellum-emphasis and mixed-period songsters suggests that publishers had brought out something that the public liked. Consumers evidently preferred either a songster that contained a large number of antebellum lyrics and few wartime texts, or one that was split between the two periods. As compilers and publishers realized this, they scrambled to bring out more of those songsters, thus causing a surge in their production.

Consumer demand might also have shaped the production of wartime-emphasis songsters. Whereas the number of antebellum-emphasis and mixed-period songsters increased noticeably during the Civil War, wartime-emphasis songsters appeared at about the same rate until 1865, when they disappeared entirely. The small but steady production of wartime-emphasis songsters (such as *Songs of the South* [1862–1864]) shows that a few consumers, whether soldiers or civilians, supported the concept of a songster dominated by Southern lyrics. Sales of this type of songster did not grow as the war progressed, but there was always enough interest to sustain the publication of one or two per year for most of the war.

If consumers were the ones who inspired compilers to make changes in songster production, and if many, perhaps most, of these consumers were Confederate soldiers, can one conclude that the contents of antebellum-emphasis and mixed-period songsters reflect the tastes of the men in gray? The high percentage of antebellum lyrics in most of the songsters is consistent with the soldiers' reputed partiality for antebellum songs. Bell Irvin Wiley, for example, notes that references connecting Confederate soldiers and secular songs often mention pieces published before the war. Moreover, of the five songs Wiley identifies as particular favorites of the Confederate common soldier, four, "Home, Sweet Home," "Annie Laurie," "Juanita" (1853), and "Lorena" (1857), are antebellum pieces. If soldiers preferred an antebellum version of the lyrics to "Dixie's Land" (1859) to one of the wartime parodies, then it, too, should be added to the examples above. By examining sheet music, songsters, and a variety of other sources, William Mahar was able to create a list of the top twenty best-selling songs of the Civil War. Each of the songs Wiley named was also identified by Mahar as either a well-known song or a best-seller.[36]

It is not surprising, during this period of great upheaval, when so many adult white males had left their homes to enlist in the Confederate army, that these men would sing or listen to familiar antebellum songs, often ones that could evoke memories of civilian life. The lyrics of many antebellum and wartime secular songs presented an idealized vision of the home and its inhabitants, frequently portraying the emotions of individuals who were parted from both. Such lyrics could resonate deeply with those enduring that same separation. Nevertheless, antebellum songs, such as "Dearest Spot of Earth" (1855), possessed an advantage that wartime songs like "Kiss Me before I Die, Mother" (1863) did not have: a history of being sung in domestic settings before the men went off to war. Songs heard during the antebellum period had had more opportunities to become attached to specific memories and to acquire layers of meaning for the listener. In a diary entry, Lieutenant Robert Patrick (1835–1866) of Louisiana directly connected antebellum songs with his recollections of home after listening to an arrangement of "Shells of Ocean" (1847):

36. Bell Irvin Wiley, *The Life of Johnny Reb: The Common Soldier of the Confederacy* (Baton Rouge: Louisiana State University Press, 1943; reprint, 1997), 152, 379n6, 421–22; Mahar, "March to the Music," 13, 15–16, 41, 43.

> There is a brass band along with our [supply] train and they are playing "Shells of Ocean" and as the familiar notes of this sweet air are gently wafted in delightful cadences over the woody hills and dewy fields of the quiet forest, numberless visions of home in happier hours and sweet reminiscences of the past crowd thick and fast upon my soul and bring to view a green spot on memory's wide waste. There is nothing in the world that reminds me more of home than those old familiar airs that I heard when life had brighter appearances than it does at present.

Such impressions were not limited to officers. Using phrases reminiscent of the lyrics of many sentimental songs, Private Grant Taylor of the Fortieth Alabama Infantry describes to his wife, Malinda, his reaction to his comrades' singing: "Even now while I am engaged in writing, some are singing some of those good old tunes that we have sung together so much, which carries my mind back far away to bygone days and happy scenes which are never more to return."[37]

Although Confederate soldiers enjoyed antebellum songs, they certainly did not object to adding new songs to their repertoires. Indeed, they embraced a few songs with unbridled enthusiasm, especially during the heady early months of the conflict. One performance of "Bonnie Blue Flag" received an overwhelming reception by a theater full of soldiers, according to Valerius Giles (1842–1915) of the Fourth Texas Infantry:

> Between the first and second acts of the play, Harry McCarty *[sic]* appeared on the stage dressed in full Confederate uniform, representing a soldier leaving home for the war, and sang his "Bonnie Blue Flag." When he came to a certain part of the song, a beautiful young girl with a bonnie blue flag in hand rushed on the stage and threw her arms around her sweetheart's neck.... Men went wild. The soldiers to a man rose to their feet, many of them standing on their seats, hats, caps, red sashes and sabers waved and flashed high over their heads.

37. F. Jay Taylor, ed., *Reluctant Rebel: The Secret Diary of Robert Patrick, 1861–65* (Baton Rouge: Louisiana State University Press, 1959), 172–73; Ann K. Blomquist and Robert A. Taylor, eds., *This Cruel War: The Civil War Letters of Grant and Malinda Taylor, 1862–1865* (Macon, Ga.: Mercer Press, 2000), 106.

Contemporaries of Giles recorded similar reactions by soldiers to wartime songs, like the positive response of General Beauregard's men to Jenny Cary's performance of "My Maryland."[38]

Wartime songs may not have dominated Confederate soldiers' repertoire, but a small number of songs apparently were performed frequently. Wiley discovered that several wartime lyrics were mentioned often in soldiers' letters and diaries: "All Quiet along the Potomac To-night" (1862), "Bonnie Blue Flag," and "My Maryland." Mahar's research confirms that each of these songs had a strong following in the South. If the songsters accurately reflect the preferences of pro-Confederate Southerners, then both Albert Pike's (1809–1891) and H. S. Stanton's wartime parodies of "Dixie" may have also been sung with some frequency by the troops. Few informants, however, include excerpts from the lyrics; therefore, it is often impossible to identify the version being sung.[39]

The figure of the disillusioned, cynical veteran who rejects overt displays of patriotism has become a standard figure in the study of combat motivation. If one accepts this view of the battle-hardened soldier, then one would assume that the Confederacy's veterans, especially those who had already displayed their patriotism by voluntarily joining the army, would feel that further declarations of their patriotism to their comrades would be superfluous, even suspect. Since most of the patriotic lyrics in Confederate songsters date to the war, this attitude might partly explain why many songsters have only a small percentage of wartime songs. Yet references to soldiers singing patriotic songs, or cheering others' performances of such pieces,

38. Mary Lasswell, ed., *Rags and Hope: The Recollections of Val. C. Giles, Four Years with Hood's Brigade, Fourth Texas Infantry, 1861–1865* (New York: Coward-McCann, 1961), 91; see also Brander Matthews, *Pen and Ink: Papers on Subjects of More or Less Importance* (New York: Longmans, Green, 1888), 143–49; and Kate E. B. Staton, *Old Southern Songs of the Period of the Confederacy: The Dixie Trophy Collection* (New York: Samuel French, 1926), 199–200.

39. Wiley, *Johnny Reb,* 152; Mahar, "March to the Music," 15, 16, 41, 42. See also "The War Song of Dixie" (New Orleans: P. P. Werlein and Halsey, 1861), P&W 7601, courtesy of the Rare Book, Manuscript, and Special Collections Library, Duke University, *Historic American Sheet Music,* July 13, 2002, http://scriptorium.lib.duke.edu/sheetmusic/; "Dixie War Song" (Augusta, Ga.: Blackmar and Bro.; New Orleans: Blackmar, 1861), P&W 6967, courtesy of the Music Division, Library of Congress; and Schultz, "Secessia's Song Books, 2:1–61.

suggest that Rebel soldiers sometimes found it proper to show their love for and commitment to the South through song.[40] Perhaps, after the initial enthusiasm for the war abated and Southerners realized that the fighting would neither be brief nor bloodless, soldiers consciously or unconsciously reserved most performances of patriotic songs for occasions that called for ritual displays of patriotism: military ceremonies such as dress parades, encounters with civilians, or encounters with Union troops. A systematic analysis of the setting and participants in performances of patriotic songs by Confederate soldiers might show whether there was any pattern to those performances.

Although soldiers certainly performed wartime songs, both the information gathered from the songsters and Wiley's and Mahar's research indicate that Confederate soldiers relied more often on antebellum lyrics than on ones written during the war. As Caroline Moseley has pointed out, many Americans of the 1860s, not just Confederate soldiers, would have been familiar with numerous antebellum songs.[41] These soldiers had spent most of their lives as American citizens, and as such they had participated in, to varying degrees, the mainstream popular culture of the United States. Furthermore, pro-Confederate Southerners would not have discarded all the songs they had learned before 1861 simply because their state had seceded. Although pro-Union lyrics and melodies, like "Yankee Doodle," were forsaken by some of the Confederacy's supporters after secession, most antebellum repertoire was retained.

The structures of the majority of the Confederate songsters do seem to have been designed to complement the preferences of the soldiers. However, to better evaluate how well the songsters did that, more contemporary sources should be explored, with an emphasis on the Southerners that comprised the bulk of the Confederate army:

40. James M. McPherson, *For Cause and Comrades* (New York: Oxford University Press, 1997), 90–92, 94–98; Schultz, "Secessia's Song Books," 1:193–95; Capt. W. C. Ward, "Incidents and Personal Experiences on the Battlefield at Gettysburg," *Confederate Veteran* 8, no. 8 (August 1900): 345; Kentuckian, "My First Promotion," *Confederate Veteran* 19, no. 1 (January 1911): 11; Francis T. Meriwether, "Reminiscences—Army of Northern Virginia," *Confederate Veteran* 21, no. 9 (September 1913): 443.

41. Moseley, "Irrepressible Conflict," 45–46.

non-elite whites.[42] Learning more about their tastes in music is vital to discovering whether songsters were aimed at all literate soldiers, or whether one or more groups within the military were the primary targets of the compilers and publishers.[43] Examining manuscripts created by and for soldiers, such as band books and songbooks, underutilized sources like court-martial records, as well as further exploration of antebellum and wartime letters and diaries, should enrich what is already known about Confederate soldiers' tastes.

Although songsters had been published on American soil for over a century before the Civil War, Confederate compilers and publishers may not have known at the beginning of that conflict whether songsters could be profitable in the Confederacy. Moreover, compilers and publishers may not have viewed soldiers as a potential market for their songsters. By the time the last Confederate soldier surrendered, this situation had changed appreciably. During the years of the war, soldiers were increasingly referred to as consumers of songsters, the number of songsters grew, and more publishers became involved in songster production. The timing of these activities suggests that, after 1862, consumers, including soldiers, began to take more interest in the songsters published by Confederate firms. As a result, compilers and publishers learned that publishing songsters was worth the financial risk. In that same period, compilers and publishers also discovered that songsters that contained a majority of antebellum lyrics, or that were divided between antebellum and wartime lyrics, were attractive to more consumers than songsters with a predominance

42. The class structure of whites in the South during the nineteenth century is a controversial topic. Historians do agree that the majority of white Southern males were farmers or agricultural workers who owned less land and fewer slaves than the planters. However, the number, composition, and name(s) of the class(es) of nonelite Southern whites are disputed. See Frank L. Owsley, *Plain Folk of the Old South* (Baton Rouge: Louisiana State University Press, 1949); David Williams, *Rich Man's War* (Athens: University of Georgia Press, 1998), 14–16; Bill Cecil-Fronsman, *Common Whites: Class and Culture in Antebellum North Carolina* (Lexington: University Press of Kentucky, 1992), 1, 12–18; J. William Harris, introduction to Charles C. Bolton and Scott P. Culclasure, eds., *The Confessions of Edward Isham: A Poor White Life of the Old South* (Athens: University of Georgia Press, 1998), xv–xvi.

43. For a summary of what is known of the music of yeoman and poor whites before the Civil War, see Bill C. Malone, "Neither Anglo-Saxon nor Celtic: The Music of the Southern Plain Folk," in Samuel C. Hyde Jr., ed., *Plain Folk of the South Revisited* (Baton Rouge: Louisiana State University Press, 1997), 21–45.

of lyrics that were published during the war. Once compilers and publishers understood what most consumers wanted in a songster, the production of songsters whose contents met consumers' expectations rose markedly.

These discoveries were vital to the development of songsters in the Confederacy. Without that knowledge, fewer firms might have become involved in songster production, and those that did probably would not have brought out as many songsters. The poor state of the Confederate economy could have given publishers little encouragement to risk their money on a publication they considered unlikely to recoup its costs. A more likely inspiration for compilers and publishers to create songsters was the mounting evidence of consumers' positive response to them.

Soldiers—the group of consumers most often linked to songsters—and songster publishers built a relationship that could be mutually beneficial. When a songster was sold, the publisher made a little money, and perhaps gained a better understanding of the kinds of songsters soldiers were willing to buy. In return, the soldier received a collection of lyrics that helped him and his comrades to entertain themselves, to express their emotions in a culturally acceptable manner, to proclaim shared values, and to strengthen their ties to their comrades, family, community, or country. By the end of the war, those songsters might have become dirty, tattered, and worn. Their physical state, however, was a testament to the satisfaction they gave to those soldiers, who, like General Robert E. Lee, could not believe in an army without music.[44]

CONFEDERATE SONGSTERS (ARRANGED CHRONOLOGICALLY)

P&W = Parrish and Willingham number.

* = Lost songster. Included are songsters that were advertised as ready for sale or whose existence is inferred from the presence of the

44. Walter Clark, *Histories of the Several Regiments and Battalions from North Carolina in the Great War, 1861–1865,* vol. 2 (Goldsboro, N.C.: Nash Brothers, 1901), 399.

extant editions. Songsters listed only as "in press" are not included in this bibliography.

† = Contents not examined by the author.

Book of Songs and Duets to Be Sung by the Little Queen Sisters, and Their Brother and Sister, at Their Popular Entertainment Given for the Benefit of the Jamison Riflemen. Charleston: Evans and Cogswell, 1861. P&W 6635.

Hopkins' New-Orleans 5 Cent Song-Book. [New Orleans]: John Hopkins, 1861. P&W 6657.

Original Songs of the Atlanta Amateurs, Containing More Truth Than Poetry. Atlanta: Intelligencer Print., 1861. P&W 6619.

**Southern Flag Song Book.* 1st ed. [Vicksburg and Natchez: H. C. Clarke, ca. 1861].

Southern Flag Song Book. New ed. Vicksburg and Natchez: H. C. Clarke, [ca. 1861].

**Bonnie Blue Flag Song Book.* 1st ed. [Augusta: Blackmar and Bro.; New Orleans: Blackmar and Co., ca. 1862].

**Bonnie Blue Flag Song Book.* 2d ed. Augusta: Blackmar and Bro.; New Orleans: Blackmar and Co., [ca. 1862].

*Mathews, Lawrence H., ed. *Camp Songs for Southern Soldiers.* Atlanta: James McPherson and Co., 1862.

Harry Macarthy's Personation Concerts: Harry Macarthy, Book No. 1. Mobile: A. G. Horn and Co., 1862. P&W 6669.

Songs of the South. Richmond: J. W. Randolph, 1862. P&W 6761.

Songs of the South. 2d ed. Richmond: J. W. Randolph, 1862. P&W 6762.

†*Southern Monthly Collection of Patriotic Songs and Heroic Poems.* Memphis: Hutton and Freligh, 1862.

Allen's Lone Star Ballads, No. 1: A Collection of Southern Patriotic Songs. Galveston and Houston: Francis D. Allen, 1863. P&W 6615.

Bonnie Blue Flag Song Book. 3d ed. Augusta: Blackmar and Bro., [ca. 1862, 1863]. P&W 6779.

Cotton Field Melodies. Augusta: Blackmar and Bro., 1863. P&W 6648.

Dixie Land Songster. Augusta: Blackmar and Bro., 1863. P&W 6651.

**Lone Star Ballad Book, No. 2 (Sentimental).* [Galveston and Houston: Francis D. Allen], 1863.

Soldier Boy's Songster. Richmond: West and Johnston, 1863. P&W 6759.

Songs of Humor and Sentiment. Richmond: J. W. Randolph, 1863. P&W 6760.

Songs of the South. Richmond: J. W. Randolph, 1863. P&W 6763.

†*Southern Flag Song Book, No. 3.* Vicksburg and Augusta: H. C. Clarke, 1863. P&W 6765.

**Stonewall Song Book: Being a Collection of Patriotic, Sentimental, and Comic Songs.* 1st ed. [Richmond: West and Johnston], 1863.

Stonewall Song Book: Being a Collection of Patriotic, Sentimental, and Comic Songs. 2d ed. Richmond: West and Johnston, 1863. P&W 6772.

**Stonewall Song Book: Being a Collection of Patriotic, Sentimental, and Comic Songs.* 3d ed. [Richmond: West and Johnston], 1863.

Stonewall Song Book: Being a Collection of Patriotic, Sentimental, and Comic Songs. 4th ed. Richmond: West and Johnston, 1863. P&W 6773.

Virginia Songster. Richmond: J. W. Randolph, 1863. P&W 6780.

Army Songster: Dedicated to the Army of Northern Virginia. Richmond: George L. Bidgood, 1864. P&W 6617.

Schreiner, Hermann L., comp. *Beauregard Songster, No. 1: Being a Collection of Patriotic, Sentimental, and Comic Songs, the Most Popular of the Day.* Macon and Savannah: John C. Schreiner and Son, 1864. P&W 6751.

**Bold Soldier Boy's Song Book.* 3d rev. ed. [Richmond: West and Johnston, 1864].

**Bold Soldier Boy's Song Book.* 4th ed. [Richmond: West and Johnston, 1864].

Captain in Gen. Lee's Army, A [Branson, Thomas A.], comp. *Jack Morgan Songster.* Raleigh: Branson and Farrar, 1864. P&W 6637.

*[Moore, William D.], comp. *New Confederate Flag Song Book, No. 1.* 1st ed. [Mobile: H. C. Clarke, 1864].

*[Moore, William D.], comp. *New Confederate Flag Song Book, No. 1.* 2d ed. [Mobile: H. C. Clarke, 1864].

[Moore, William D.], comp. *New Confederate Flag Song Book, No. 1.* 3d ed., enl. Richmond: A. Morris; Mobile: H. C. Clarke, 1864. P&W 6685.

[Moore, William D.], comp. *New Confederate Flag Song Book, No. 1.* 4th ed., enl. Mobile: H. C. Clarke, 1864. P&W 6686.

*[Moore, William D.], comp. *New Confederate Flag Song Book, No. 1.* 5th ed. [Mobile: H. C. Clarke], 1864.

**New Confederate Flag Songster, No. 2.* [Mobile: H. C. Clarke], 1864.

Punch Songster: A Collection of Familiar and Original Songs and Ballads. Richmond: Punch Office, 1864. P&W 6720.

Musical Gentleman of This City, A, comp. *Rebel Songster: Containing a Choice Selection of Sentimental, Patriotic, and Comic Songs.* Richmond: Ayres and Wade, 1864. P&W 6724.

Songs of Humor and Sentiment. Richmond: J. W. Randolph, 1864.

North Carolina Lady, A [Moore, Mrs. Marinda Branson], comp. *Songs of Love and Liberty.* Raleigh: Branson and Farrar, 1864. P&W 6684.

Songs of the South. Richmond: J. W. Randolph, 1864. P&W 6764.

Southern Soldier's Prize Songster: Containing Martial and Patriotic Pieces, (Chielfy [sic] *Original,) Applicable to the Present War.* Mobile: W. F. Wisely, 1864. P&W 6767.

Tentler, A. A., comp. *Southern Songster: Arranged Expressly for Camp.* Richmond: Tentler and Baker, 1864.

Stonewall Song Book: Being a Collection of Patriotic, Sentimental, and Comic Songs. 5th ed. Richmond: West and Johnston, 1864. P&W 6774.

**Stonewall Song Book: Being a Collection of Patriotic, Sentimental, and Comic Songs.* 6th ed. [Richmond: West and Johnston], 1864.

**Stonewall Song Book: Being a Collection of Patriotic, Sentimental, and Comic Songs.* 7th ed. [Richmond: West and Johnston], 1864.

**Stonewall Song Book: Being a Collection of Patriotic, Sentimental, and Comic Songs.* 8th ed. [Richmond: West and Johnston], 1864.

**Stonewall Song Book: Being a Collection of Patriotic, Sentimental, and Comic Songs.* 9th ed. [Richmond: West and Johnston], 1864.

Stonewall Song Book: Being a Collection of Patriotic, Sentimental, and Comic Songs. 10th ed. Richmond: West and Johnston, 1864. P&W 6775.

Taylor, J. C. R., comp. *Taylor's Southern Songster, No. 1: Containing All the Favorite Songs and Ballads of the Day.* Charleston: A. E. Miller and Co., 1864. P&W 6777.

*Taylor, J. C. R., comp. *Taylor's Southern Songster, No. 2.* [Charleston: A. E. Miller and Co.], 1864.

*Taylor, J. C. R., comp. *Taylor's Southern Songster, No. 3.* [Charleston: A. E. Miller and Co.], 1864.

Cavalier Songster: Containing a Splendid Collection of Original and Selected Songs: Comp. and Arranged Expressly for the Southern Public. Staunton, Va.: n.p. [ca. 1864], P&W 6642.

Schreiner, Hermann L., comp. *Gen. Lee Songster: Being a Collection of the Most Popular Sentimental, Patriotic, and Comic Songs.* Macon and Savannah: John C. Schreiner and Son, 1865. P&W 6752.

Stonewall Song Book: Being a Collection of Patriotic, Sentimental, and Comic Songs. 11th ed., enl. Richmond: West and Johnston, 1865. P&W 6776.

Stonewall Song Book: Being a Collection of Patriotic, Sentimental, and Comic Songs. 12th ed., enl. Richmond: West and Johnston, 1865.

Bold Soldier Boy's Song Book. [Richmond: West and Johnston, ca. 1865]. P&W 6633.

Hopkins' New-Orleans 5 Cent Song-Book. [New Orleans]: John Hopkins, [ca. 1865]. P&W 6656.

**Jack Morgan Songster, No. 1.* [Augusta: Blackmar and Bro., 1864?].

**Southern Flag Song Book, No. 2.* [Vicksburg?: H. C. Clarke, ca. 1861–1863].

Southern Flag Song Book. [n.p.: H. C. Clarke?, n.d.]. P&W 6766.

**Southern Songster.* [Richmond: J. W. Randolph, 1862?].

Across a Great Divide

IRISH AMERICAN MUSIC AND MUSICIANS OF THE CIVIL WAR ERA

Michael Saffle

Between 1800 and 1920, well over four million men and women emigrated from Ireland to the United States. Among them were Catholics and Protestants, wealthy speculators and impoverished farmers, university graduates and illiterate laborers—all of them Irish. More than 260,000 of them arrived between 1820 and 1840, and still more during the decades that followed; the historian Roger Daniels suggests the number exceeded 780,000 between 1841–1850.[1] These last years, of course, were those of the Famine in Ireland; in America, the 1840s and 1850s immediately preceded the outbreak of hostilities between

The author would like to thank Virginia Polytechnic Institute and State University, Blacksburg, and the Center for Ulster Migrations, Cultures, and Societies for intellectual and financial support that made it possible for him to attend the "Music of the Civil War Era" conference in Shepherdstown, West Virginia, in March 2002.

1. Roger Daniels, *Coming to America: A History of Immigration and Ethnicity in American Life* (New York: Harper and Row, 1990), 129–30. Daniels's precise figure is 780,719. See also Patrick J. Blessing, "Irish Emigration to the United States, 1800 to 1920: An Overview," *Irish Studies* 4 (1984): 13. In the pages that follow, *Irish* refers both to those peoples also known as "Scots-Irish," "Scotch-Irish," or "Ulster-Scots," as well as to those peoples identified by Peter Van der Merwe as "Catholic Irish" (see Van der Merwe, *Origins of the Popular Style: The Antecedents of Twentieth-Century Popular Music* [Oxford: Clarendon, 1989], 45–49). Prior to the 1830s in the United States, "Irish" music was more often called "Scotch-Irish" or "Scotch" and "Irish"; later it was usually called "Irish." In the pages that follow, *Scots-Irish* is used to identify those individuals and their descendants whose ancestors migrated from Scotland to Ireland before coming to America, and *Catholic Irish* is used to identify those individuals and their descendants of Roman Catholic affiliation. Except in titles and quotations, the words *Scots, Scotch,* and *Irish,* especially insofar as they pertain to musical sources and styles, appear in quotation marks.

the Union and the Confederacy in 1861. These antebellum immigrants and their descendants, together with their music, contributed in a variety of ways to American culture of the decades before, during, and immediately after the War Between the States. Put it another way: immigrants from Ireland crossed a great divide to come to the United States and make places for themselves and their music among nineteenth-century Americans of various ethnic, religious, and cultural backgrounds.

Peoples everywhere, including the Irish, have emigrated to America either because of unfortunate experiences at home, or because they sought a better life abroad, or both. This requires qualification. Consider Patrick Ronayne Cleburne, one of many nineteenth-century Irish immigrants to the United States—and one, interestingly enough, celebrated in Civil War song. Cleburne was born in 1828 west of Cork, the son of a surgeon trained in Dublin; his early circumstances were prosperous ones. Yet Cleburne came to America in 1848 because he happened to fail an examination. Unable to matriculate at a medical school in Ireland, he settled first in New Orleans and then worked in several other cities, including Cincinnati, as a pharmacist before finally qualifying as a doctor. We remember him today because his militia company became part of the Fifteenth Arkansas Volunteers and fought in several battles. In 1864 Cleburne, who by then was a major general, was killed in action at the battle of Franklin, Tennessee. As the lyrics of the anonymously written song "Patrick Cleburne" have it:

> On Richmond's plain his captive train
> Outnumbered the host he led,
> And he won his stars on the field of Mars
> Where glorious Johnston bled! . . .
> And they'll tell with pride how Cleburne died,
> In the land of the free and the brave,
> And his sword of might was a beam of light
> Though it led to an Exile's grave. (*IS,* 21)[2]

2. Throughout this essay, most of the textual quotations from Civil War songs are taken from *The Civil War Songbook,* ed. Richard Crawford (New York: Dover, 1977); Irwin Silber, ed., *Songs of the Civil War* (New York: Columbia University Press, 1960); and Derek Warfield, *Irish Songster of the American Civil War* (self-published, 2000). Page citations are provided parenthetically, abbreviating the three

The details of the battle itself—"Richmond," "Johnston," and so on—do not concern us here. Relevant, instead, are these facts: that a *song* commemorates Cleburne's death and that the words of this song reflect *characteristic* Irish American experiences and values. Among these are bravery and loyalty, a consciousness of the sufferings of Ireland's peoples, hope for a newer and more prosperous Ireland to come (or for greater prosperity and acceptance of and among Irish Americans), and the expression of these sentiments in music. The historian William Williams writes that "most Irish immigrants [to the United States] after 1820 generally shared some degree of national identity, with an accompanying dislike of England; a sense of patriotism easily extended to embrace America; a strong allegiance to the Roman Catholic faith; and political experience that enabled them to grasp quickly the mechanisms of the American democratic process."[3] The lyrics to "Patrick Cleburne" refer neither to Catholicism nor to political processes, but they do refer to national identity, a dislike of England, and patriotic sentiments, and they allude to the contributions made by Irish Americans to their adopted land during the Civil War.

The pages that follow constitute an attempt to simultaneously confirm, elaborate upon, and—occasionally—correct previous opinions of Irish American music and musicians, particularly insofar as the Civil War era is concerned. Consider, for example, Derek Warfield's statements that "The American Civil War [began] the process of the integration of the 'Famine' Irish into American life"; that the war served as a "proving ground for many leaders, North and South" as well as "the graveyard for many more"; and especially that the ballads and songs "written by those who fought and lived through those years," that is, 1861–1865, together with "the military music of both sides," were "influenced *more by Irish music* than any other."[4] Like other generalizations, Warfield's require amplification (and, in some instances, qualification) if they are to be fully appreciated. There can

sources as *CWS, SCW,* and *IS,* respectively. Additional antebellum musical editions are identified by title, publisher (or place of publication), and date in the text itself.

3. William H. A. Williams, *'Twas Only an Irishman's Dream: The Image of Ireland and the Irish in American Popular Song Lyrics, 1800–1920* (Urbana: University of Illinois Press, 1996), 16.

4. Warfield, *Irish Songster,* 12 (italics added).

be no doubt that they merit careful and enthusiastic attention. Of the ten categories identified by Bruce Kelley earlier in the present volume, seven of them—those associated with music personalities, popular song and dance, music and culture, military and civilian bands, the collection and description of relevant musical works and associated documentation, new beginnings, and music publishing—involve Irish American music, musicians, and musical activities.

It is impossible to evaluate, even to review, all that is or should be known about Irish American aspects of these categories in a single article. Nevertheless, the present essay suggests answers to certain questions about Irish American music and musicians in the years before, during, and immediately after 1861–1865. Among the questions are: What was Irish American music of the antebellum and Civil War eras like? How did it reflect or assist in the process of assimilation? Which Irish American ballads, songs, and military music were popular in the North, the South, or both? Finally, how did Irish American music and musicians reflect upon and contribute to several important aspects of the Civil War itself?

Although Celtic scholars were among the first to document traditional Old World songs and dances, we shall probably never really know much about Ireland's music prior to the eighteenth century. In 1724, however, *A Collection of the Most Celebrated Irish Tunes,* compiled by John and William Neal, was published in Dublin; it was subsequently pirated by Dermot O'Conner, then living in London. The collection's contents also appeared in arrangements for flute, oboe, and violin. John Gay's *The Beggar's Opera* (1728) employed some familiar "Irish" tunes; so did the *Carolan* anthology of 1748. It was in 1792, however, at the Congress of Harpers in Belfast, that Edward Bunting took down much of the music he began publishing four years later in Dublin as *A General Collection of the Ancient Music of Ireland,* also known as *Ancient Irish Music.* It was from Bunting's work that Thomas Moore, a self-taught pianist who participated in the revolt of 1798, took some of the material he subsequently published in his *Irish Melodies,* issued in ten volumes between 1808–1834.[5] Handel,

5. For additional information about early editions of traditional Gaelic melodies, see Nicholas Carolan, "*'The Most Celebrated Irish Tunes': The Publishing of Irish*

Haydn, and other European art composers were acquainted with Ireland's airs. Beethoven, for example, drew in his own arrangements upon "Eileen Aroon," a melody that may date from medieval times. As Russell Sanjek explains, the English publisher George E. Blake—who settled in Philadelphia at the end of the eighteenth century—printed New World editions of Moore's *Melodies* "in exact duplication of both decoration and typography." The songs themselves, "already well known in America," eventually "played a definitive role in the contribution" Moore and his associates made to American music.[6]

Of Irish-influenced Civil War songs, the most familiar today are probably the Confederate anthem "The Bonnie Blue Flag" (and its parodies, including "The Homespun Dress" and "The Bonnie White Flag"), "Pat Murphy of the Irish Brigade," "The Yellow Rose of Texas," and "When Johnny Comes Marching Home." With the exception of "Johnny," however, tunes such as "Danny Boy," "My Wild Irish Rose," and "When Irish Eyes Are Smiling" are better known today, at least among older Americans. Some, although not all, of these last tunes are comparatively recent inventions: nineteenth- and early twentieth-century American simulations of "Irishness."[7] In fact, most of the "Irish" songs Americans sing today date from the 1870s or even later. "Sweet Rosie O'Grady," for example—credited to Maude Nugent, although it may have been composed by her husband, Wiliam Jerome—appeared first in 1896. These and similar Tin Pan Alley

Music in the Eighteenth Century (Cork, Ireland: Irish Traditional Music Society, 1990); and Francis O'Neill, *Irish Minstrels and Musicians, with Numerous Dissertations on Related Subjects* (Chicago: Regan, 1913; reprint, Darby, Pa.: Norwood, 1973), 136ff (see especially chapter 14). An excellent synopsis of Irish and Irish American music from Moore through the mid-nineteenth century appears in Charles Hamm, *Yesterdays: Popular Song in America* (New York: Norton, 1979), 42–59.

6. See "The Irish Songs," in *The Beethoven Companion,* ed. Thomas K. Scherman and Louis Biancolli (Garden City, N.Y.: Doubleday, 1972), 801–5; and Russell Sanjek, *American Popular Music and Its Business: The First Four Hundred Years,* vol. 2, *From 1790 to 1909* (New York: Oxford University Press, 1988), 51.

7. Not all of the more familiar Irish American songs appear in every modern collection. On the other hand, Crawford's *Civil War Songbook* contains facsimiles of such slightly less well-known numbers as "The Drummer Boy of Shiloh"—which, in its melodic leaps, quick ascents, and slower descents, "tipping" rhythmic figures, and designated or implied cadenzas (at fermatas), incorporates characteristic Irish features. The more recent, familiar melodies, including "Kathleen Mavourneen," "Oft in the Stilly Night," and "When Johnny Comes Marching Home," may be found in *Popular Irish Songs,* ed. Florence Leniston (New York: Dover, 1992).

constructs lie outside the confines of the present essay. It is worth noting, however, that the very existence of these numbers testifies to increased acceptance in the United States of "Irish" ethnicity and values after 1865 and especially up to 1924, when the Immigration Act signaled a new chapter in the story of Irish American identity and "integration." In this sense, even tawdry "Irish" ditties document the uneven but increasingly successful process of Irish American assimilation that began before the Civil War and was much influenced by it.

There can be no question that authentic "Irish" music—whatever "authentic" means—was familiar to many antebellum Americans.[8] Some of this music, like the men and women who made it, was initially restricted to the Appalachian highlands, where many eighteenth-century immigrants from Ireland settled. During the earlier twentieth century, Irish American music very much influenced "old timey" and "bluegrass" styles. During the nineteenth century, however, and especially after 1840, most immigrants from Ireland settled in American cities, where the music they made rapidly became intermingled with other ethnic strains. No wonder many early "Irish" songs and instrumental numbers were actually composed for commercial consumption by individuals of French, German, and Jewish descent.[9] "The Last Rose of Summer" (also known as " 'Tis the Last Rose" or " 'T the Last Rose"), for example, was associated with both "Ned of the Hill" and "The Grove [or Groves] of Blarney"; was reputedly sung in honor of Edmund Ryan, an early bard; and has been attributed both to Edward Bunting and to Thomas Moore, who borrowed from Bunting in his *Irish Melodies.* "Kathleen Mavourneen," composed by Frederick Nicholls Crouch, was long ago "declared by some

8. Authenticity has been hotly debated among musicologists as well as by anthropologists and folklorists. In *Authenticities: Philosophical Reflections on Musical Performance* (Ithaca, N.Y.: Cornell University Press, 1995), Peter Kivy argues the pros and cons of various approaches to playing and singing "ancient" European art musics especially of the seventeenth and eighteenth centuries. Another important discussion appears in Richard Peterson's *Creating Country Music: Fabricating Authenticity* (Chicago: University of Chicago Press, 1997). For Peterson, whose chapter 6 is entitled "Authenticity: A Renewable Resource," the genuineness of country music may reside in artifacts, traditions, or consensus that a particular kind of music accurately embodies the concerns and enthusiasms of those who sing, play, and listen to it.

9. Consider *Songs from O'Malley,* published somewhere in the United States in 1842 and under the name of one "Patricio Zandtpatternische."

not to be Irish at all!"[10] Whatever its origins, however, "Kathleen Mavourneen" became one of the best-loved antebellum American parlor songs and was familiar on both sides of the Mason-Dixon Line. During the early 1850s Gold Rush in California, miners called on a visiting female vocalist to sing the song "over and over again," until the woman wished it "had never been written."[11]

As Ken Emerson reminds us, the echoes of Thomas Moore and his collaborator John Stevenson are everywhere: "Tara, Scarlett O'Hara's beloved plantation in *Gone with the Wind,* conjures up Moore's 'The Harp that Once Through Tara's Halls,' while The Five Satins' classic doo-wop ballad 'I'll Remember (in the Still of the Night)' inevitably evokes, a century and a half later, Moore's 'Oft in the Stilly Night.'"[12] Some numbers, of course, are more "Irish" than others. In contradistinction to Jon Finson, for example—who describes "The Yellow Rose of Texas" (*SCW,* 76–78) in terms of its "references to 'darkies'" and its polka-like rhythms, even as he acknowledges its "nostalgia for the beauty of the lost country" (a most important aspect of Irish American song, as we shall see below)—Williams observes that the same song, although less clearly and unquestionably Gaelic than many others, has something of traditional balladry about it, recalling such "surprisingly similar" melodies as "An Irish Mother's Lament."[13] So do dozens of other songs composed before and during the Civil War. The fact is, Williams could have gone much farther, into the present day: the rock band Metallica has borrowed "Irish" tunes, and so has Peter Schickele. "Oft of an E'en ere Night Is Nigh," attributed to "P. D. Q. Bach" and included by Schickele in that imaginary composer's *Three Folksong Upsettings,* also looks back, albeit playfully, to Moore's publications.

10. Francis O'Neill, *Irish Folk Music: A Fascinating Hobby, with Some Account of Allied Subjects* (Chicago: Regan, 1910; reprint, Darby, Pa.: Norwood, 1973), 47.

11. Quoted in Philip D. Jordan, *Singin' Yankees* (Minneapolis: University of Minnesota Press, 1946), 185.

12. Ken Emerson, *Doo-Dah! Stephen Foster and the Rise of American Popular Culture* (New York: Simon and Schuster, 1997), 45.

13. Jon W. Finson, *The Voices That Are Gone: Themes in Nineteenth-Century American Popular Song* (New York: Oxford University Press, 1994), 194; Williams, *'Twas Only an Irishman's Dream,* 37. Observations about the character, popularity, and significance of Irish American songs are scattered throughout the literature; in addition to the sources cited below, see Richard Crawford, *America's Musical Life* (New York: Norton, 2001), 247–49.

How well known was "Irish" music, of whatever kind, in nineteenth-century America? Quite well known, if one judges from the titles of surviving sheet-music publications. In addition to reprints of Moore's melodies and other European collections, these include *The Harp of Columbia, or The American Warbler: Being a New Selection of Patriotic, Irish, Sentimental, and Comic Songs,* published in Baltimore in 1825, and *The Mammoth Songster: A Splendid Collection of All the Modern Negro, Sentimental, and Irish Songs,* published in Philadelphia in 1853. Occasionally, "Irish" songs were lumped together with other numbers from, or associated with, the British Isles. Consider *The Blackbird, being a Choice Collection of the Most Popular American, English, Irish, and Scotch Songs*—a volume published by Mack, Andrus, and Woodruff of Ithaca, New York, in 1836. One anthology, described by Peter van der Merwe as "neatly summing up the popular American taste of the time," was called *Marsh's Selection, or, Singing for the Million, containing the Choicest and Best Collection of Admired Patriotic, Comic, Irish, Negro, Temperance, and Sentimental Songs Ever Embodied in One Work;* it appeared in print in 1854.[14]

These antebellum collections and others like them were printed mostly in the North, where the lion's share of music-publishing houses was located. After April 1861, however, "Southern music publishers . . . quickened their activities tremendously during the early months of the war," when "the outpouring of song from the Confederacy bordered on the phenomenal."[15] By 1864, Confederate printing houses in Atlanta, Charleston, and elsewhere had brought out an

14. Van der Merwe, *Origins of the Popular Style,* 49. Nicholas Tawa raises the question of whether "any of the melodic commonplaces [in nineteenth-century American parlor songs] are ascribable to any one of the national musics from the British Isles," then goes on to observe both that "it would be hazardous indeed to speak of specifically Irish or Scottish traits," and that "what seems Irish may also appear in the melodies of some Italian songs—an observation made by a few contemporary writers on music." Nicholas E. Tawa, *Sweet Songs for Gentle Americans: The Parlor Song in America, 1790–1860* (Bowling Green, Ohio: Bowling Green University Popular Press, 1980), 163. But Tawa's principal concern is with parlor songs "in general," not so much songs containing more or less clear-cut, even self-acknowledged "Irish" characteristics and subjects. Furthermore, Tawa himself not only acknowledges the presence of "Irish" markers in antebellum American song but also points out the envy American composers experienced over the success of "Irish" music in their country.

15. Ronald L. Davis, *A History of Music in American Life,* vol. 2, *The Gilded Years, 1865–1920* (Huntington, N.Y.: Robert Krieger, 1980), 266.

impressive number of Irish American titles. Among these forgotten publications were series issued by Blackmar and Brothers of Augusta, Georgia, which included, predictably, "The Bonnie Blue Flag," and the several editions of "Kathleen Mavourneen" issued by George Dunn and Company of Columbia, South Carolina. Nor should we overlook those postwar, albeit almost entirely Northern songs, that cast a positive light on Irish Americans' patriotism. Consider "Richmond Jail," dedicated to "Michael Corcoran of the Irish Brigade," published in 1865 in New York (discussed below). Consider, too, *The Annie Laurie Melodist* and *The Irish Boy's Return Songster,* both of them published for the first time in New York in 1857 and reprinted in 1868. The last title, by the way, would have been understood after Appomattox in terms of "drummer boy" as well as "returning" to Ireland herself.

It is scarcely surprising that "Irish" music should have permeated America's antebellum and Civil War cultures. As Nicholas Tawa notes, a desire "for uncomplicated music coupled with a cultural memory impressed with the sound of traditional melody," combined with envy on the part of many composers over the success enjoyed by Moore's volumes, inspired the melodic characteristics of "The Last Rose of Summer" and other favorites.[16] Virtually everyone, it seems—from a rural New Jersey journalist, who in 1830 "spoke up for honest songs 'with pure and simple melody,' to Henry Wadsworth Longfellow, who loved symphonies and the opera but also admired "the simple and expressive"—enjoyed the tunes to which Tawa alludes.[17] In examining the lyrics of one of Stephen Foster's most obscure and silliest numbers, "The Song of All Songs"—a conflation of titles evidently well known in 1863, when the composition itself appeared in print—we find references to what were (or may have been) a number of Irish and Irish American melodies: "Annie of the Vale," "At Lanigan's Ball," "Jenny's Coming o'er the Green," "No Irish Need Apply," "Oft in the Stilly Night," and so on. The anthologist Sigmund Spaeth exaggerates his inability to identify "hardly any of [these] songs . . . today"; two of the titles quoted by Foster, "No Irish" and

16. Tawa, *Sweet Songs for Gentle Americans,* 163.

17. Quoted in Nicholas E. Tawa, *High-Minded and Low-Down: Music in the Lives of Americans, 1800–1861* (Boston: Northeastern University Press, 2000), 29–30.

"Oft," are discussed in the present essay.[18] Yet Spaeth is correct in maintaining that we possess only a fraction of the music, "Irish" and otherwise, familiar to many nineteenth-century Americans.

The tunes we do possess, whether newly composed or copied from "ancient sources," seem "to haunt the languid musical syntax, and help to give it its perpetual note of melancholy," as Robert Welch observes in his book *Irish Poetry from Moore to Yeats.* Their subjects, he reminds us, largely involve "a continual remembering" of Ireland's dead, and "a keeping faith with their memory." In some verses, this remembering and keeping faith seems bitter, even anguished. In Kerby Miller's opinion, Ireland's peoples "could not accept emigration as the voluntary choice it [often] was . . . but rather only as a cruel and bitter fate forced upon them by tragic circumstance. Thus the general sense of nostalgia so prevalent in nineteenth-century American popular culture coincided with the more profound sense of exile and loss that Irish [men and women] brought with them to America."[19] In sentimental numbers, on the other hand, we more often encounter bittersweet reminiscences of lost or distant sweethearts.

Tawa observes that Moore's influence extended to Foster and to a host of other antebellum composers, all of whom "took as their 'most frequent subject' . . . a dream of security, of a vaguely defined home from the past, of a friendless present." As Charles Hamm has pointed out, Irish American song characteristically expresses a persistent theme "of nostalgia, of longing for a lost home, childhood, and friends"; this theme, appropriate to the circumstances of immigrants in a new land, struck a responsive chord among nineteenth-century Americans of all ages and races. No wonder Moore's *Irish Melodies,* together

18. Sigmund Spaeth, *Read 'Em and Weep: The Songs You Forgot to Remember* (Garden City, N.Y.: Doubleday, Page, 1926), 48. Emerson suggests that Foster's "half-sensical" verses may actually have been written by John F. Poole, "who parodied 'Jenny's Coming o'er the Green' as 'Whiskey in Decanter Clean' for George Christy [of Christy's Minstrels] and contributed 'No Irish Need Apply' " to Tony Pastor's *New Comic Irish Songster,* yet another "song book" without music, which was published in 1863 by the New York firm of Dick and Fitzgerald. Emerson, *Doo-Dah!* 290.

19. Robert Welch, *Irish Poetry from Moore to Yeats* (Totowa, N.J.: Barnes and Noble, 1980), 11; Miller paraphrased in William H. A. Williams, "From Lost Land to Emerald Isle: Ireland and the Irish in American Sheet Music, 1800–1920," *Eiré/Ireland* 26, no. 1 (spring 1991): 24. See also Kerby Miller, "Assimilation and Alienation: Ireland's Response to Industrial America, 1871–1920," *Irish Studies* 5 (1985): 103.

"with the songs of Stephen Foster," share the distinction of "being the most popular, widely sung, best-loved, and most durable songs in the English language of the entire nineteenth century."[20]

Unfortunately, most surviving antebellum "songs" and song collections contain only words or, at most, words and musical snippets.[21] In order to identify characteristic features of antebellum and Civil War–era Irish American melodies, we are forced to rely upon a limited number of print sources: (1) Moore's publications; (2) songs composed by Catholic Irish immigrants or their descendants, of whom Patrick Gilmore is probably the most celebrated example; (3) songs composed by Scots-Irish immigrants or their descendants, of whom Foster is the most celebrated example; (4) songs that invoke Ireland but may have been or were in fact invented by members of other immigrant ethnic groups; and (5) songs that merely seem to have something "Irish" about them. In the last two categories we find titles and lyrics containing names such as "Patrick" and "Norah," or anglicized Gaelic words such as "colleen" and "mavourneen," or dialect formulas (replacing "of" with "o'," for instance). More than a few lyrics, of course, refer explicitly to Ireland as a nation as well as to many of its individual cities, towns, political figures, and historical events. Foster's songs are sometimes more or less definitely "Irish," sometimes not; their creator also composed waltzes, novelty numbers, and songs that invoke African Americans.

Musicologists have criticized printed music as an unreliable or unrepresentative source of information. For one thing, sheet music has almost always embodied elitist values in terms both of price and the presupposition of "cultivated" musical ability on the part of publishers and purchasers alike. For another, printed music can be difficult to date, especially in the United States prior to 1853, when our own Copyright

20. Nicholas Tawa, *A Music for the Millions: Antebellum Democratic Attitudes and the Birth of American Popular Music* (New York: Pendragon, 1984), 38; Hamm, *Yesterdays,* 61, 44.

21. Exceptions include not only the well-known works of Foster, Hays, and other parlor-song composers, but also such early anthologies as *A Selection, from the Ancient Music of Ireland, Arranged for the Flute or Violin, some of the most Admired Melodies, adapted to American Poetry* (Petersburg, Conn.: Yancy and Burton, 1824), which contains a few full-fledged songs as well as many unaccompanied melodies. *The Annie Laurie Melodist* (New York: n.p., 1869) contains complete melodies; *The Irish Boy's Return Songster,* mentioned above, contains only indications of tunes.

Act became law. Most problematic, in some ways, is the fact that many published scores preserve little or nothing of performance practices; they give us the notes (and lyrics) but nothing more.

Among the few exceptions to this last rule are the monographs of Francis O'Neill, a turn-of-the-last-century Chicago police captain and pioneering ethnomusicologist. In reprinting two versions of "The Blackbird," a familiar folk song, O'Neill observes that "an air so universally known . . . would find no mention in a cursory sketch of this kind [i.e., in O'Neill's *Irish Folk Music,* which is anything but cursory] except that we desire to invite attention to Sergt. O'Neill's [Francis O'Neill's father's] unique traditional version which he learned from his father [Francis O'Neill's grandfather]. It has been often remarked, and I believe not without justice, that the song could not very well be sung to the music of it as commonly printed." Evidently a vigorous tradition of melody making and improvisational performance, which extended to immigrants and their Irish American descendants, survived among Gaelic "bards" well into the nineteenth century. Especially intriguing is O'Neill's observation that printed versions of the tune differ greatly from real-life versions. Also intriguing, as well as disappointing, is the disappearance of such traditions. On one occasion, O'Neill observes, he was listening to his father play the violin when "The Proposal" (also identified as "He Asked Me Name the Day")—a tune the elder O'Neill had forgotten "since early youth"—came to the captain's father "like a flash one afternoon. . . . For fear of again losing it I grasped Sergt. O'Neill's bow-hand, lest his strains unhinge my memory. This unpublished melody, which possesses marked individuality, came dangerously near passing into oblivion."[22]

Not, of course, that "traditional" (and, later, "popular") songs were intended to be performed in only canonical ways. As Phillips Barry observed as long ago as 1911, "Whereas the singer of 'My Rosary' or 'The Lost Chord' is in duty bound to reproduce with exact fidelity the words and notes of the archetype, no such injunction is laid on the singer of . . . 'The Little Red Lark.' He is left free, according as the inspiration of singing may lead him, to roam with the multitude of his kind through the devious paths of communal re-creation. Art-song

22. O'Neill, *Irish Folk Music,* 75.

is static; folk-song is dynamic . . . [and] an idea, of which we can get by the process of actualization, traceable as a history." In other words, any attempt to identify unmistakable "Irish" aspects of early American sheet music is necessarily problematic. "Irishness," like folk song, is truly an "idea" that manifests itself through the historical processes of actualization and change. Certainly it has long been a vague idea, geographically and culturally speaking; if it were not, terms such as "Irish," "Scots," and "English" could not have so often been lumped together.[23]

Not all Irish American music can be considered "folk" music; certainly Stephen Foster's parlor songs cannot. Some of Moore's *Irish Melodies,* on the other hand, were derived from transcriptions of live "folk" performances, even though Moore and others like him made little or no effort to record precisely how what they heard had been played and sung. Fortunately, the outlines of a few tunes have been jotted down and published with regard to ornamentation, phrasing, and the like. Compare, for example, Bunting's arrangement of "The Blackbird" (mentioned above), with that of Francis O'Neill's grandfather: Bunting's tune dates from 1803, the elder O'Neill's from memories of his grandson's childhood, although the later version was published only shortly before World War I.[24]

Other melodies, of course, were published as early as the 1820s in more or less "authentic" versions and became popular songs; "The Girl I Left behind Me," for example, was a favorite with Civil War bands (it was also known as "Brighton Camp"). Anonymous in origin,

23. Phillips Barry, "Irish Folk Song," *The Journal of American Folk-Lore* 24, no. 93 (July–September 1911): 333. Whether traditional practices can be separated from contemporary circumstances, from "popular culture and all its mutations," is a telling question. They probably cannot; even if they can be, the result may well be "a stagnant artifact" rather than a living art; see Sally Sommers Smith, "The Origin of Style: The Famine and Irish Traditional Music," *Eiré/Ireland* 32, no. 1 (spring 1997): 122. Attempts to distinguish between "Scots" or "Scotch" music and the various musical traditions of Ireland, at least from a nineteenth-century American perspective, have been unsuccessful. One scholar has suggested merely that Scottish song, often lumped together in antebellum anthologies with Irish, Negro, German, and other ethnic varieties, were "sunnier" and more often conjured up "a more settled, more satisfying, even idyllic existence" than Irish songs; see Williams, *'Twas Only an Irishman's Dream,* 79.

24. Both melodies are reprinted in O'Neill, *Irish Folk Music,* 342–43.

the lyrics of this song seem to date from about 1770; the music, "unquestionably a genuine folk-tune, was 'taken down' by A. O'Neil, harper, A.D. 1800," according to Spaeth.[25]

Based on these and other antebellum Irish American tunes, it is possible to identify a few fairly reliable musical markers of "Irishness," original or simulated, including: (1) rising melodic figures, often leaping upward by a sixth or even an octave; (2) a tendency for melodies to begin "high" and descend slowly, or for them to leap quickly upward, then more slowly descend; (3) the presence of short, repeated motifs within, rather than necessarily at the beginnings or ends, of phrases; (4) suggestions of improvised ornamentation; (5) frequent use of "tipping" (rapidly repeated pairs of identical notes) and "popping" (rapidly presented pairs of adjoining notes), especially in jigs; (6) melodies entirely or largely pentatonic or hexatonic (tunes built from no more than five or six notes of the scale); and (7) suggestions of chromatic inflection—for example, D-flat and D-natural within a few notes of each other in Bunting's version of "The Blackbird."

Many nineteenth-century American parlor songs, not all of them "Irish," possess these characteristics. In fact, any one of these markers may appear almost anywhere in the antebellum literature. Upward leaps of a sixth, for example, abound in "Black Eyed Susianna," published anonymously by Fiot of Philadelphia in 1846. This song is anything but "Irish," for the lyrics clearly simulate an African American dialect, with such phrases as "And ob all de gals I lub de bes."[26] Also, "cultivated" songs are likely to include chromatic inflections, with no "Irishness" implied. "Scots" songs can often be distinguished from other kinds by the "Scotch snaps"—the sixteenth-note/dotted-eighth rhythmic figures—that appear throughout such tunes as "He Stole My Heart Away."[27]

"Jeanie with the Light Brown Hair," on the other hand—and, in Hamm's opinion, a melody "inconceivable" had there been no *Irish Melodies* to precede it—possesses several of the markers outlined above. Foster's melody, which begins high and slowly descends, is almost entirely hexatonic; there are several upward leaps of a minor

25. Spaeth, *Read 'Em and Weep,* 16.
26. See Tawa, *Music for the Millions,* 170–71.
27. Reprinted in Hamm, *Yesterdays,* 60.

Example 1. Music to "Jeanie with the Light Brown Hair," by Stephen Foster, *Fosters's Melodies,* No. 26 (New York: First, Pond, 1854).

sixth, as in the lyrics "a vapor" in measure 7; elsewhere, too, there are pauses for cadenzas, which give the performer an opportunity to improvise—the last an uncommon feature of traditional German tunes. As Finson explains, the influence of *Irish Melodies* on "Jeanie" reveals itself "not only in the extraordinary, isolated musical leaps . . .

but also in the cadenzas prefacing the penultimate line of each stanza." He neglects to identify all of its markers, but this does not mean he fails to recognize them in other songs. To Wilfrid Mellers, Foster's accompaniment calls to mind "an eighteenth-century British arrangement (and urbanization) of a celtic folk-tune," and he acknowledges other Gaelic touches in this beautiful melody, including its "'pentatonic' flavour," its "Irish" simplicity, and the "little cadenza" that begins with a fermata on "vapour" and ends with "the tenderest cadential thirteenth [an A above the dominant C, later in the song] on the word 'summer.'"[28] Several of the same characteristics appear in Lady John Scott's "Annie Laurie," which dates from the late 1830s and opens with an upward leap of an octave, followed by a slow descent.

Now consider "The Last Rose of Summer," a melody in part composed by Moore and arranged by Stephenson but also based on the traditional tune "Groves of Blarney" and "borrowed" by Friedrich von Flotow for *Martha.* Again, this is a melody that ascends comparatively quickly and descends comparatively slowly. Note the upward leap of a minor sixth on the words "last rose" in measure 5 and the ornaments on "of" and "blooming alone" in measures 6 and 7; there's even a place designated by John Stevenson and Henry Bishop, Moore's posthumous arrangers in this edition, for a cadenza in measure 16. Note too the repeated melodic figures in this and many other traditional tunes as well as several of Foster's songs. There is little chromatic inflection in the tune itself (the accompaniment is Stevenson's and Bishop's work), nor is it altogether hexatonic—although the note D-sharp in the key of E Major appears only as an ornament. Suggestions of tipping appear in many of the ornamented figures, while suggestions of popping appear everywhere; consider the repeated G-sharps that

28. Hamm, *Yesterdays,* 219; Finson, *Voices That Are Gone,* 37; Wilfrid Mellers, *Music in a New Found Land: Themes and Developments in the History of American Music* (New York: Alfred A. Knopf, 1965), 248. Gestures of these kinds are often overlooked as "Irish" today, because they became part of American popular song as a whole. Think of "Somewhere Over the Rainbow," with its initial octave leap; subsequent upward leaps of a sixth; slow melodic descents; and penultimate "break" just before the final phrase, after which a cadenza—or at the very least, a seemingly spontaneous "lingering"—suggests an opportunity for improvisation. Judy Garland emphasizes this break, or possibly inserts it, in the 1939 soundtrack for *The Wizard of Oz.* Finally, both "Jeanie" and "Somewhere" evoke a wistfulness we know was often associated especially with Irish American sentimental song.

Example 2. Music to " 'Tis the Last Rose of Summer," based on "Groves of Blarney," an Irish folk tune. Transcribed by Thomas Moore; arranged by Sir John Stevenson and Sir Henry Bishop (Dublin: M. H. Gill and Son, 1891).

connect "faded" and "and" in measure 11, and the repeated Es that connect the words "and" and gone" between measures 11 and 12.

Tipping and popping, of course, are much more often present in livelier numbers. Their presence, however, is no guarantee of "Irishness"; "Black Eyed Susianna," for instance, contains plenty of popping.[29] Only in snappier numbers, such as "The Bonnie Blue Flag" (*CWS,* 17–20) and "When Johnny Comes Marching Home" (*CWS,* 113–16), do we find tipping (in "Flag," on the word "brothers" at the end of the opening phrase) as well as modal inflections (in "Johnny," on the chords accompanying the popping "Hurrahs").

Older, possibly more traditional tunes—"The Blackbird" among them—also feature several of these gestures. So do folk songs that originated in the British Isles but were collected several generations ago in Appalachia. These include "The Sons of Liberty," which in one of its versions is pentatonic and incorporates strong rising figures, repeated phrases, and hints at ornamentation.[30] Still other features also appear scattered throughout the ballads collected during the early decades of the twentieth century by Francis James Child, Cecil Sharp, and a host of other "songcatchers" of the Southern Highlands. And, as we have seen above, they appear in at least a few popular songs of the late nineteenth and twentieth centuries.

Finally, there is "mood." The emotion generated by any piece of music is difficult to describe. Certainly there is no uniquely "Irish" affect, just as there is nothing unmistakably "Irish" in a great many Irish American dances, marches, and parlor songs. Nevertheless, "Irishness" often seems to be present in Irish American music. Occasionally this is linked with high spirits, as in jigs and reels; more often, perhaps, it seems to be present in melancholy songs of vanished love and fatherland. The songs described immediately above involve these subjects: lost sweetness, distant love (whether distant in time, place, or memory), and, especially in "Sons," an Ireland never to be seen again.

29. Peter Van der Merwe is not the only scholar to raise the issue of "who influenced whom" during the first few centuries of American musical history. Early nineteenth-century Irish Americans may well have borrowed musical gestures from slave songs and dances, and vice versa. This does not mean, however, that all or even most antebellum parlor songs are necessarily "Irish" or "African," much less both at the same time.

30. Reprinted in Cecil J. Sharp, *English Folk Songs from the Southern Appalachians,* ed. Maud Karpeles (London: Oxford University Press, 1932), 224–25 (song no. 162).

These subjects appear either separately or combined with references to battle and to "General Washington and his bold men." As we have already seen, these features became commonplaces of nineteenth-century American popular music, and they reappear in more than a few twentieth-century celebrations of lost love and home.

Irish American immigrants were not always appreciated by eighteenth- and early-nineteenth-century "natives." Often they were ridiculed, even despised. "No Irish Need Apply," a song still occasionally performed today, at once documents such prejudice and an attempt to overcome it. The composition's title was taken from an advertisement for domestic help that ended with the phrase in question. Although the advertisement had actually appeared in a London newspaper, the sentiment was shared by many Americans. Nevertheless, Kathleen O'Neil, who wrote and published "No Irish" in 1863, used the anti-British sentiments of wartime Yankee audiences "to suggest that the catch-phrase was un-American." By such stratagems did O'Neil and other composers "win more tolerance of immigrants in the urban, industrial North" at the height of the Civil War.[31]

The earliest immigrants from Ireland often ended up standing on the bottom rung of America's "egalitarian" social ladder: they became mountain farmers. Later, many of them went to work in big-city sweatshops; still later, and mostly after 1865, a few of them became policemen and politicians. Often Irish immigrants of every stripe and occupation were likened to African Americans "with regard to laziness, dirtiness, lying, pilfering, stupidity, and so on—all the vices ascribed to subject peoples since the beginning of time." At best, as Hamm observes, nineteenth-century Irish Americans long remained "laborers, small farmers, or tradesmen." Their "popular image was of a rough, rowdy, hard-drinking people, who willingly became part of the new nation but at the same time retained an inordinate fondness for, and pride in, their home country."[32]

One Irish American antebellum stereotype was the playful but drunken and often foolish "Paddy," the figure who inspired the old joke "What can possibly be dumber than a dumb Irishman?" (One

31. Finson, *Voices That Are Gone,* 290–91.
32. Van der Merwe, *Origins of the Popular Style,* 48; Hamm, *Yesterdays,* 43.

answer: "A smart Swede.")[33] Another, however, was less often mocked: this was "Patrick," the lovelorn or war-torn exile. Still another was buxom "Bridget" or "Molly" or "Kate."[34] The Irish belle, in fact, enjoyed a treasured (albeit imaginary) existence especially in song: she was the "ideal sweetheart" of antebellum America, at once rural, virginal, and marriageable—a girl "who asked for neither wealth nor position." Simple and trusting, "but not stupid," her beauty was offset by an unrealistic "passive, child-like innocence that seldom suggested the emotions of a mature woman." All of these stereotypes—"Paddy" remains perhaps the most familiar—have evoked fond as well as furious responses in many Americans.[35]

In the South as well as in the North, immigrants recently arrived from Ireland ranked at the very bottom of the social order. According to James Gannon, they were regarded by the "better" classes as "uneducated, drunken, brawling social misfits who bred epidemic disease and destitute children," and in 1853 they were blamed for a yellow fever epidemic in New Orleans. Imagine, as Gannon describes them, these "clannish Celts huddled together in their Catholic churches, political clubs, neighborhood saloons, and budding labor unions, hoping to eventually be accepted as true Americans and loyal Southerners." In the industrial North, music critics of the 1850s—among them, Boston's John Sullivan Dwight—went so far as to sug-

33. Included by Carl Sandburg in *The People, Yes* (New York; Harcourt, Brace and World, 1964), 114 (no. 51).

34. Variations on "Kate" were especially common, including "Katy," of "Katy McFerran" by Hays; and "Kathleen," of both "Kathleen Mavourneen" and "I'll Take You Home Again, Kathleen." Regarding the last song, Finson correctly points out that, although it contains a "faint hint" of the longing for home so common in Irish American verse and song, the "general mention of the sea voyage and the Irish name 'Kathleen' are all the information" its composer, Thomas P. Westendorf, provides as markers of "Irishness." Finson, *Voices That Are Gone,* 288–89. A less common variant was "Kitty," celebrated in "Kitty O'Neal: Irish Ballad" (New York: William Hall and Son, 1848), published, in this early and unusual instance, complete with tune and keyboard accompaniment as well as words.

35. Williams, *'Twas Only an Irishman's Dream,* 39. One description of "Pat, Paddy or Teague" mentions "an atrocious Irish brogue," "blunders and bulls in speaking," as well as the fiery red hair, rosy cheeks, and fondness for whiskey associated with a "simian bestiality" and "pugnacity"; see Mick Moloney, "Irish Ethnic Recordings and the Irish-American Imagination," in *Ethnic Recordings in America: A Neglected Heritage* (Washington, D.C.: American Folklife Center, 1982), 87. Moloney deals exclusively with the post–Civil War American theater. Things may well have been worse prior to 1861.

gest that "forsaken boys and girls, with strong Irish accent," who slept in the "carts and coal boxes" of New York City's slums, might be redeemed through the influence of "free concerts"! Far more damaging to all concerned were the 1863 Draft Riots, which struck "a severe blow" to the reputation of New York City's Irish American community. Although some Irish Americans struggled to rescue children from the mob, others looted and pillaged; George Templeton Strong, a contemporary diarist and music enthusiast, proclaimed that "the atrocities these Celtic devils perpetrated can hardly be paralleled in the history of human cruelty."[36]

We have already seen that talented immigrants and second-generation Irish Americans fought against stereotypes and poverty with songs such as "No Irish Need Apply." This and similar ditties "were sung in the music halls of New York where Irish performers played such an important role." One of the best-known antebellum entertainers was Joe English, whose nightly turns covered a wide range of topical fare. In "Paddy and the Know-Nothings," as Irwin Silber observes, "English ridiculed anti-Irish prejudice, has warm words for Irish heroism, and winds up, naturally, singing the praises of 'Little Mac.'"[37] Other Irish American performers returned as successes to their native land. Immigrant Dion Boucicault and American-born Dan Bryant (born Daniel Webster O'Brien)—respectively, the lyricist and the composer of the song "Pat Malloy"—achieved success through organizing and appearing in traveling minstrel shows. In May 1865, immediately after the Civil War, Bryant "sailed for Europe, and in Dublin, Ireland, . . . gave several performances of Celtic characters." The same year Boucicault (also known as "Bourcicault") collaborated with E. H. House in order to provide a patriotic number for *Arrah-Na-Pogue,* a play he himself wrote and produced with Bryant. The song was "The Wearing of the Green," beloved still

36. James P. Gannon, *Irish Rebels, Confederate Tigers: The 6th Louisiana Volunteers, 1861–1865* (Campbell, Calif.: Savas, 1998), xi; Dwight quoted from the *New York Musical Review* in *Dwight's Journal of Music* for 1854, and in Robert R. Grimes, S.J., *How Shall We Sing in a Foreign Land? Music of Irish Catholic Immigrants in the Antebellum United States* (Notre Dame, Ind.: University of Notre Dame Press, 1996), 181; Strong quoted in Edward K. Spann, "Union Green: The Irish Community and the Civil War," in *The New York Irish,* ed. Ronald H. Bayor and Timothy J. Meagher (Baltimore: Johns Hopkins University Press, 1996), 204–5.

37. Williams, *'Twas Only an Irishman's Dream,* 92; Silber, *Songs,* 178.

by Americans of many ethnic backgrounds.[38] The success of Stephen Foster's songs also must have softened the hearts of many, at least insofar as plaintive tunefulness was concerned.

"By the end of the Civil War," as Williams notes, a "more positive side to the stereotype of the Irish" had begun to emerge in American society—facilitated both by parlor ballads, "based on romantic images" of exile and lost homeland, and even by the "somewhat benevolent" comic songs of the best performers: "Neither the images of soulful Patrick, the romantic exile from Erin, nor good-humored Paddy disturbed Americans as much [as some critics have claimed]. While the negative side of the stereotype might have predominated for much of the nineteenth century, the positive aspects provided a kind of beachhead within the popular culture, in song and on the stage, which the Irish themselves would gradually expand."[39]

Only slowly did anti-Irish prejudices give way during the antebellum decades. After the outbreak of hostilities at Fort Sumter, however, hatred and distrust diminished more rapidly in both North and South. In several cases this change in opinion was facilitated by song as well as battle.

Consider the establishment of the Sixth Louisiana Volunteers shortly after the Civil War began. On May 24, 1861, the *New Orleans Daily Picayune* saluted the Volunteers as a fine body of men comparable "with any yet raised in our city.... [One] Mr. Michael O'Connor has been greatly instrumental in raising this corps, and justly deserves the title of 'Father of the Brigade.' He has been one of our best citizens, and for the past sixteen years an exempt fireman." In the *New Orleans Delta* for Sunday, May 19, 1861, we find these words: "They may boast in the North of their 79th Regiment [the passage should probably read "69th Regiment"; see below] ... but we can vouch for 4,000 Irishmen in this city, ready and willing to enter the Brigade and

38. Edward Le Roy Rice, *Monarchs of Minstrelsy, from "Daddy" Rice to Date* (New York: Kenny, 1911), 50. For additional information about John Brougham, Tyrone Power (not to be confused with the film star), Barney Williams, and other antebellum "Paddy actors" similar to Joe English in some of their exploits, see Williams, *'Twas Only an Irishman's Dream,* 66–77; on Boucicault, see 97–101. See also Finson, *Voices That Are Gone,* 287.

39. Williams, *'Twas Only an Irishman's Dream,* 88.

fight for the South to our Cannon's mouth." The Sixth Louisiana may have been "the most thoroughly Irish regiment" of all that fought in the Civil War; of the 980 soldiers in that unit whose birthplace is recorded, more than 450 were born in Ireland, and "another 100 men, undoubtedly sons of immigrants, bore common Irish surnames."[40]

On the battlefield, Confederate Irish Americans turned out in surprising numbers and were quickly accepted as equals. Although comparatively few Irish American fighting units were organized among Southern troops, at least one unit—the Tenth Tennessee Volunteers—was larger even than the famed "Irish Brigade" assembled in New York State. Other "green flag" units were organized in Virginia, Georgia, and possibly Missouri (the Seventh Missouri Infantry).[41] One celebrated Confederate officer of Irish American heritage was Billy Mahone of Virginia. Another, Patrick Cleburne (discussed at the beginning of this essay)—the "Stonewall Jackson of the West"—served in the Arkansas militia and died in battle in Tennessee.

In all, as many as 160,000 Civil War combatants were immigrants from Ireland or their descendants. Because more Irish Americans lived in Northern cities, the greater number of "Irish" regiments were on the Union side. Among these were the 9th Connecticut Infantry, the 23rd Illinois Infantry, the 35th Indiana Infantry, the 9th and 28th Massachusetts Infantry, the 10th Ohio Infantry, the 24th and 116th Pennsylvania Infantry, and the 17th Wisconsin Infantry. Most famous of all was the "Irish Brigade," composed in large part of the 69th New York Infantry, together with members of the 88th and 155th New York Infantry Regiments.[42]

40. Gannon, *Irish Rebels, Confederate Tigers,* xii, xiii.

41. See William L. Burton, *Melting Pot Soldiers: The Union's Ethnic Regiments* (Ames: Iowa State University Press, 1988), 151.

42. These and other units are described in Burton, *Melting Pot Soldiers,* 112–56 (chapter 6, "The Irish Regiments"). The Brigade's history and character is described in a variety of publications, including Joseph G. Bilby, *The Irish Brigade in the Civil War: The 69th New York and Other Irish Regiments of the Army of the Potomac* (Conshohocken, Pa.: Combined, 1998); D. P. Conyngham, *The Irish Brigade and Its Campaigns: With Some Account of the Corcoran Legion, and Sketches of the Principal Officers* (New York: William McSorley, 1867); and Paul Jones, *The Irish Brigade* (Washington, D.C.: Robert B. Luce, 1969). Jones's lively and engaging synopsis is largely undocumented and lacks an index; both Jones and Bilby concentrate almost exclusively on military engagements and accomplishments. Conyngham's firsthand account provides information about certain "civilian" experiences as well.

Not every Irish American fought bravely, of course. Claims that "all Irishmen are alike" and "all fought courageously for the Union" reinforced ethnic stereotypes of "the Irish" as "happy-go-lucky, even simple-minded" fellows "who saw the war as a lark" and drank whiskey whenever they could find it. In fact, many Irish Americans did drink, on and off the battlefield. Others did not. Some Irish American soldiers deserted their Northern posts, while others fought on "for the same reasons their compatriots fought—to support their friends and comrades and to preserve the Union." A few soldiers were at once noble and debased, reflecting the human condition. James Mulligan, commander of the Twenty-third Illinois Infantry (known, like its New York counterpart, as the "Irish Brigade") and a battlefield hero, may have declined promotion to general in 1861 because "ethnicity was extremely important to him" and he wanted to stay with his fellow Irish Americans. A year later, his military ambitious stymied, Mulligan "blamed the absence of a star on anti-Irish prejudice in Washington" and even inveighed against President Lincoln for freeing "the niggers."[43] Nevertheless, the very existence, as well as the frequent military successes, of Irish American soldiers enrolled in these and other units, unquestionably served to lessen anti-Irish prejudices and helped promote the careers of more than a few officers and even a few generals.

A great many Irish American Union soldiers were Democrats by affiliation and lost heart as the war progressed, and Lincoln, the nation's first Republican president, proved increasingly successful and popular. Others, however, either cast aside such political convictions or never adopted them in the first place. D.P. Conyngham, a captain

43. Burton, *Melting Pot Soldiers,* 152, 153, 137–38. "The 69th New York seem to be drunken rowdies," according to firsthand observer Rufus R. Dawes. Dawes, *A Full Blown Yankee of the Iron Brigade: Service with the Sixth Wisconsin Volunteers* (Marietta, Ohio: E. R. Alderman, 1890; reprint, Lincoln: University of Nebraska Press, 1962), 21. They were not the only unit celebrated for drinking too much: on one occasion, seventy-five Irish American members of the "Fire Zouaves" New York regiment left their camp at night, became intoxicated, and were dismissed from the ranks; see Burton, *Melting Pot Soldiers,* 153. This behavior should not surprise us; whiskey was used to "encourage" civilians to enlist as common soldiers. Even the celebrated Michael Corcoran, himself a saloon keeper as well as an officer, was involved in several alcohol-related incidents; one of them finally killed him.

with the Irish Brigade, explained that many of his immigrant compatriots not only were concerned with "the safety of the great Republic, the home of their exiled race," but also "wanted to learn the use of arms and the science of war, with the hope of one day turning them to practical use in his own country."[44]

Perhaps this was propaganda; it is unwise to generalize about motives, however, especially on the part of individual soldiers dead these 140 years. Gannon suggests the range of personal motives and standards of performance when he reminds us that the Sixth Louisiana "produced heroic leaders in men such as Isaac Seymour and William Monaghan, just as it produced a coward in Nathaniel Offutt and a turncoat in John Conley."[45]

Occasionally, Civil War battlefields, soldiers, and music became conjoined in history. Some regiments and regimental leaders, for example, were celebrated in song. Consider the Irish Brigade, especially the Sixty-ninth New York (previously the Sixty-ninth New York State Militia, one of the few Civil War units that predated 1861), whose members were compared to the heroes of Troy in the words of the anonymous "The Boys of the Irish Brigade":

> What for should I sing you of Roman or Greek,
> Or the boys we hear tell of in story,
> Come match me for fighting, for frolic or freak,
> An Irishman's reign in his glory.
> For Ajax and Hector and bold Agamemnon,
> Were up to the tricks of our trace, O?
> But the rollicking boys for war, women and noise,
> Are the boys of the Irish Brigade, O. (*IS,* 19)

Or consider the career of General Thomas "Fightin' Tom" Sweeney. Born in Cork County in 1820, Sweeney fought in both the Mexican and Yuma wars as well as at the Battle of Shiloh, where he was wounded but survived to serve as an Honor Guard at President Lincoln's funeral. The words of "Sweeney at Shiloh" represent this brave Irish American as an almost superhuman hero, the savior of "Grant's waning glory; And Sherman's laurels too" (*IS,* 41).

44. Conyngham, *Irish Brigade,* 5–6.
45. Gannon, *Irish Rebels, Confederate Tigers,* 317.

Many Irish Americans become New World patriots and successful soldiers, but a few of them never gave up hope of returning to a "free" Ireland. In 1850s America the Fenian movement, led by the same Michael Corcoran who later commanded the Irish Brigade, kept hopes of a Free Ireland alive in immigrant hearts and minds. The most ardent Fenians included Corcoran, Thomas Francis Meagher, and Robert Nugent of the Sixty-ninth New York: officers who "worked diligently to associate [their] regiments with Irish nationalism and to persuade the larger society that Irish-Americans fought both for the Union and for Irish independence."[46] These feelings are exemplified in the lyrics of "The Song of the Irish Legion," which proclaim both American and Irish political enthusiasms:

> Ye boys of the sod, to Columbia true,
> Come up, lads, and fight for the Red, White, and Blue!
> Two countries we love, and two mottoes we'll share,
> And we'll join them in one on the banner we bear:
> Erin, mavourneen! Columbia, agra!
> E pluribus unum. Erin go bragh.[47]

As always, politics entered into things. Thus Archbishop John J. Hughes of New York urged Lincoln to make Corcoran a general, basing his plea "not on Corcoran's merits or achievements, but on what was already a familiar and effective argument of ethnic politics: [that] the promotion . . . would soothe the injured feelings of Irish-Americans."[48] Other soldiers, who struggled without the intervention of presidents and princes of the church, were more moderate in their enthusiasms. Peter Welsh, a member of the Twenty-eighth Massachusetts and a Fenian sympathizer, wrote on June 1, 1863:

> I know pretty well in what light people view soldiering in Irland[.] Nor do i wonder that such a feeling exists[,] For i consider an Irishman who volunterly enlists in the British service merits the utter contempt of his countrymen. . . . In this country it is very different[.] Here we have a free government just laws and a Constitution which guar-

46. Burton, *Melting Pot Soldiers,* 153.
47. Quoted in Burton, *Melting Pot Soldiers,* 112.
48. Burton, *Melting Pot Soldiers,* 116.

> entees equal rights and privelages to all[.] Here thousands of the sons and daughters of Irland have come to seek a refuge from tyrany and persecution at home[.] . . . If Irland is ever free the means to acomplish it must come from the shores of america[.][49]

These attitudes and actions, bolstered by certain patriotic songs and the deeds recorded in them, helped Americans accept immigrants from Ireland as "real" citizens. "The Irish Jaunting Car," for example, a well-known traditional tune, served as the basis for "The Bonnie Blue Flag," a Confederate anthem. Inspired by Irish American patriotism, Southern patriots also produced a parody known as "The Bonnie Green Flag," which ridiculed anti-Irish prejudice in the North. Union musicians responded with "The Soldiers Return," a "cultivated" parlor song equipped with a comparatively elaborate keyboard introduction, a melody full of upward-sixth and octave leaps, slow descents, chromatic inflections, and "Ad Lib[itum]" pauses for improvisatory inspiration. More than one song achieved success on both sides of the Mason-Dixon Line. "The Drummer Boy of Shiloh," for example, was published simultaneously in both Louisville, Kentucky, and Chicago in 1863. This song also exemplifies the upward melodic leaps, tipping rhythmic figures, chromatic inflections, and opportunities for interpolated cadenzas as well as expressions of loyalty and loss ("I've loved my country as my God; To serve them both I've tried" [*SCW,* 140–42]).

In many respects the Civil War was a bad time for composers. Although Foster wrote almost one-fourth of his songs during 1863, when the conflict was at its height, he also wrote his brother Henry that "pay, in these times, especially in music, is very poor." He and his partners in song, including the lyricist George Cooper, soldiered on, however. Although it is scarcely one of Foster's best efforts, "Willie Has Gone to the War" dates from about this time. The song was purchased for ten dollars by Frank Brower for Henry Wood's minstrel company, which was a direct competitor of Dan Bryant's troupe

49. *Irish Green and Union Blue: The Civil War Letters of Peter Welsh, Color Sergeant, 28th Regiment, Massachusetts Volunteers,* ed. Lawrence Frederick Kohl (New York: Fordham University Press, 1986), 100–101.

and one of many ensembles that performed music by and about Irish Americans throughout the dark days of the mid-1860s.[50]

If Foster did much to disseminate Gaelic melody among antebellum Americans, Patrick Starsfield Gilmore did as much or more to establish a reputation for Irish American musicians as bold, brave, and visible. Born in 1829 in Athone, Ireland, Gilmore caught "band fever" at an early age, asked for cornet lessons, and in 1845, at the age of sixteen, joined a regimental band. Two years later he traveled with the band to Canada; he moved to America in 1849, migrating to Boston, and went to work at the Ordway Brothers Music Store, where he organized a minstrel company with himself as cornet soloist. Soon afterward he organized a military band for Boston's Charlestown Militia Company.

In 1852 Gilmore was offered the position of bandmaster with the Boston Brass Band, an ensemble "composed mainly of professors, musical composers and artists, each one highly accomplished in the use of his particular instrument"—as *Gleason's Pictorial Drawing-Room Companion,* a contemporary periodical, observed in 1851. He also went into business with Joseph M. Russell; for a time they published music under the name Gilmore & Russell. At about the same time, Gilmore was offered the position as director of the Salem Light Infantry Regiment, with a salary of "one thousand a year and all he [could] . . . make" (the last phrase referring to income from concerts and other gigs). This was in 1855, when an average government bureaucrat earned less than six hundred dollars per year.[51]

After Fort Sumter fell, Gilmore's band became involved in escorting regiments to their training camps. Soon afterwards, enrolled as members as the Twenty-fourth Massachusetts Volunteer Regiment, these musicians were assigned to General Burnside's army, at the

50. Quoted in Emerson, *Doo-Dah!* 282, 286–87.

51. Kenneth E. Olson, *Music and Musket: Bands and Bandsmen of the American Civil War* (Westport, Conn.: Greenwood Press, 1981), 224, 225. See also ibid., 64–65, where Olson refers to the cost of banners for New York's Irish Brigade. Conyngham witnessed the first presentation of these colors, which he described as "a deep rich green, heavily fringed, having in the centre a richly embroidered Irish harp, with a sunburst above it and a wreath of shamrock beneath. Underneath, on a crimson scroll, in Irish characters, was the motto, 'They shall never retreat from the charge of lances' "; see Conyngham, *Irish Brigade,* 56.

time fighting in Virginia. Like many regimental bandsmen, Gilmore was discharged in 1862; he returned to Boston, where in 1863 he was asked by Governor Andrew of Massachusetts to reorganize completely all the state militia bands.

The events that made Gilmore famous may have been inspired by the large-scale concerts of Louis-Antoine Juillien and his orchestra during their American tour. Wherever his idea came from, Gilmore put it into action: on March 4, 1864, in New Orleans, he organized a concert of some five thousand children (some say ten thousand) who, together with all regimental bands in the city and surrounding area, celebrated the inauguration of Governor Michael Hahn for a "Free and Restored Louisiana." For the rest of his life, Gilmore became "the Irishman who gave the most 'American' concerts," and certainly the biggest ones, the nation had ever witnessed. The same year, or perhaps in 1863, he composed "When Johnny Comes Marching Home" and published it, for some reason, under the pseudonym "Louis Lambert." It may even have been Gilmore's arrangement of "John Brown's Body" that prompted Julia Ward Howe to write the words for the "Battle Hymn of the Republic."

As a Civil War musician, Gilmore once played "Dixie" for Confederate soldiers waiting for transportation on Roanoke Island, North Carolina, on their way to Northern prisons. He was reprimanded for impertinence, but the event contributed to his manly legend. He is also known to have entertained Governor Hicks of Maryland at Annapolis and General Burnside in Newbern with such numbers as "The Last Rose of Summer." As a member of his regiment wrote home in April 1862: "I don't know what we should have done without our band. It is acknowledged by everyone to be the best in the division. Every night about sun down Gilmore gives us a splendid concert, playing selections from the operas and some very pretty marches, quicksteps, waltzes and the like, most of which are composed by himself or . . . a member of his band. . . . Thus you see we get a great deal of *new* music, notwithstanding we are off here in the woods."[52]

Members of Gilmore's regimental band were not flawless performers; occasionally they didn't even try to play well. Alfred Roe,

52. Quoted in Bell Irvin Wiley, *The Life of Billy Yank: The Common Soldier of the Union* (New York: Doubleday, 1971), 158.

historian of the Twenty-fourth Massachusetts Volunteers, wrote that they "could produce discords, as when their application for furlough was disapproved." Then, as he went on to explain, they would march "across the parade ground," whence "there came from their brazen instruments notes that no one would have believed them capable of blowing." On happier occasions, however, "the spell disappeared and harmony as of old prevailed."[53] Such lapses must have been temporary; Gilmore's organizations were generally good enough to earn praise from a host of witnesses and helped confirm his postwar reputation as a leading figure of American music.

After the war, although the heroics of individual Irish Americans were largely forgotten, Gilmore's fame grew. The mammoth band concerts he organized—the musical portion of the National Peace Jubilee, held at Boston in 1869, may serve as an example—wrung praise from no less a critic than John Sullivan Dwight, who perhaps compromised his "cultivated" musical standards in honor of the bandmaster's patriotic record. Praising one concert, Dwight confessed that the selections, "light and popular, but good of their kind," helped raise money for the benefit of Boston's sanitary officers (mostly Irish Americans at the time), and that the concert as a whole constituted "a noble gift of one man's heart and energy to the defends of the sacred cause"—the last an allusion to the bandmaster's war work. "As for Mr. Gilmore," Dwight concluded, "he has fairly earned all the reward which a grateful people appear eager to bestow. If the laudations of the newspapers do not turn his head—and so far we know he takes it sanely, modestly and simply—it is infinitely to his credit."[54]

The mere presence of music was always welcome among Civil War soldiers. Musical performances, however, were often anything but

53. Alfred S. Roe, *The Twenty-fourth Regiment, Massachusetts Volunteers, 1861–1865* (Worchester, Mass.: Twenty-fourth Veteran Association, 1907), 412.

54. John Sullivan Dwight, "The National Peace Jubilee," *Dwight's Journal of Music* 33, no. 8 (July 3, 1869): 60. The most exhaustive summary of Gilmore's career remains Marwood Darlington, *Irish Orpheus: The Life of Patrick S. Gilmore, Bandmaster Extraordinary* (Philadelphia: Olivier-Maney-Klein, 1950). Valuable observations about Gilmore also appear in several of the works cited above, as well as Frank J. Cipolla, "Patrick S. Gilmore: The Boston Years," *American Music* 6 (1988): 281–92; and "Patrick S. Gilmore: The Boston Years and Beyond," in *Kongressbericht Abony/*

"accomplished." On one occasion, as Rufus Dawes records in his history of the Sixth Wisconsin (not an Irish American unit, by the way), one Captain Bragg asked him "if I did not want two of his men." Dawes goes on to explain that he "was anxious to muster in as many as possible, and did want badly two men. He said that one of his men wanted to serve his country as a fifer and the other as a drummer. The fifer could not fife, neither could the drummer drum. But none of my men in Company 'K' could perform such service, and they were all desirous to serve as soldiers in the line . . . and so I took them in. Captain Bragg got nothing for his men, but he settled perplexing questions about the [quality of the] music in Company 'E.' "[55]

Issues of performance quality aside, Irish American troops, especially those with Fenian sympathies, seem to have longed for any kind of music that recalled to them their homeland, their oppression under the British, and their hopes of better lives to come. Also inspiring was anything that reminded them of their religious convictions. This brings us to antebellum Irish American *Catholic* composers, publishers, and performers: a subject discussed at length by Robert Grimes, who describes in detail the activities of musicians and music publishers, especially in Boston, to transform the music of Irish immigrants through the publication of cheap editions, modern music education, and other techniques.[56] In addition to their work on behalf of prewar religious institutions and publishing houses, however, Irish Catholic musicians played a limited but important role in Civil War ceremonies and worship services.

That Irish Americans in both the Union and the Confederacy sometimes enlisted out of religious pride is almost certain; this was especially true after Union victories in 1862–1863 and Lincoln's Emancipation Proclamation following the Battle of Antietam, when many immigrants and their families in the North abandoned their conditional loyalty to a Republican administration and threw themselves

Ungarn 1994, ed. Wolfgang Suppan (Tutzing, Germany: Hans Schneider, 1996), 183–87; Stephen P. Gilmore, "Patrick Sarsfield Gilmore: America's Prototypical Impresario," *Journal of Band Research* 34 (fall 1998): 69–100; and Jere Humphreys, "Strike Up the Band! The Legacy of Patrick S. Gilmore," *Music Educators Journal* 74, no. 2 (October 1987): 22–26.

55. Dawes, *Full Blown Yankee,* 15.

56. Grimes, *How Shall We Sing?* see esp. 178ff.

wholeheartedly behind the winning side. Moreover, and to a greater extent than some historians once proposed, they demanded tolerance for their religious beliefs. And tolerance, even respect, was increasingly granted, especially during and after the war. Thomas O'Connor points out, for example, that in 1861 Harvard College conferred an honorary degree on Catholic Bishop Fitzpatrick, a man who had "several good friends among the members of Harvard's board of overseers," but whom "none would have dared propose... for such an honor" during the turbulent 1850s, when the school question, the slavery issue, and the Know-Nothing movement were causing so much controversy. Even in 1861, O'Connor continues, "it might not have been possible... had it not been for 'the loyalty shown by [Fitzpatrick] and by the Irish who offered... themselves freely for the army.'"[57]

Concerning actual Civil War Irish American Catholic music making, we have only a few records. One of the most complete was left us by Maria Lydig Daly of New York City, who attended Sabbath services with the Sixty-ninth New York Regiment as a personal guest of Colonel Corcoran. "I have never saw anything in my life that impressed me so much," Daly asserted. "It was a picture such as I never saw equaled. Four thousand men were confirmed and as many more took the sacrament. I could scarcely restrain my tears, for I felt it was like a mass for the dead." Corcoran, described as "a genuinely religious man," was also musically included: he "introduced singing into his regiment, in which all of the men and officers [were]... expected to take part"; at evening parade "'John Brown's Soul is Marching on,' chorused by a thousand men... [gave]... a Cromwellian earnestness to this war, in at least one camp."[58]

Another of these accounts deserves close attention. Written by William Corby, a priest and army chaplain, it depicts at some length a military mass celebrated in September 1864:

> Precisely at ten o'clock... [and as] soon as the priests are ready, the *Asperges me* is announced, and, instead of a grand choir, such as is

57. Thomas H. O'Connor, *The Boston Irish: A Political History* (Boston: Northeastern University Press, 1995), 93.

58. Maria Lydig Daly, *Diary of a Union Lady, 1861–65* (New York: Funk and Wagnalls, 1962), 60; on Corcoran, see *Dwight's Journal of Music* 20, no. 16 (January 18, 1862): 335 (quoted in part in Olson, *Music and Musket,* 191).

> heard in the royal cathedrals of Christendom, the bugles, followed by the report of numerous guns, announce the beginning. Then, under the direction of Gen. Meagher, at the *Introibo* various military bands discourse solemn music until after the *Credo,* when, again, by a sign from the Master of Ceremonies to the Officer of the Day, another discharge, a grand salute of guns, testify to *Credo in unum Deum*—I believe in one God. The bugle follows with its well-known notes, "tara-taran-tara," and again the bands play. Now their music is soft, low, and sweet, suitable to the devotion that immediately disposes the faithful for the more sacred portion of the Mass. The *Sanctus! sanctus! sanctus!* rouses all to a fixed attention and is accompanied by a sudden rattle of dozens of kettle-drums, with an occasional thundering sound from the bass drums. Shortly after this comes that moment of moments in the offering of the sublime mysteries. The preparatory is over, and now you see men bow down in deep devotion as the priest leans over the altar and takes up the Host. Here, at a sign from the Master of Ceremonies, the bugle notes, "tara-taran-tara," ring out over the tented fields, and the same grand evidence of respect and faith is given by the sound of cannon and the roll of musketry, as the sublime words, full of power and purpose—the supreme words of Consecration—are pronounced. Soft music is again in order at intervals, until the end, which is proclaimed in turn by guns, drums, and bugles that prolong a grand *finale.*

Worth noticing especially is the conclusion of this event, at which time "Maj.-Gen. Hancock . . . spoke in the highest terms of the bravery and devotedness of the Irish Brigade" and "Gen. de Trobriand . . . said that his Irishmen claimed *him* as one of their own, stating that his name was in reality only slightly Frenchified from the original *(O'Brien)* which caused prolonged merriment." This celebration, Corby concluded, "throws additional light on the character of the Irish Brigade."[59]

59. William Corby, *Memoirs of Chaplain Life: Three Years with the Irish Brigade in the Army of the Potomac,* ed. Lawrence Frederick Kohl (New York: Fordham University Press, 1992), 266–68.

Civil War Music and the Common Soldier

The Experiences of Charles Wellington Reed

Eric A. Campbell

The late Bell Irvin Wiley, who was considered the preeminent authority on the Civil War soldier, wrote, "On the march, sitting about the campfire, riding trains or transports, at home on furlough—wherever Yankees assembled—the strains of popular tunes were sure to be heard. More than American fighters of any other period, the men who wore the blue, and the butternut Rebs who opposed them, deserve to be called singing soldiers."[1] Music was indeed important, even indispensable, to the Civil War soldier. This was especially true considering that the average soldier, Union or Confederate, was primarily a "citizen-soldier." This essay covers the importance of music to the common Civil War soldier through the eyes and words of one particular volunteer, Charles Wellington Reed.

Reed was an extraordinary individual on many levels. He was multitalented, gifted as both artist and musician. Reed's artistic talents later led to his direct connection with one of the most famous pieces of Civil War literature, John Billings's 1887 classic, *Hardtack and Coffee, or the Unwritten Story of Army Life.* This book not only eloquently described the everyday trials of the average Civil War soldier but also contains over 220 of Reed's illustrations, many based on his wartime drawings. Although Reed is better known today for his artwork, his interest and talent in music were notable; he was the "First Bugler" of the Ninth Massachusetts Battery, and it was also reported that he "had a splendid voice" for singing. Reed also was extraordinary for his personal bravery, and his "most distinguished gallantry at

1. Bell Irvin Wiley, *The Life of Billy Yank* (Indianapolis: Bobbs-Merrill, 1952), 157.

the battle of Gettysburg" was recognized in 1895 when he was awarded the Medal of Honor.[2]

Although Charles Reed was an exceptional individual in many ways, he was representative of the average soldier who served during the Civil War. On the day of his enlistment, August 2, 1862, Reed was twenty-one, just slightly younger than the average Union soldier. Like the majority of his comrades, Reed was literate, native born, white, and from a lower-middle-class background. Physically, at 5 feet 11 inches and 150 pounds, Reed was slightly taller and heavier than the average soldier, who was 5 feet 8¾ inches and 143½ pounds. His "light" complexion, blue eyes, and "light" hair also matched the most prevalent groups in those categories.[3]

His military service, in many ways, also was typical of the average Union soldier who fought in the Eastern Theater. Following its mustering in, the Ninth Massachusetts Battery was assigned, as were many of the units recruited in 1862, to the defenses of Washington. Reed and his comrades spent the next eleven months getting acclimated to military life through constant drilling and training. The Ninth Massachusetts Battery subsequently was assigned to the Army of the Potomac on June 25, 1863, and was promptly thrust into the midst of the Gettysburg Campaign. The battery's baptism of fire came one week later on July 2 at Gettysburg.[4]

Reed continued to serve with the Ninth Massachusetts Battery for the next sixteen and a half months, participating in every major campaign during that time period, including the Bristoe Station Campaign of October 9–20, 1863; the Mine Run Campaign of November 25–December 3, 1863; the 1864 Overland Campaign, which included the battles of the Wilderness, Spotsylvania Court House, North Anna,

2. John Billings, *Hardtack and Coffee, or the Unwritten Story of Army Life* (Boston: George M. Smith, 1887) (Billings was an artilleryman in the Tenth Massachusetts Battery); Charles W. Reed obituary, *Boston Globe,* April 30, 1926; F. H. Ainsworth to Charles Reed, August 16, 1895, Charles Wellington Reed Medal of Honor File, National Archives (hereinafter cited as NA).

3. Charles W. Reed Military Service Record, National Archives (hereinafter cited as MSR, NA); Wiley, *Billy Yank,* 303, 307, 313; Gregory A. Coco, *The Civil War Infantryman* (Gettysburg, Pa.: Thomas Publications, 1996), 7; description of Reed in "Letter, Order, Descriptive, Morning Report Book, Ninth Battery," NA.

4. Levi Baker, *History of the Ninth Massachusetts Battery,* (Framingham, Mass.: Lakeview Press, 1888), 19–21, 24–53, 213.

Charles Wellington Reed. *Library of Congress.*

Bethesda Church, and Cold Harbor; and the Petersburg Campaign, which included the initial assaults on June 17–18, 1864, and the battles of the Weldon Railroad, Peeble's Farm, and Hatcher's Run.[5]

On November 19, 1864, the army at long last took advantage of Reed's artistic talent and detailed him as an "assistant topographical engineer" to the Army of the Potomac's Fifth Corps staff. He served in this capacity for the rest of the war, recording and mapping the Hicksford Raid of December 7–13, 1864, and the Battle of Second Hatcher's Run, February 5–7, 1865. Reed mustered out on June 6, 1865, having served his country for nearly three years, and he returned home a hardened man, wise beyond his twenty-four years and, like most veterans, changed forever by the war.[6]

Reed was intelligent, articulate, observant, insightful, humorous, industrious, and modest. These qualities are evident in his wartime letters and drawings, many of which have been preserved. This extensive and unique collection, which consists of more than 180 letters and hundreds of drawings, provides the modern researcher with a wealth of information on the role and activities of Union field musicians during the war. Charles Wellington Reed is therefore an ideal subject in a discussion of Civil War music, for all of his attributes, both ordinary and extraordinary, make him the perfect witness and commentator on the influence music had on the average Civil War soldier. Although he was literate, Reed sometimes erred in spelling, capitalization, and punctuation, which will become apparent when reading excerpts from his letters.

MUSIC AS ENTERTAINMENT

Music was a popular form of amusement and recreation in the mid-nineteenth century. When the soldiers marched off to war (most were leaving home for the first time), their love of music went with them, both as comfort and entertainment. These men also quickly

5. Ibid., 91–92; Frederick Dyer, *A Compendium of the War of the Rebellion* (Des Moines, Iowa: Dyer, 1908), 1246.

6. Charles W. Reed MSR, NA; Eric A. Campbell, ed., *"A Grand Terrible Dramma": From Gettysburg to Petersburg: The Civil War Letters of Charles Wellington Reed* (New York: Fordham University Press, 2000), 294–305 (hereinafter cited as *GTD*).

learned that military service was composed of little fighting and lots of boredom, so music served as a way of passing the long hours. Bell Irvin Wiley ranked music as the soldiers' second most popular pastime after reading.[7] Reed's letters testify to the importance of music to the soldiers; they describe performances that range from formal band concerts to impromptu solo or group vocal concerts performed by the soldiers themselves.

MILITARY BANDS

In describing the use of formal bands, Wiley wrote, "When not on the march . . . bands commonly gave twilight concerts which were greatly enjoyed by the soldiers. On holidays and other festive occasions the bands gave special programs. Now and then they serenaded high-ranking officers, much to the pleasure of the rank and file. . . . Not the least appreciated of the bands' performances were those given during the course of fatiguing marches." In 1861 nearly every Union regiment went to war with its own band, but in July 1862 a law was passed prohibiting bands below the brigade level. This law improved the musical quality of the brigade bands, since each took the best of their regimental musicians, but it also meant that the frontline soldiers enjoyed their music less often.[8]

Because music was so important to Charles Reed, he was careful to note in his letters the rare band appearances he did have an opportunity to enjoy. During his entire service he only recorded eight instances of when he witnessed military bands perform. The first was in October 1862, two months after he enlisted. To his sister Helen Tilton he wrote, "the Band which accompanied the 13th N.H. Reg that arrived here Thursday is playing Sacred Music. the first I have heard since I have been out here, it is splendid."[9]

7. Paul Glass, *Singing Soldiers (The Spirit of the Sixties): A History of the Civil War in Song* (New York: Grosset and Dunlap, 1968), xi–xx; Wiley, *Billy Yank,* 157.

8. Wiley, *Billy Yank,* 157–58; U.S. War Department, *The War of the Rebellion: A Compilation of the Official Records of the Union and Confederate Armies* (Washington, D.C.: U.S. Government Printing Office, 1880–1901) series 3, 2:278 (General Order No. 91, section X, dated July 29, 1862) (hereinafter cited as *OR*).

9. *GTD* 36, 194, 201, 214, 228, 283, 308, 326. The Thirteenth New Hampshire Regiment was mustered into service on September 20, 1862, and was assigned to the

Reed's next reference to a military band revealed how rarely they were seen and heard by the enlisted men. It came in his diary entry of March 27, 1864, over one and a half years later. According to Reed, "Col Shermer reg't 2200 strong came into Reserve Art[illery] with a band, a desirable aquistion." Reed was referring to the arrival of the Fifteenth New York Heavy Artillery Regiment at Brandy Station, Virginia, the location of the army's winter encampment. Fresh from the Washington defenses, where they had spent their entire military service, the regiment, along with many other units manning those fortifications, was reinforcing the Army of the Potomac in preparation for the upcoming 1864 spring offensive. Reed described the reaction to the band's arrival in more detail in an April 13, 1864, letter to his sister Emma Gowing: "A regiment of heavy artillery New Yorkers commanded by Col. Schirmer a german, in fact the men are all germans came into [camp] a short time ago bringing a band with them which makes it quite pleasant for us[.] we have been deprived of music ever since leaving Centerville and hailed the comeing of this band with delight."[10]

Some of the most remarkable moments concerning Civil War bands occurred on the battlefields. There are numerous recorded episodes where Union and Confederate musicians exchanged songs or actually engaged in competitions, one band attempting to better the other's rendition of a particular song. Reed witnessed and recorded one such scene during the 1864 Overland Campaign near Spotsylvania Court House. On the night of May 20, he wrote in his diary: "In the evening the musical department engaged in a duel[.] the Rebs performing Dixie, Bonnie blue flag, Get out of the Wilderness, Etc. ours Kingdom coming and National airs. quite interesting." Reed also mentioned

capital defenses. During the war the regiment served with the Army of the Potomac, the Union operations along the North Carolina coast, and eventually the Army of the James (see Dyer, *Compendium,* 1315–16).

10. *GTD,* 194, 201. Colonel Louis Schirmer commanded the Fifteenth New York Heavy Artillery, which had mustered into service in December 1861 and was immediately sent to the Washington defenses. General Grant ordered the transfer of many of these heavy artillery batteries from their fortifications to the Army of the Potomac, assigning them as infantry. Arriving at the front at nearly full strength, Schirmer's regiment was larger than some veteran brigades already with the army. The regiment served as infantry throughout the remainder of the war, being mustered out in August 1865 (see Dyer, *Compendium,* 1386–87).

the performance of bands a few times during the siege of Petersburg in late 1864. In all of these instances, bands were used as a form of entertainment to boost the men's morale.[11]

Reed witnessed and recorded another use of military bands—for formal military exercises—in March 1865. This incident was rather unusual, however, for he described the performance not of Union musicians, but of a Confederate band near Petersburg, Virginia. In a letter dated March 8, 1865, to his sister Emma, he wrote:

> I accompanied one of the Signal boys to a Signal Station a short time ago and [upon] climbing . . . was amply repaid for my pains by a glorious view of the enemy's line and country south west of Petersburg. I took a scetch of a portion of their works taking in the famous lead works, with the aid of a powerful telescope which brought the objects out as plain as if I were standing with in fifty yards of them. while [there] I saw a reb inspection which was done up in style by them in their lines[.] they had a band of music and the wind blowing in our direction we could catch the airs they were playing.[12]

Reed's last mention of bands in his wartime correspondence briefly described one of the "festive occasions" for which they performed. This incident occurred at Arlington Heights, Virginia, on May 25, 1865. The war was over and the Grand Review of the Union Armies in Washington had just been completed. The Union soldiers were celebrating their imminent return home when Reed penned to his sister Helen, "The troops are yelling and screeching with joy at the prospect of getting off tomarrow. immense fires burning, bands playing, and exploding ammunition. a novel idea is going on every man is placing candles on the outside of every tent. thousands upon thousands, cheer upon cheer, resounding and sweling through the night air. Oh I wish you could see it."[13]

INSTRUMENTAL MUSIC AND SINGING

While military bands were popular with the rank and file, this pleasure was rarely enjoyed. Thus the men were forced to rely upon their

11. Glass, *Singing Soldiers,* xvi; *GTD,* 214, 228, 283.
12. *GTD,* 308.
13. Wiley, *Billy Yank,* 157; *GTD,* 326.

personal talents to create their own music; ad hoc instrumental music and singing were therefore common throughout the camps of both armies.

Concerning Union soldiers, Wiley wrote: "Some Yanks on leaving home for the war took violins, guitars and other instruments along with them and entertained their comrades at informal camp sessions." In describing the pastimes of Union soldiers, Union veteran John Billings recalled,

> In some of the tents vocal or instrumental music was a feature of the evening. There was probably not a regiment in the service that did not boast at least one violinist, one banjoist, and a bone player in its ranks—not to mention other instruments generally found associated with these—and one or all of them could be heard in operation, either inside or in a company street, most any pleasant evening. However unskilled the artists, they were sure to be the centre of an interested audience.

The writings of Charles Reed bear out these statements. In several letters he mentioned incidents of his fellow soldiers playing instruments, including a cornet, a guitar, and a violin. In a letter dated January 27, 1864, Reed provided a detailed description of a typical camp scene, which included the mention of both instrumental music and singing: "at evening, after the fatigue work of the day is completed and supper discussed the men gather round their doors, some smoking and discussing the news of the day, a little knot enjoying a sing another party having a friendly box or some other rough game, others promenadeing, a merri burst of laughter here, a little animated conversations there altogether making a spirited and agreeable scene."[14]

Throughout his wartime correspondence Reed recorded thirteen instances of singing or instrumental music. The majority of these related to vocal music, which is not surprising, as the majority of soldiers, no matter what their musical ability, could and did sing. Singing came naturally to these men, who had sung routinely at home before the war. When a soldier was granted a rare furlough home, singing was commonly engaged in with family and friends. Reed described to

14. Wiley, *Billy Yank,* 157; Billings, *Hardtack and Coffee,* 69–70; *GTD,* 169, 178, 203.

one of his sisters a visit he had with family friends in New Jersey while he was returning to his unit following a furlough: "I received a right hearty welcome and enjoyed a charming afternoon there. . . . [W]e talked over old time, discussed scetches, made a few in an album, had music, Etc."[15]

Bugles lack valves and thus the ability to produce the full range of chromatic notes required to play melodies; because of this limitation, bugles were not considered an instrument for entertainment. Although Reed's main duty in the military was as a bugler, he was forced to find other outlets for his musicianship. Reed found occasions to sing throughout the war, mostly as a pastime. An excellent example comes from a letter he wrote to his seven-year-old niece, Gracie May Tilton. In answer to her inquiry as to what he most needed or wanted, Reed wrote,

> You ask in your last note what I should most like to have. Above all things I should like to catch hold of you and give you a hearty good squeeze, with a lot of smacking kisses but as that is an impossibility now in shape of reality you must take the will for the deed. The next that I most desire . . . a Colledge Song Book which would be very acceptable as a New Years gift from you. I am about forming a quartete to enjoy our evenings with. it is very pleasant to have a quiet little sing now and then, and as that book has the four parts in it, it will be easy to learn from.

Reed took his singing seriously, even to the point of practicing regularly. In his diary entry for Friday, February 19, 1864, he recorded: "in the evening Sergt Parks joined me in my singing excercises making it more interesting."[16]

Reed and his comrades also used singing as a way to establish relationships with civilians who lived near their camps. One such occasion occurred in January 1863, when the Ninth Massachusetts Battery was assigned to the outer defenses of Washington, near Centreville, Virginia. Reed and a fellow comrade visited a farmer who was loyal to the Union and on whose land their fort was located. Reed described this in a letter to his sister:

15. Wiley, *Billy Yank,* 157; *GTD,* 323.
16. *GTD,* 66–67, 179.

> last Wednesday evening a "Non Com" and myself called on a Va farmer who was an honest hospitable fellow. an English Scothman . . . I should judge by his dialect and amused us immensely by his many droll anecdotes. . . . [T]here were two young Lassies . . . they were decidedly modest. . . . Conversation began to flow quite pleasantly. . . . I was amused at the witty repartees brought out by my comrade. . . . I let him do as much talking as he liked and held myself in readines as a resecue force, in case he should fall out. . . . Singing was proposed and we sang a few songs which pleased the old folks very much. . . . [W]e . . . soon after departed with the conclusion that we had a good time. . . . I was obliged to play taps at half past eight. . . . We do enjoy singing very much. Johnie sings now and then.[17]

MILITARY USES OF MUSIC

Reed's mention in the last passage to being "obliged to play taps" leads to a discussion of the military use of music, primarily bugle calls, to regulate and control the soldiers in camp and on the battlefield. In camp, and at the most basic level, music had a tremendous impact on the soldiers' existence, for it set and controlled their daily routine. John D. Billings's *Hardtack and Coffee* includes a chapter entitled "A Day in Camp," which described a typical day for a light artillery battery as the soldiers responded to the various bugle calls that dictated their regimen. The use of these calls was so obvious and accepted that Billings felt no need to interpret their meanings. He simply stated, "Beginning the army day . . . the first bugle-call blown was one known . . . as the *Assembly of Buglers.*" This call was followed thereafter by "Assembly," "Reveille," "Stable Call," "Breakfast Call," "Sick Call," "Watering Call," "Fatigue Call," "Drill Call," "Boots and Saddles," "Dinner Call," "Water Call," "Stable Call," "Attention," "Assembly," "Retreat," "Assembly of the Guard," "Attention," "Assembly," "Tattoo," and finally "Taps."[18]

Operating as a kind of "public address system" on behalf of the commanding officers, these bugle calls controlled the men's movements and actions during their every waking moment from morning until night. Thirty-nine bugle calls were listed in the *Instruction for*

17. Ibid., 73–74.
18. Billings, *Hardtack and Coffee,* 165–97.

Field Artillery, the standard operational and training manual of the time. These calls became so ingrained into the men's subconscious that they sometimes instantly produced certain emotions or responses. One example comes from the reaction the men had to "Assembly of the Buglers." According to Billings, "It was the signal to the men to get out of their blankets and prepare for the morning roll-call, known as Reveille. At this signal, the hum of life could be heard within the tents. 'Put the bugler in the guard house!'—'Turn out!'—'All up!'—and other similar expressions, mingled with yawns, groans, and exclamations of deep disgust, formed a part of the response to this always unwelcome summons." "Taps," played at the end of the military day, evoked a different set of emotions and memories, as Billings related:

> Well do I recall, after the lapse of more than twenty years, the melodious tones of this little bit of army music coming to our ears so consecutively from various parts of the army as to make continuous vibrations for nearly fifteen minutes, softened and sweetened by varying distances, as more than a thousand bugles gave tongue to the still and clear evening air, telling us that . . . a hundred thousand men had come out of their rude temporary homes—possibly the last ones they would ever occupy—to respond to their names, and give token, that though Nature's pall had now overshadowed the earth, they were yet loyally at their posts awaiting further orders for their country's service.

These bugle calls were so regular the men invented a little ditty to describe them:

> I hear the bugle sound the calls
> For *Reveille* and *Drill,*
> For *Water, Stable,* and *Tattoo,*
> For *Taps*—and all was still.
> I hear it sound the *Sick-Call* grim,
> And see the men in line,
> With faces wry as they drink down
> Their whisky and quinine.[19]

So important were these calls to the training and daily routine of a military unit that when Captain Archille De Vecchi formed the Ninth

19. Board of Artillery Officers, *Instruction for Field Artillery* (New York: D. Van Nostrand, 1864), xviii–xix; Billings, *Hardtack and Coffee,* 164, 165, 195.

Massachusetts Battery in August 1862, one of the first positions he sought to fill was that of chief bugler. The man De Vecchi recruited was Charles Wellington Reed. In a letter to his sister, Reed related that the captain "wants me to enlist at once, as he wants the men to learn the bugle calls immediately." Soon, Reed was able to use his musical ability to attain the position of chief bugler, a post that gave him some benefits, which he detailed in this same letter: "the pay will be $21.00 a month and I shall receive $145.00 in advance. . . . I shall have a horse to myself and equipments complete should wear a sabre and would be quartered with the staff officers . . . have plenty of time to scetch and Etc." Altogether, these were much better conditions than the average private experienced during the Civil War.[20]

Shortly after he enlisted, Reed recounted learning the various bugle calls: "when I entered the Battery I did not know a single Artillery call but now know most of them by heart[.] as soon as the other Buglers learn I shall have nothing to do but see that the calls are played at the proper hours[.] I have been highly complimented on my playing." These various calls not only had to be taught to the other buglers, but also had to be recognized by the rank and file and by the officers as well. In a December 1862 letter to his mother, Reed wrote, "I have been practicing the Bugle calls in the Captains tent this evening for the benifit of the officers which was quite amusing as they make some mistakes and laugh at each other heartily."[21] Obviously, if the officers failed to recognize a particular call on a battlefield, it would not be nearly as "amusing" as Reed related here.

Though Captain De Vecchi apparently showed some latitude with his officers, he tolerated no excuses for the buglers themselves. Less than two months after being mustered into service, Reed described the fate of an incompetent bugler: "Mr Nash the second Bugler has been replaced in the ranks for his confounded lazynes[.] he would'nt practise and the consequence was he always made blunders[.] so all the duty devolved uppon me, in camp and in the field. Captain was in a rage about it, and appointed another man in his place."[22] Capt. John Bigelow, the officer who took command of the battery following

20. *GTD,* 10.
21. Ibid., 16, 58.
22. Ibid., 27.

De Vecchi's resignation in February 1863, also realized the importance of these bugle calls. Bigelow felt not only that the calls set the daily routine of his camp, but also, and more importantly, they were a tool he could utilize to establish discipline within the battery.

When Bigelow took command, the battery was in disarray. De Vecchi had not been much of a disciplinarian, and the battery had been pulling garrison duty outside of Washington for over six months. Bigelow recalled finding the battery "demoralized and unhappy because the men felt they were only playing soldiers, for which they had not enlisted." The new commander had little in common with Reed or with the other men in the battery. Bigelow was a two-year combat veteran; further distancing him from his men, he had been born and raised in a wealthy upper-class Boston family and was a graduate of Harvard.[23]

Realizing the importance of discipline, Bigelow insisted on the unquestioning obedience of orders, and he had his men strictly adhere to military protocol, including the practice of regular roll calls. Of course, it was Charles Reed who performed most of the bugle calls to summon forth the men. In a March 9, 1863, letter to his sister Helen, Reed related his new commander's policy and its effect on the men. According to the young bugler, "he has been order[ing] eight roll calls a day. in fact they are regular dress parades which precede all the drill calls, stable, and water calls which keeps the men cleaning up only to be besmeared with mud again from morning till night, and then drilling and turning out for roll call in the everlasting mud is anything but condusive to the health of the men."[24]

ON THE DRILL FIELD

Bigelow also insisted on the constant training of the gun crews and horses, which involved the use of bugle calls for battery maneuvers and battlefield commands. Of the thirty-nine bugle calls described

23. John Bigelow, *The Peach Orchard, Gettysburg, July 2, 1863* (Minneapolis: Kimball-Storer, 1910), 62; Lee Harrington, "John Bigelow, from Harvard to Gettysburg," unpublished paper, University of Massachusetts, Boston, May 1884.

24. Letter, Order, Descriptive, Morning Report Book, Ninth Battery, Orders 79, March 5, 1863, NA; *GTD,* 84.

Captain John Bigelow. *U.S. Army Military History Institute.*

in the *Instruction for Field Artillery,* twenty-four dealt with battery maneuvers or battlefield commands. While many commands could be given verbally, the *Instruction for Field Artillery* suggested that "Trumpet or bugle signals are used instead of commands whenever they can be advantageously introduced." Thus Reed and his fellow buglers were responsible for signaling such commands as "To Horse," "Walk," "Trot," "Gallop," "Forward," "Commence Firing," and many others. Like the calls that set camp routine, these signals became second nature to the men. In *Hardtack and Coffee,* the old artilleryman Billings described the use of these bugle signals and the reaction it brought forth from both soldier and beast: "As the drilling of a battery was done for the most part by sounding the commands upon a bugle, it became necessary for cannoneers and drivers to learn the calls; and this they did after short experience. Even the horses became perfectly familiar with some of these calls, and would proceed to execute them without the intervention of a driver." Reed likewise related one drilling incident in a March 1864 letter to his mother: "yesterday we had a review, and I had the honor of having charge of the musical department 'to wit' ten buglers. previous to the review, the buglers of this brigade have been assembled at stated periods for exercise, and by order of the commandant; under my supervision and by the time of the review we were able [to] give the musical exercise appertaining to a review quite creditably."[25]

ON THE BATTLEFIELD

During combat operations, Reed's position always placed him in the zone of greatest danger. After the heavy fighting of the 1864 Overland Campaign in Virginia, Reed wrote to his sister Emma, "My duty in a fight is to go in with the Captain . . . at the front, in fact I have been in every fight with the battery while the other bugler is keept in the rear with the caisons." One bugle call, above all others, that created an instant reaction among the men was "Boots and Saddles." Years later John Billings described the emotional response to this

25. Board of Artillery Officers, *Instruction for Field Artillery,* xviii–xx, 52; Billings, *Hardtack and Coffee,* 186; *GTD,* 191.

call: "The signal . . . Boots and Saddles [was] a call whose tones . . . sent the blood of artillerymen . . . coursing more rapidly through the veins when it denoted that danger was nigh, and seeking encounter."[26] After John Bigelow took over the Ninth Massachusetts Battery in the spring of 1863, the soldiers had this call ingrained in them as the new commander drilled them over and over.

Because of his strictness, insistence on military regulation, and high-society upbringing, Bigelow was hated by the men of the Ninth Massachusetts Battery. The bugler wrote home that his new commander was "a regular aristocrat" who did not have "the feelings for his men as a slave owner for his slaves. . . . he is worse than any regular that ever breathed." Though disliked intensely by the men, Bigelow and his methods apparently worked, for the battery experienced a slow but steady improvement in morale, discipline, and confidence. One soldier later wrote, "Our camp, from headquarters to stables, felt a new influence." Even Reed stated that "laterly he has relaxed his strictness. . . . I think he understands his business. . . . I think his strictness was to make the men know what he is." Another member of the battery recalled, "we felt we were making rapid strides toward a position in which we can be efficient in any place." Little did these men realize that they would get a chance to prove this statement true that very summer near a Pennsylvania crossroads town called Gettysburg.[27]

GETTYSBURG

The role played by the Ninth Massachusetts Battery at Gettysburg is one of the better-known episodes of that famous battle. This event, viewed through the experiences of Charles Wellington Reed, provides a perfect example of the initiation of men to combat and the role of the bugler on a Civil War battlefield.

This story actually began with the arrival of the Army of the Potomac outside the outer defenses of Washington, D.C., in the middle of June 1863. The Union army was moving northward in reaction to

26. *GTD,* 248; Billings, *Hardtack and Coffee,* 183–84.

27. *GTD,* 84 (Reed's statement was made in a March 9, 1863, letter to his sister Helen Tilton); Baker, *History of the Ninth,* 45; *GTD,* 86; Baker, *History of the Ninth,* 46.

the second Confederate invasion of the war. Charles Reed, never having seen this many soldiers at the same time, was impressed. On June 17 he wrote, "We have been having stirring times within the last week.... [A] great portion of the army has been here and gone.... [A] stream [of] troops pouring in here all begrimed with dirt and dust... you can form no idea what soldiering is unles you have seen the Army of the Potomac." Reed and his comrades would soon find themselves a part of that army. Attempting to strengthen its numbers in preparation for the impending battle, the army gained reinforcements from the capital's garrison troops. On June 25, the Ninth Massachusetts Battery became a part of this massive army. At the time, the battery consisted of 104 officers and enlisted men, 110 horses, and six smoothbore Napoleon cannons. The men soon discovered they had been assigned to the First Volunteer Brigade, Artillery Reserve, commanded by Lieutenant Colonel Freeman McGilvery.[28]

Though well drilled and disciplined, the battery was not acclimated to campaigning and found their initiation to hard marching difficult. Despite their sufferings, the men stoically endured and kept pace with the rest of the army. They arrived on the battlefield around 10:30 a.m. on July 2, 1863. The battle had begun the day before as elements of both armies clashed by accident outside of Gettysburg, with the end result being the retreat of the Union forces to a range of hills and ridges located south of town. Major General George Gordon Meade, commanding the Army of the Potomac, had decided to await Confederate movements and was arranging his battle line for a defensive struggle. The Artillery Reserve thus was placed behind the lines and held in readiness to be used when and where it was most needed. Charles Reed and the rest of the Ninth Massachusetts Battery settled down for a long and restless wait.[29]

The principal Confederate attack began around 3:30 p.m. as Southern troops under Lieutenant General James Longstreet struck the Union left flank. Defending this area was the Third Corps, Army of

28. Edwin B. Coddington, *The Gettysburg Campaign: A Study in Command* (New York: Charles Scribner's Sons, 1968), 75; *GTD,* 49; *OR* series 1, vol. 27, pt. 3, p. 972 (hereinafter all citations are from series 1); John W. Busey and David Martin, *Regimental Strengths and Losses at Gettysburg* (Baltimore: Gateway Press, 1982), 114.

29. Baker, *History of the Ninth,* 54; *OR,* vol. 27, pt. 1, p. 872; Coddington, *Gettysburg Campaign,* 338; Baker, *History of the Ninth,* 55–56.

the Potomac, commanded by Major General Daniel Sickles. Earlier that afternoon this flamboyant commander, in one of the most controversial decisions of the battle, had pushed his corps approximately three-fourths of a mile forward to an advanced and overextended position. Now in desperation, Sickles sought reinforcements to bolster his thin line.[30]

A readily available source from which to draw reinforcements was the Artillery Reserve. The long wait for the Ninth Massachusetts Battery ended around 4:00 p.m. when a call for reinforcements reached McGilvery. Reed blew "Assembly" and, according to Bigelow, "drivers mounted and within five minutes we were off at a lively trot, following our leader to the left, where the firing was getting to be the heaviest." Four days later Reed described how he felt while moving toward his first battle: "I must say I was surprised at myself in not experienceing more fear than I did as it was it seemed more like going to some game or review."[31]

McGilvery halted his brigade by General Sickles's headquarters near the Abraham Trostle farmstead. The men waited as McGilvery conferred with Sickles. According to Bigelow, "A spirited military spectacle lay before us; General Sickles was standing beneath a tree close by, staff officers and orderlies coming and going in all directions; at the famous 'Peach Orchard' angle on rising ground, along the Emmetsburg Road . . . smoke was curling up from . . . the deep-toned booming of [Union] guns . . . while enemy's shells were flying over or breaking around us."[32]

Reed, probably excited by the momentous event unfolding before him and realizing its importance, decided to record the scene. Incredibly, despite being under fire for the first time, he pulled out his sketch pad and began to draw. He recalled that "at the foot of the hill on which we took position were Major Gen Sickles headquarters under a tree. we halted here a few minutes giveing me time to take a scetch of him. one of his Aids was already wounded by a piece of shell

30. Coddington, *Gettysburg Campaign,* 345–46, 371, 374, 386.

31. Bigelow, *Peach Orchard,* 52; *OR,* vol. 27, pt. 1, pp. 234–35, 872, 881; Baker, *History of the Ninth,* 56; *GTD,* 114 (Reed was writing to his mother and his sister Helen Tilton).

32. Bigelow, *Peach Orchard,* p. 52; *OR,* vol. 27, pt. 1, p. 881; Baker, *History of the Ninth,* 56.

in the back and a surgeon was doing it up." Soon after, McGilvery ordered his batteries to take up positions along the Wheatfield Road, east of the famous Peach Orchard. They moved up under fire into an "open and exposed" area along the road. As the guns readied for action, Reed remembered that he "assumed a more serious aspect" toward the battle. It is no wonder that his attitude changed: more than one hundred Union and Confederate cannons were thundering away in and around the Peach Orchard. Reed described the overwhelming noise produced by this artillery: "such a shrieking, hissing, seathing I never dreamed was imagineable. it seemed as though it must be the work of the very devil himself.... [T]heir fire about this time was tremendous[.] there were five Batterys of us in a line... besides other artillery in different positions the roar of which was deafening."[33]

Soon after taking position, Reed recounted what happened next. "Captain ordered me to the rear saying there was no need of my being there. my first action was to obey and rode back two or three rods." Although neither Bigelow nor Reed ever explained the reasoning behind this order, a possible explanation might have been the tremendous noise. The thunderous tumult around the Peach Orchard made even bugle calls useless. Thus, looking out for the welfare of his men, Bigelow might have ordered his bugler to the rear for his safety. But as Reed rode to the rear, he changed his mind, "but somehow 'I could'nt see it.' I was bound to see a fight and might be of some use after all so I disobeyed orders by turning round going up to the bat'ry again." Reed could not have known what an important decision this would turn out to be, not only for himself but for Captain Bigelow as well. Immediately upon returning to the battery, Reed realized he had made the correct decision: "I was right for presently Major McGilvrary... came up and set me at it in the shape of transmitting orders from one bat'ry to another, which suited me to a T as I had a wider field under my eyes and could see what was going on farther to our right and left."[34]

As more Confederate units were ordered into the assault, the battle grew in size and moved steadily closer to the Peach Orchard. Soon

33. *GTD,* 114; *OR,* vol. 27, pt. 1, p. 881; Bigelow, *Peach Orchard,* 52–53; *GTD,* 114; Harry Pfanz, *Gettysburg: The Second Day* (Chapel Hill: University of North Carolina Press, 1987), 303, 312.

34. *GTD,* 131.

Reed's sketch of Major General Daniel Sickles and his staff. Reed drew this while under fire on July 2, 1863. *Library of Congress.*

the Ninth Massachusetts Battery and the other batteries along the Wheatfield Road came under infantry attack. Leading the Confederate assault were the twenty-two hundred South Carolinians of Brigadier General Joseph B. Kershaw's brigade. According to Reed, "they... steadily advanced on us giving us such a shower of balls that it was dangerous to be safe!" At this same time Reed had a close call. "I had just been along the line of batterys," he wrote, "with an order from the Col to double shott the guns with canister and returning a shell tore up the ground in front of my horse at which he halted so suddenly... as to almost throw me out of the saddle." Near 6:00 p.m., two Confederate brigades struck the Union line in the Peach Orchard. Leading this attack was Brigadier General William Barksdale's Mississippi brigade. In a short but terrible struggle, the Third Corps line collapsed. McGilvery, realizing his unsupported batteries were vulnerable to capture, rode down the Wheatfield Road and ordered them to retreat. A Union officer near the Peach Orchard vividly described this withdrawal, as the batteries pulled back one at a time: "A glance to my left at that moment revealed a thrilling battle picture. The shattered line was retreating in separated streams[,] artillerists heroically clinging to their still smoking guns.... The positions of these batteries showed broken carriages, caissons and wheels, while scores of slain horses and men lay across each other in mangled and ghastly heaps."[35]

Despite the chaos occurring to their right, the men of the Ninth Massachusetts Battery were oblivious to their worsening situation. Reed, who by this time had returned to the battery, wrote, "we were so intent upon our work that we noticed not when the other batterys left." McGilvery's arrival soon drew their attention to Barksdale's approaching line.[36]

35. Coddington, *Gettysburg Campaign,* 393–94; Joseph B. Kershaw, "Kershaw's Brigade at Gettysburg," *Battles and Leaders of the Civil War* (New York: Century, 1884), 3:334; *GTD,* 114, 133; Coddington, *Gettysburg Campaign,* 405–6; Francis Moran, "A Fire Zouave, Memoirs of a Member of the 73rd New York," *National Tribune,* November 6 and 13, 1890. Barksdale's brigade numbered approximately sixteen hundred. The other Confederate brigade was Brigadier General William Wofford's Georgia brigade (approximately fourteen hundred men). See Busey and Martin, *Regimental Strengths,* 139, 141.

36. *GTD,* 114; Eric A. Campbell, "'Baptism of Fire': The Ninth Massachusetts Battery at Gettysburg, July 2, 1863," *Gettysburg Magazine* 5 (July 1991): 65.

The Ninth Massachusetts was on the far left of McGilvery's line and was the last battery to get the order to retreat. Bigelow instantly was faced with a dilemma. If his guns stopped firing, the Confederates to his front would quickly close in and "every saddle would be emptied in trying to limber up." Yet if he stayed and fought, his battery would be overwhelmed by Barksdale's Mississippians to his right. Desperate to save his guns, Bigelow ordered a risky maneuver called "retire by prolonge firing."[37]

Despite the risks involved, Bigelow gave the necessary commands, the prolonges were attached, and the retreat began. They had over four hundred yards to retreat, without support and while under fire from Confederate infantry and artillery. Reed recalled that "the Rebs as soon as they saw us limber up threw up a number of sharpshooters who fired on [us] with... deadly effect[.] we fired retireing slowly." Under tremendous pressure, from left, front, and right, the battery steadily fell back, keeping the advancing Confederates at a safe distance. Their only escape route was a single gateway through a stone wall near the Trostle farm buildings.[38]

After what must have seemed an eternity, the battery finally reached the Trostle house. They halted under cover of a slight rise of ground. Bigelow immediately ordered the battery to limber up to complete their escape. McGilvery, meanwhile, had discovered a large and dangerous gap in the Union line along Cemetery Ridge. Realizing he needed more time to organize a new line of defense to cover this gap, the artillery colonel galloped back to Bigelow's guns and ordered the stunned captain to "hold your position at all hazards, and sacrifice your battery if need be." Later, Reed summed up the situation in a letter, writing, "we were left in a most critical position."[39]

The final desperate stand of the Ninth Massachusetts was an extraordinary display of leadership, bravery, and above all incredible discipline. Fighting in its first battle, the battery now found itself

37. *OR,* vol. 27, pt. 1, p. 882; Bigelow to Battlefield Commission, February 20, 1901, "Position of Troops," 2:32; Bigelow, *Peach Orchard,* 55. "Retire by prolonge firing" is a maneuver that allows a battery to retreat and fire at the same time. A prolonge, or rope, is attached from the gun to the limber. After the gun is fired, the horses pull the limber, and thus the gun, backward, while the crew reloads the gun. The horses are stopped, the gun is fired, and the process is repeated.

38. Bigelow, *Peach Orchard,* 55–56; *GTD,* 114–15; Baker, *History of the Ninth,* 61.

39. Bigelow, *Peach Orchard,* 56; Baker, *History of the Ninth,* 60; *GTD,* 114.

literally crammed into the corner of the stone wall with only a narrow gateway offering an escape route. Even worse, the battery was without infantry support, low on ammunition, facing greatly superior numbers, and had a severely limited field of fire. Bigelow called the "position . . . an impossible one for artillery." Despite the odds, the men immediately obeyed Bigelow's orders to unlimber and prepare for action.

Attacked from three directions—Kershaw's skirmishers from the left and Barksdale's troops from the center and right—the battery stood its ground for nearly thirty minutes. Bigelow recalled the turmoil of confusion that engulfed the battery: "The enemy crowded to the very muzzles of [the guns] but were blown away by the canister. Sergeant after Sergt., was struck down, horses were plunging and laying about all around, bullets now came in on all sides, for the enemy had turned my flanks. The air was dark with smoke. . . . The enemy were yelling like demons." Sensing the end was near, the captain ordered his two left guns to limber up and escape. As the first cannon reached the lane, it overturned, blocking the gateway. While the men scrambled to right it, the crew of the trailing gun looked in desperation for a way out. A few men "tumbled the top stones off the wall" before the drivers led the horses "directly over the wall." Reed remembered "the horses jumping and the gun . . . going over with a tilt on one side and then a crash of rocks and wheels." Amazingly, the cannon made a successful escape.[40]

Bigelow later recalled that, throughout this entire fight, "Bugler Reed sat by me on his horse, a conspicuous mark, during the trying ordeal." Hoping to save whatever he could, the captain, trailed by his bugler, "rode down to the stone wall" and ordered his cannoneers to "make a better opening" for the remaining four guns. "I sat on my horse calling the men," Bigelow wrote, "when my bugler, on my right, drew his horse back on his haunches, as he saw six [Confederates] . . .

40. Baker, *History of the Ninth,* 60–61; Bigelow, *Peach Orchard,* 56; Bigelow, *Peach Orchard,* 56–57; Bigelow to John Bachelder, n.d., John Bachelder Papers, New Hampshire Historical Society (hereinafter cited as NHHS); Bigelow to John Bachelder, n.d., Bachelder Papers, NHHS; Bigelow, *Peach Orchard,* 57; "Artist Reed Given a Medal by the U.S. Government for His Brave Deed at Gettysburg," *Boston Daily Globe,* August 13, 1895.

taking deliberate aim at us."[41] Years later, Reed recalled, "I saw the enemy skirting down the stone wall on our side and called to the captain to look out." Although Reed's quick reaction saved him, his warning to his commander came too late—Bigelow was hit twice. One bullet passed through the captain's side above his hip, tearing a five-inch gash in the muscles of the stomach, and the other struck the little finger on his left hand. His horse, also hit twice, staggered to the rear and Bigelow fell near the wall, dazed. Reed and Bigelow's orderly were quickly at their commander's side.[42]

As he "drew himself back to the stone wall," Bigelow recalled seeing "the Confederates swarming in on our right flank." Hand-to-hand fighting engulfed the battery as the men began to use handspikes and rammers to defend their guns. Bigelow also remembered seeing Confederates "standing on the limber chests, and shooting down cannoneers" from behind. Realizing that "Longer delay was impossible," the captain told Reed to sound "Retreat." Years later a newspaper reporter who had interviewed Bigelow described this scene as it was told to him: "The moment the notes of the bugle ring out the men turn, and, leaping the wall, run for their lives, surrounded by swarms of Confederates."[43]

The Ninth Massachusetts Battery was shattered, losing three of four officers, six of eight sergeants, nineteen enlisted men, eighty horses, and four of its six guns. They had sacrificed themselves just as they had been ordered, yet it was not a sacrifice made in vain. As Bigelow "glanced anxiously to the rear," he "saw the longed for batteries just coming into position." McGilvery's new artillery line was nearly completed.[44]

41. John Bigelow to the Adjutant General, June 19, 1895, Charles Reed Medal of Honor File, NA; Bigelow, *Peach Orchard,* 57.

42. "Artist Reed Given a Medal by the U.S. Government for His Brave Deed at Gettysburg, *Boston Daily Globe,* August 13, 1895; John Bigelow Pension Record, NA; John Bigelow to the Adjutant General, June 19, 1895, Charles Reed Medal of Honor File, NA.

43. "How the Battle Was Won," *Minneapolis Saturday Journal,* August 13, 1895; Baker, *History of the Ninth,* 81, 216; Bigelow, *Peach Orchard,* 57; Bigelow to Bachelder, n.d., Bachelder Papers, NHHS.

44. Baker, *History of the Ninth,* 63–64; return for July 1863, Monthly Returns, Regimental Papers, Ninth Massachusetts Battery, NA.

As the remainder of the battery scattered to the rear, Bigelow "told . . . the orderly and myself to leave him and get out as best we could." The bugler, however, "didn't do just that." Instead Reed, as he had done earlier in the battle, disobeyed orders. Years later, Bigelow described the actions of his faithful bugler: "he remained with me . . . called my orderly and had him lift me on to his horse; then taking the reins of both horses in his left hand, with his right hand supporting me in the saddle, took me at a walk [to the rear]." Reed was attempting to lead both horses toward McGilvery's new line of artillery. They had nearly four hundred yards of open ground to cross and, as Reed recalled, "the captain was so weak and the orderly's horse so frightened that all I could do was keep him on at a walk." Reed also remembered the "shells singing all around us." Bigelow recalled what happened next: "Before I was half way back . . . Lieut. Dow, commanding [the Sixth Maine Battery] sent an Officer . . . urging me to hurry, as he must commence firing on the men . . . who had my Battery. I told him to fire away, I could not hurry; so Dow opened with shell, while we were in his front." Now caught between the fire of the opposing lines, Reed managed to keep his wounded commander upright and control both horses. Bigelow never forgot his bugler's bravery, "Bugler Reed did not flinch; but steadily supported me; kept the horses at a walk although between two fires and guided them, so that we entered the Battery between two of the guns that were firing heavily."[45]

45. "Saved His Captain at Gettysburg," unknown newspaper, unknown date, Charles Reed Collection, LC; John Bigelow Pension Record, NA; John Bigelow to the Adjutant General, June 19, 1895, Charles Reed Medal of Honor File, NA; Eric A. Campbell, " 'We Saved the Line from Being Broken': Freeman McGilvery, John Bigelow, Charles Reed, and the Battle of Gettysburg," in *Unsung Heroes of Gettysburg: Programs of the Fifth Annual Gettysburg Seminar* (Gettysburg, Pa.: Gettysburg National Military Park, 1996), 58–59; "Saved His Captain at Gettysburg," unknown newspaper, unknown date, Charles Reed Collection, LC; John Bigelow Pension Record, NA; John Bigelow to the Adjutant General, June 19, 1895, Charles Reed Medal of Honor File, NA; John Bigelow to the Adjutant General, June 19, 1895, Charles Wellington Reed Medal of Honor File, NA. Charles Reed's modesty is clearly evident here, for in his only wartime description of this act of bravery he wrote to his mother and his sister Helen Tilton, "Captain fell from his horse when he was struck, was placed on another and as we were in no condition to contest the ground any longer we left[.] I assisted the Captain to a place of safety" (*GTD,* 115, 116).

Reed's act of gallantry revealed the drastic change in the relationship between these two men. Coming from completely different social and economic classes, it is no wonder that less than five months before, when Bigelow took over the battery, Reed thought his new commander was a tyrant and "a regular aristocrat." Yet at Gettysburg, Charles Reed had twice disobeyed orders to leave the field and had willingly risked his own life to save his commander. This selfless act brought these two men from vastly different backgrounds together and made them friends for life.[46]

Thirty-two years later, in 1895, John Bigelow attempted to repay this debt to his former bugler by nominating Charles Reed for the Medal of Honor. The medal was awarded on August 19, 1895, by "direction of the President" for "most distinguished gallantry in action at the battle of Gettysburg, Pennsylvania, July 2, 1863." Bigelow wrote to Reed a few days later to congratulate him, stating, "I feel that the Government honors itself in honoring You." On a more personal level, Bigelow believed that Reed had not only saved the captain from a stint in a Confederate prison but, more importantly, had also saved his life: "the obligation still remains with myself. Had I been left, where I fell, even though the Mississippians would probably have spared me, Dow's [Sixth Maine] searching canister and Shells would not have done so."[47]

The Civil War changed Charles Wellington Reed forever. Music, in its many forms, had both regulated his life in the military and provided a direct connection to his civilian life and home, but it could not stave off the inevitable changes that the war would bring to him. This fact was immediately clear after his first experience of combat. Charles Reed had ridden onto the battlefield at Gettysburg with a naïveté, a sense of adventure, towards war. After the battle, he eloquently described the revelation he experienced:

> During the din of battle my feelings were curious and various but the one idea I entertained could not be shaken off until the fight had ceased for the day. It appeared to be a grand terrible dramma we were

46. *GTD,* 84.
47. John Bigelow to Charles Reed, August 17, 1895, Charles Reed Medal of Honor File, NA.

enacting and the idea of being hit or killed never occurred to me. but when I saw the dead, wounded, and mutilated pouring out their lifes blood groaning and crying piteously for assistance then the terrible sense of the reality came upon me in full force. the novelty had vanished. I could only turn my thoughts to him who see's and controls all, with silent thanks-giveings and weep for the many, many dead and maimed.[48]

48. *GTD,* 131.

Music Inspired by the Battle of Gettysburg, 1863–1913

MARK A. SNELL

It was three in the afternoon on July 3, 1863. A thick blanket of white smoke hung in the wide, shallow valley between Seminary and Cemetery ridges. The great bombardment of the Union position on Cemetery Ridge no sooner had ended than the strains of a Confederate band could be heard in the distance. Some twelve thousand Southern infantrymen were preparing to assault the center of the Army of the Potomac's defenses, and it was hoped that the bandsmen's martial airs would steel the gray- and butternut-clad soldiers for the onslaught. But no amount of musical inspiration could prepare the men from Virginia, North Carolina, South Carolina, Alabama, Mississippi, Tennessee, and Georgia for what lay ahead. More than five thousand Confederate soldiers would become casualties of the attack. Pickett's Charge, as it came to be called, was the grand finale of the dramatic overture known as the Battle of Gettysburg. Total casualties exceeded fifty-one thousand, making it one of the bloodiest battles in American history.[1]

Naturally, such a momentous event spawned countless volumes of history, some penned shortly after the battle, some before the end of the war, and thousands since 1865.[2] The battle also became the subject

1. Edwin B. Coddington, *The Gettysburg Campaign: A Study in Command* (New York: Charles Scribner's Sons, 1968), 503; U.S. National Park Service, *Gettysburg: Official Map and Guide* (Washington, D.C.: Government Printing Office, 2000).

2. Richard B. Sauers's *The Gettysburg Campaign, June 3–August 1, 1863: A Comprehensive, Selectively Annotated Bibliography* (Westport, Conn.: Greenwood Press, 1982) lists 2,757 articles, books, and monographs that have been written about this campaign. In the twenty years since Sauers's bibliography was compiled, hundreds more have been published.

of poetry, paintings, novels, documentary films, board games, computer games, and of course, a feature-length Hollywood movie. It is little known, however, that the Battle of Gettysburg inspired composers and lyricists, some of whom wrote their music even before all of the fallen were properly buried. This essay will examine some of the musical compositions written during the fifty-year period between 1863 and 1913, the latter date marking the semicentennial of the battle and the year before the beginning of a much more terrible conflagration.

By November 1863, four months after the momentous battle, most of the Union dead had been collected and interred within a seventeen-acre plot of land adjacent to Gettysburg's civilian burial ground, Evergreen Cemetery. President Abraham Lincoln was asked to make some dedicatory remarks after Senator Edward Everett of Massachusetts delivered the keynote address. It was a formal and solemn affair, with music provided by the U.S. Marine Band, Birgfield's Band, and the National Union Musical Association of Baltimore (popularly known as the Baltimore Glee Club). Tucked between Everett's two-hour oration and Lincoln's remarks, a hymn—composed for the occasion by Benjamin B. French—was performed by the Baltimore Glee Club. French, a longtime Washington bureaucrat, titled his work "The National Consecration Chant or Hymn." Wilson G. Horner, director of the Glee Club, set the words to music.[3]

When Horner rose to direct his vocalists, he held a small American flag, which he used as a conductor's baton.[4] "The National Consecration Chant" was written in 4/4 time for bass, baritone, alto, and soprano voices. When the piece was later published, its cover inscription read, "The following beautiful lines were chanted at the dedication of the National Cemetery, Gettysburg, Pa., Nov. 17, 1863, by the National Union Musical Association of Baltimore, at the close of Mr. Everett's, and just before President Lincoln's Address. The deep pathos of the poetry—the words of which, being clearly enunciated, were distinctly heard by the assembled thousands—the occasion, and the surroundings, made it a solemn feature of the day, mov-

3. *Washington Morning Chronicle,* November 21, 1863, quoted in John B. Horner, *Lincoln's Songbird: Wilson G. Horner, a Brief Life of Melody and Harmony* (Gettysburg, Pa.: Horner Enterprises, 1998), vi.

4. Ibid.

ing very many to tears."[5] Although the sheet music does not specify the tempo at which it is to be performed, the nature of the music and the solemnity of the occasion naturally dictate that the piece is to be sung slowly and deliberately. The verses emphasize the themes of sacrifice, freedom, the rule of law, and mourning:

> 1. 'Tis holy ground, This spot, where in their graves, We place our country's brave, Who fell in Freedom's Holy cause, Fighting for liberties and laws; Let tears abound.
>
> 2. Here let them rest, And summer' heat, and winter's cold, Shall glow and freeze above this mould, A thousand years shall pass away, A nation still shall mourn this clay, Which now is blest.
>
> 3. Here where they fell, Oft shall the widow's tear be shed, Oft shall fond parents mourn their dead, The orphan here shall kneel and weep, And maidens where their lovers sleep, Their woes shall tell.
>
> 4. Great God in Heaven! Shall all this sacred blood be shed, Shall we mourn our glorious dead? Oh, shall the end be wrath and woe, The knell of Freedom's overthrow, A country riven?
>
> 5. It will not be! We trust, O God! Thy gracious power To aid us in our darkest hour. This be our prayer: "O Father, says A people's Freedom from its grave; All praise to Thee!"

The sixteenth president of the United States next delivered his famous address, which was followed by another work written specifically for the occasion, "Dirge," a patriotic piece of four verses, written by James G. Percival with music by Alfred Delaney. The lyrics of the first, second, and fourth verses emphasize the nobleness of death for a righteous cause and the rewards that awaited in heaven for those Union soldiers who died on the battlefield, but the third verse made an analogy to ancient Greece:

> Not in Elysian Fields, by the oblivious river,
> Not in the Isles of the Blest, over the blue rolling sea;
> But on Olympian heights shall dwell the devoted forever;
> There shall assemble the good, the wise, valiant, and free.

5. B. B. French and W. G. Horner, "National Consecration Chant or Hymn" (Baltimore: Henry McCaffrey, 1864).

These lyrics were particularly appropriate to the location and the occasion, since the cemetery was designed in the Greek Revival style of landscape architecture then in vogue in the United States, and Edward Everett—who himself played an important role in America's Greek Revival—even pointed out in his oration that the Athenian dead at the Battle of Marathon, like the Union dead at Gettysburg, were buried on the battlefield where they fell. The dirge was musical evidence of the American idea that the United States was a second Athens.[6]

Delaney composed the music for several other Civil War songs, including another Gettysburg piece appropriately titled "Gettysburg!" which was part of a collection of six "songs and odes" published in 1863 under the series name "Songs of the Loyal." The collection included "My Love Is on the Battlefield," "The Nation Shall Not Die," "The Young Volunteer," "The Christian Commission," and "The Son Who Was His Mother's Pride." Robert Morris wrote the lyrics to "Gettysburg!" and the song was dedicated to General George G. Meade, the victorious commander of the Army of the Potomac. Written in 6/8 time and performed at a lively pace, one can almost imagine the sounds of the galloping horses as Confederate cavalry came riding across the Mason-Dixon Line, especially in the first verses: "The boldest and the bloodiest raid the Southern Legions ever made, / Was when their countless thousands strayed to Gettysburg! To Gettysburg! / Laden with spoils upon each back, a wolf-like and ferocious pack." The end of the first verse, however, informed the audience that the Rebels eventually paid the price for their invasion: "How few e're found the homeward track From Gettysburg! From Gettysburg! / How few e're found the homeward track From Gettysburg! From Gettysburg!"[7]

Several ballads written shortly after the battle touched the heartstrings of listeners by capitalizing on the great loss of life sustained by

6. Alfred Delaney, "Dirge Sung at the Consecration of the Soldiers' Cemetery at Gettysburg" (Philadelphia: Lee and Walker, 1863). The piece was written in C major, in common time, and for four voices. Delaney dedicated his composition to Pennsylvania's wartime governor, Andrew Curtin. Everett's role in America's Greek Revival is discussed in Garry Wills, *Lincoln at Gettysburg: The Words That Remade America* (New York: Touchstone/Simon and Schuster, 1992), 41–62.

7. Alfred Delaney and Robert Morris, "Gettysburg!" Songs for the Loyal series (Philadelphia: Lee and Walker, 1863).

the two armies. One piece supposedly was based on a poignant episode about a dying Union soldier. According to the text on the cover of the sheet music, "On the battlefield at Gettysburg, among many of our wounded soldiers was a young man the only son of an aged mother. Hearing the surgeon tell his companions that he could not survive the ensuing night, he placed his hand upon his forehead, talking, continually of his mother and sister, and said to his comrades assembled around him, 'Break it gently to my mother.'" The words to "Break It Gently to My Mother" were written by Mary Griffith and the music by Frederick Buckley. Buckley was a popular violinist and a member of "Buckley's Serenaders," the musical family who first performed this piece. Frederick died in October 1864 and did not live to see the end of the Civil War.[8]

An additional ballad featured as its subject another heretofore-unknown American who also made the supreme sacrifice but who was *not* a soldier. On July 3, Virginia Wade was baking bread in her sister's home on the outskirts of Gettysburg when a bullet pierced the door and struck the young woman, killing her instantly. "Jenny" Wade thus became the only civilian killed during the Battle of Gettysburg. Her musical tribute, "Jenny Wade: The Heroine of Gettysburg," was published in 1864, with lyrics by Albert Anderson and music by Rudolph Wittig. The song extolled the virtues of a "woman true" that was cut down by "traitors" while she was fulfilling her duty to the Republic. "She was making bread for our army during the battle, having refused to leave the house, which was in range of both armies," reads the narrative on the cover of the sheet music, "and she was shot through the heart." In reality, Jenny was just unlucky enough to get in the way of an errant bullet. Not surprisingly, the Confederates were described in harsh terms, while Jenny was portrayed almost as a goddess of liberty. Written in common time for piano and voice, the song was to be performed at a moderately slow tempo. It contained four verses and a refrain. The third verse and refrain display the song's attitude about the Confederates and Jenny:

8. Mary Griffith and Frederick Buckley, "Break It Gently to My Mother" (Boston: Henry Tolman, 1863); *The New Grove Dictionary of American Music* (1986 ed.), s.v. "Buckley," by Robert B. Winans.

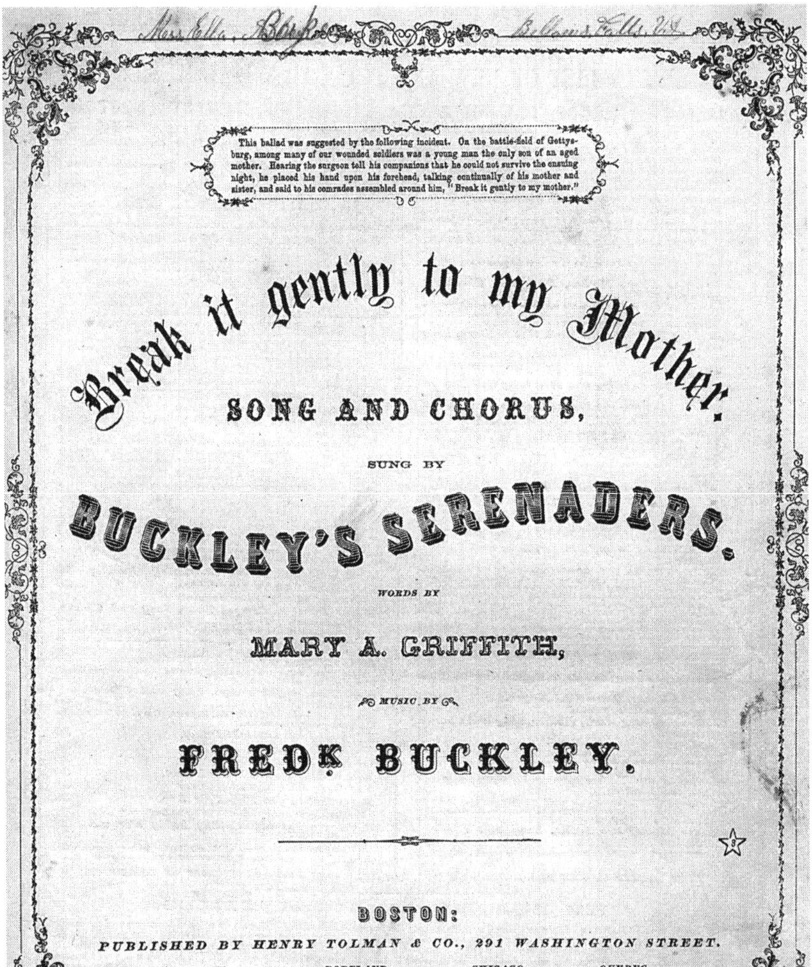

Cover to "Break It Gently to My Mother." *Collection of Walter L. Powell.*

When to the north wind rebels threw
Their noisome traitor rag,
The courage of a woman true
Upheld our dear old flag.
Wher-e're that starry flag shall wave,
Mid clouds or on the plain,
Remember'd be thy hallow'd grave,—
For home and country slain.

In the quiet church-yard sleeping,
With the bravest fitly laid,
Moans the wind through willows weeping
O'er the grave of Jenny Wade.[9]

The refrain, however, used a good deal of poetic license. Jenny was not laid to rest in a "church-yard"—she was buried in the town cemetery—nor did willows grow over her grave.

Although the Battle of Gettysburg had caused the death of one young woman and thousands of young men, the passing of one particular Union soldier became a cause célèbre across the North. During the afternoon of July 1, two corps of the Army of the Potomac—the First and the Eleventh—were beginning to retreat under the weight of an overwhelming Confederate assault. Two divisions of the Eleventh Corps were heading back toward Cemetery Hill, where a third division already was digging defensive positions. Sensing that the rest of his corps needed help, the Union division commander on Cemetery Hill sent one of his brigades to the other side of Gettysburg to fight a delaying action while the rest of the corps escaped. This lone brigade quickly was overrun and soon was flying rearward to Cemetery Hill. One soldier from that brigade, a member of the 154th New York Infantry, was shot during the retreat and lay mortally wounded. Before he died, he pulled out a photograph of his children for one last look. When he was found several days later, his lifeless hands still clutched the photograph next to his heart. One recent historian has written: "He was only one of thousands of dead men strewn about Gettysburg's fields, but he was special. Of all

9. Albert Anderson and Rudolph Wittig, "Jenny Wade: The Heroine of Gettysburg" (Philadelphia: William R. Smith, 1864). The song was dedicated to George G. Meade.

the blackened, bloated, contorted corpses on the battleground, his death pose spoke of devotion. In the silence of death, he spoke of love."[10]

Unfortunately, the soldier bore no identification. The story was so touching that the children's image was reproduced all across the Northern states, and newspaper editors published the moving account time and time again. Wilson Horner, the director of the National Union Musical Association of Baltimore, composed the music for a song written by W. H. Hayward, titled "The Unknown Soldier Song (Who Is He?)." Published in 1864, it was dedicated to "the orphans of the brave soldiers who have fallen in defence of their country." Its six verses spoke of duty to country, love of flag and family, and the plight of the poor widow and children. Eventually, a woman living in western New York discovered that the celebrated photograph was the same one she had given her husband, Sergeant Amos Humiston. By the time Horner published "The Unknown Soldier," Humiston's identity already had been ascertained.[11]

The story of the nameless soldier touched everyone's heart, including a composer named James G. Clark, who had made a name for himself as a popular songwriter and performer during the antebellum period. Clark had entered a contest sponsored by the *American Presbyterian* newspaper to compose song lyrics concerning the Humiston incident. Announcing Clark as the winner, the *American Presbyterian* proclaimed, "Out of several pieces sent to us on the death of Sergeant Humiston, we unhesitatingly give the preference to the following simple, sweet verses, very well adapted to music, which the author has already provided for them, and will soon publish." James Clark's "The Children of the Battle Field" was published in April 1864. Fine print on the sheet music announced, "The net proceeds of the sales of this music are reserved for the support and education of the Orphan Children."[12]

10. Mark H. Dunkleman, *Gettysburg's Unknown Soldier: The Life, Death, and Celebrity of Amos Humiston* (Westport, Conn.: Praeger, 1999), xi.

11. W. H. Hayward and Wilson Horner, "The Unknown Soldier—Who Is He?" (New York: William A. Pond, 1864); Dunkleman, *Gettysburg's Unknown Soldier,* xi.

12. Dunkleman, *Gettysburg's Unknown Soldier,* 169; James G. Clark, "The Children of the Battle Field" (Philadelphia: Lee and Walker, 1864).

Cover to "The Children of the Battlefield." *Collection of Walter L. Powell.*

The song was dedicated to Dr. J. Francis Bourns of Philadelphia, who took an early interest in identifying the soldier and later sold copies of the photograph, called *cartes de visite,* or CDVs, to raise money for the orphans and widow. Interestingly, the Humiston family claimed that they never received a penny from the sales of either the music or the CDVs. This is particularly ironic, especially considering the final line of each of the song's three verses: "O! Father, shield the soldier's wife, And for his children care." The song became so popular that Clark made it part of his regular repertoire and published a second edition in October 1864.[13]

In addition to the pieces that focused on the battle's human-interest stories, several compositions were written to commemorate the victory itself. James Cox Beckel, a Philadelphia organist, was fifty-two years old at the time of the battle and was best known as a composer of sacred music and teacher of organ method. In his composition entitled "Battle of Gettysburg," Beckel used his "artistic license" to alter the outcome of the battle: at one point, he imagined militiamen from New York and Pennsylvania assaulting the rear of the Army of Northern Virginia, culminating with a Union counterattack by the entire Army of the Potomac. Had this episode actually occurred—and Abraham Lincoln wished it had—the Civil War might have come to a close in 1863. Styled a "programmatic" composition, meaning that it described a particular story or historical event, it began with a section called "March of the Grand Army of the Potomac under Major Genl. George Gordon Meade into Pennsylvania July 1st 1863." The other episodes of the battle that Beckel featured in his composition were identified within the score, such as the "Rebels approaching under Gen. Lee," the death of General John Reynolds, and the arrival of the Union Fifth and Sixth Corps, who "come up bravely to the tune of Yankee Doodle." The pianist was given clues about the "special effects" that the music was supposed to create, such as flying artillery shells, troops approaching from a distance, the sound of drums beating, "terrific cannonading," and even "Three Grand Hurrahs and a Tiger," indicating Union men cheering and growling in a victory celebration. The piece is typical for this

13. Dunkleman, *Gettysburg's Unknown Soldier,* 171–73.

genre, with dramatic changes in dynamics, meter, and tempo. Beckel's "Battle of Gettysburg" undoubtedly sparked the imaginations of many listeners.[14]

As the war continued, so too did more compositions about the Battle of Gettysburg but mostly from a Northern perspective. Considering the outcome of the battle, it is not surprising that Southern composers did not rush to publish songs about Gettysburg. John Prosinger, a professor at Hollins Institute in Virginia, wrote a piano piece titled "Picket's *[sic]* Charge March," which was published by B. Duncan and Company of Columbia, South Carolina. Prosinger dedicated the march to the Army of Northern Virginia—although the cover of the sheet music said it was "dedicated to the Northern Army of Virginia." Not only did he get the name of the army wrong, he also misspelled General George Pickett's name![15]

In 1864 T. C. Porter and J. B. Kevinsky published a piece for voice and piano called "The Rocky Hills of Gettysburg." As with other Northern songs about the battle, the Union soldiers were heroic and selfless, while Confederate soldiers were portrayed as haughty traitors, as evinced by the lyrics of the first and third verses:

> Oh dark the day, and dark the hour,
> When treason in her height of power,
> With all her gathered legions came,
> To waste the North with sword and flame!
> Right onward, swift exultant, proud,
> With burning wrath and curses loud,
> Up to yon chain of hills they crowd;
> The rocky hills of Gettysburg.
>
> In nameless graves the traitors sleep,
> Where none shall ever come to weep;
> But for her martyred sons, with tears,
> A monument the nation rears,

14. F. O. Jones, ed., *A Handbook of American Music and Musicians* (1886; reprint, New York: Da Capo Press, 1971), s.v. "Beckel, James C."; James C. Beckel, "Battle of Gettysburg" (Philadelphia: Winner, 1863).

15. John Prosinger, "Picket's Charge March" (Columbia, S.C.: B. Duncan, [ca. 1864]). This march was the only Southern composition that I could find during the course of my research that even touched on the Battle of Gettysburg.

And age to age shall pass it down,
The story of their bright renown,
And everlasting fame shall crown
The rocky hills of Gettysburg.[16]

Another song written in 1864 also paid tribute to the Union defenders of Gettysburg while it castigated the "traitor hoards" of the Army of Northern Virginia. Titled "The Heroes of Gettysburg; or, A Dirge for the Brave," it was dedicated "to the friends of the heroes who fell in the Battle at Gettysburg." James A. Scott wrote the music and Max J. Coble penned the lyrics. Coble was a Gettysburg native who in 1861 had enlisted in Cole's Maryland Cavalry and served as "First Bugler." The song's seminal performance was by the Glee Club of Company C, Cole's Maryland Cavalry. Coble sang lead and was accompanied by his fellow troopers who sang the chorus and played guitar, violin, and flute. Sadly, Coble was captured before his music was published, and he died from disease later that year as a result of his incarceration in Andersonville Prison.[17]

The song included six verses and two different choruses, and its tempo was marked "grave." The piece was sung softly at the beginning, increased in volume at the end of the verses, and was played and sung forcefully during the chorus:

16. J. B. Kevinsky and T. C. Porter, "The Rocky Hills of Gettysburg" (Philadelphia: Lee and Walker, 1864). The song was dedicated to "the Officers and Soldiers of the Army of the Potomac."

17. Max J. Coble and James A. Scott, "The Heroes of Gettysburg; or A Dirge for the Brave" (Philadelphia: Lee and Walker, 1864); the cover of the sheet music included the dedication and the makeup of Company C's glee club. On Coble, see C. Armour Newcomer, *Cole's Cavalry: Or Three Years in the Shenandoah Valley* (n.p., 1895; reprint, Freeport, N.Y.: Books for Libraries Press, 1970), 15. The Adams County Historical Society in Gettysburg has a photograph of Coble and Thaddeus Welty just before they enlisted. It is part of the J. Howard Wert Collection. Wert was a young Gettysburg schoolteacher at the time of the battle; he later joined the Union army and was wounded at the Battle of Petersburg. On the back of the photo, Wert wrote, "Here is a photo of two young men of Gettysburg taken at the time they enlisted in the Union Army, April 1861. The one on the left is my cousin, Thaddeus Welty, the other Max J. Coble, a talented young musician, who wrote the music to James A. Scott's 'Heroes of Gettysburg,' and who was so starved in the foul prison of Andersonville that he died a few days after his exchange whilst on a steamer that was conveying him to Annapolis."

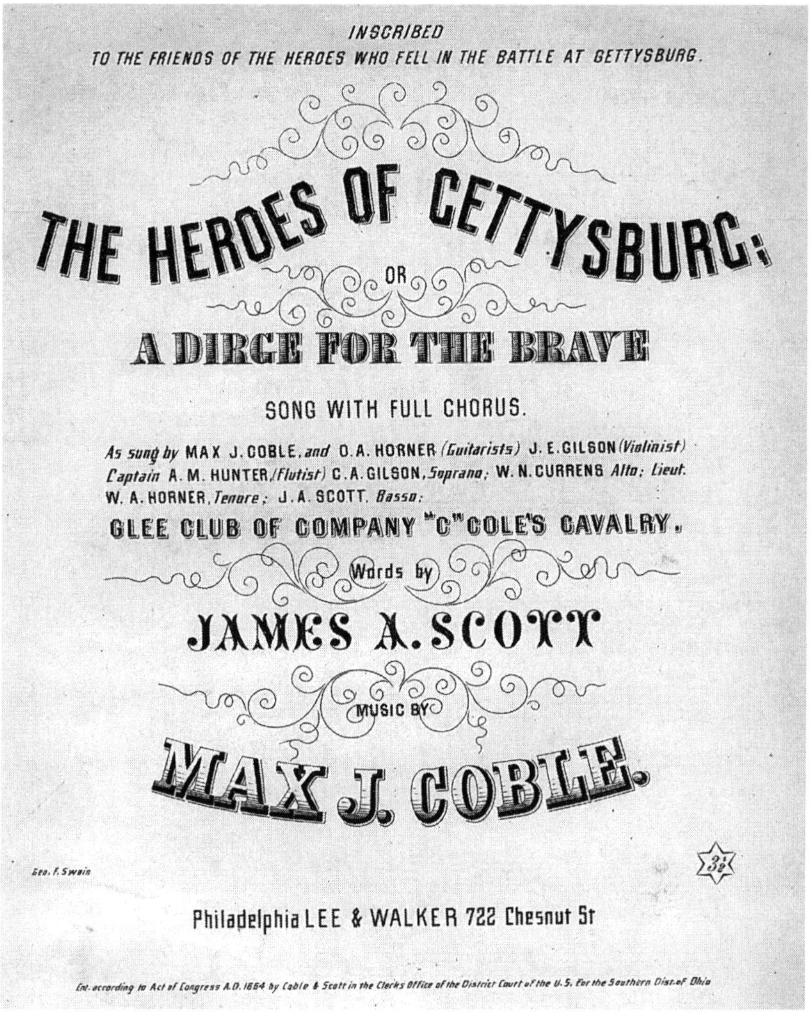

Cover to "The Heroes of Gettysburg." *Collection of Walter L. Powell.*

1. From the bloody Rappahannock,
Where in myriads lie!
Those who perished for the nation,
That it might not die!
Came our glorious patriot army,
Here again to meet
Traitor hordes in shock of battle,
And their hopes defeat.

(First Chorus)
Up! shake off thy slumber,
Mighty nation, rise!
Marshal forth thy hearts for battle
Under Freedom's skies.

2. And they fought as those fight only
Who defend the right;
When the cause of truth and justice
Serves with double might;
'Till the foe, dismayed and beaten
Were compelled to yield,
With their broken columns flying
From the bloody field.

(First Chorus)

3. And the spot is now immortal
Where our heroes died,
'Mid the awful roar and carnage
Of the battle's tide.
Their dear memories in the nation
Never shall decay;
It shall bear in fond remembrance,
Gettysburg's proud day.

(Second Chorus)
Pause! The earth is holy
Where our heroes lie!
And the winds are ever wisp'ring
Of their victory.

The lyrics touched the old familiar theme that the Union defenders were heroes and martyrs, the Confederate invaders were traitors, and the field of battle was now a shrine to the fallen brave who wore the blue.

When the Civil War ended in the spring of 1865, the need for patriotic music diminished. The soldiers returned home and composers found other subjects upon which to base their titles and lyrics. In 1880, however, lyricist Irenaeus D. Foulon harkened back memories of the battle to make a political point. That year, the presidential election pitted two former Union generals against each other. The

Music to "The Heroes of Gettysburg." *Collection of Walter L. Powell.*

Republican candidate, James Garfield, was a veteran of the Civil War's western theater and thus did not fight at Gettysburg. Winfield Scott Hancock was the Democratic contender. As the commander of the Army of the Potomac's Second Corps, Hancock defended the center of the Union position on Cemetery Ridge on July 2 and 3. The postwar Republicans loved to wave the symbolic "bloody shirt" of fallen Union soldiers to reinforce the fact that the Democratic party's antebellum stronghold was in the South. Even though Hancock was seriously wounded defending the Union at Gettysburg, the lyricist of the song titled "The Veteran's Vote" opined that Hancock had become a turncoat: "Then he [Hancock] wore the Union blue / Now he's donned the Rebel gray." Charles Kunkel wrote the music of "The Veteran's Vote." Lyrics were even supplied in German so that the thousands of German immigrants who had served in the Union army could understand the verses. "The Veteran's Vote" (or *"Die Stimme des Veteranen"*) was part of "The Boys in Blue Series" of Republican campaign songs for the election of 1880. "The Veteran's Vote" was "Respectfully dedicated to the Veterans of the War of the Rebellion."[18]

As the years passed and the physical and symbolic wounds healed, veterans of both sides began returning to the fields of strife. Northern veterans came in droves to Gettysburg, scene of their first clear-cut victory in the eastern theater. They began erecting monuments and memorials to honor the sacrifices they made in 1863. In 1887, the first reunion of Union and Confederate veterans of Pickett's Charge occurred at Gettysburg. Perhaps opportunistically, two years earlier C. H. Burton composed a guitar piece entitled "Gettysburg," and in 1886 Septimus Winner, a well-known bandleader, composer, and music publisher, wrote "The Gettysburg March." Not to be outdone, Louis Conterno, another bandleader, wrote his own piece, also called "The Gettysburg March," in time for the twenty-fifth anniversary in 1888. Finally, James C. Beckel, now seventy-seven, published in 1888 another programmatic piece with the ponderous title "The Battle of Gettysburg: Major General Geo. E. Pickett's Celebrated Charge at the Battle of Gettysburg, July 3, 1863." Unlike his first "Gettysburg" composition, this one was somewhat sympathetic to

18. Irenaeus D. Foulon and Charles Kunkel, "The Veteran's Vote" (St. Louis: Kunkel Brothers, 1880).

the Southerners, especially now that Beckel's sheet music could be sold in the Southern states. In this composition, Beckel once again stretched his artistic license, claiming that 3,500 men in Pickett's division had been killed, when in reality only 499 had been killed or mortally wounded.[19]

With the passing of the twenty-fifth anniversary, composers' interest in the battle waned. In 1913, the fiftieth anniversary of the battle was observed with a grand reunion of surviving Union and Confederate veterans. The U.S. government and the Commonwealth of Pennsylvania sponsored the event. More than fifty-three thousand veterans returned, and tens of thousands of spectators came to see them. President Woodrow Wilson gave a speech. Military bands played the old martial airs and, of course, songs were written especially for the occasion.[20]

The cover of one piece of sheet music proudly announced that it was written specifically for the "Gettysburg Semi-Centennial Reunion." Titled "Grand Old Gettysburg Boys," the lyrics were composed by Mrs. Findley Braden and the music by W. A. Webb. The words at the very top of the cover sheet claimed that it was the "National Peace Song." The lyrics themselves reflect the spirit of reconciliation and friendship that pervaded the anniversary celebration, as exemplified by the first verse:

> They come today from far away,
> To camp on once contested ground,
> In blue and gray, long after fray,
> Where only peace and rest are found.

19. C. H. McD. Burton, "Gettysburg," in *The Compositions of C. H. McD. Burgon for the Guitar* (Philadelphia: William H. Bonner, 1885); Septimus Winner, "The Gettysburg March" (Philadelphia: Sep. Winner and Son, 1886); for more on Winner, best known as the composer of "Listen to the Mocking Bird," see *The New Grove Dictionary of American Music* (1986 ed.), s.v. "Winner, Septimus," by Nicholas E. Tawa; Louis Conterno, "Gettysburg March" (Brooklyn: Joseph Mocs, 1887); James C. Beckel, "The Battle of Gettysburg . . ." (Chicago: National Music, 1888). Casualty figures were found in Jeffry Wert, *Gettysburg: Day Three* (New York: Simon and Schuster, 2001).

20. For a detailed description of the reunion, see Commonwealth of Pennsylvania, *Fiftieth Anniversary of the Battle of Gettysburg: Report of the Pennsylvania Commission* (Harrisburg, Pa.: Wm. Stanley Ray, State Printer, 1914), and Stan Cohen, *Hands across the Wall: The 50th and 75th Reunions of the Gettysburg Battle* (Charleston, W. Va.: Pictorial Histories Publishing), 1997.

And hand grasps hand, as oft they stand
Comparing notes about the past;
God in command a happy land,
And blest reunion now at last.[21]

Another "reconciliation" song was "Gettysburg," by James Wisler and Vivian Brooks. The song is a typical Tin Pan Alley arrangement with a syrupy, ragtime accompaniment. The lyrics are absolutely dreadful:

Fifty long years all told,
On these green fields were formed,
Facing each other bold,
In battle lines we stormed.
Up from the South they came,
Down from the North we marched,
Clad in blue, musket true,
They in gray, with no delay.

(Chorus)
Never shall thy glory cease;
Gettysburg, Gettysburg,
Never more in days of peace.

The battle fierce did rage,
O'er meadow, valley, plain,
Round top, big Round Top small,
Join in the deadly combat.
Culp's Hill with shot and shell,
Man and tree alike now tell,
Broken branch, leaded tree,
Broken army and leaded limb.

(Chorus)

Now on these fields you see,
Many a Monument, Marker, tow'r
Culp's Hill off to the East,
Cemetery Hill near by.

21. Mrs. Findley Braden and W. A. Webb, "Grand Old Gettysburg Boys" (Doylestown, Pa.: Braden Publishing, 1913).

Seminary Ridge West,
All tell of war in the past,
Thus shall they ever stand,
Emblems of peace, ended war.

(Chorus)[22]

The fiftieth anniversary of the battle came and went, and the next year the world was plunged into a much more terrible conflict. In 1917, the United States entered the First World War, which soon had American composers and lyricists writing a whole new generation of war music with tunes such as "Over There," "K-K-K-Katy," and "Good-bye Broadway, Hello France." The Gettysburg battlefield itself was turned into a large U.S. Army training camp. This war, like all those before it, proved not to be the "war to end all wars."

Music written in remembrance of—or about—the Battle of Gettysburg had evolved from compositions written immediately after the battle as a musical tribute to the fallen Union soldiers; to music that, thematically, told the story of the battle or one of its episodes from the viewpoint of one side or the other (normally the side of Union); to songs of reconciliation that were intended to heal the wounds and diminish the scars of the past. Although composers might return to the fields of Gettysburg for inspiration, it seems apparent that after the fiftieth anniversary in 1913, the Battle of Gettysburg had played its final cadence—with perhaps only a few widely scattered exceptions—as the subject of popular music.[23]

22. James Wisler and Vivian Brooks, "Gettysburg" (Washington, D.C.: H. Kirkus Dugdale, 1913).

23. A search of several sheet-music databases, including Peabody Institute's "Lester S. Levy Collection of Sheet Music," yielded only one "Gettysburg" composition written after 1913. Published in 1917, E. T. Paull's "Battle of Gettysburg" was labeled a "Descriptive March." It was similar in structure to James C. Beckel's programmatic pieces. See E. T. Paull, "Battle of Gettysburg" (New York: E. T. Paull Music, 1917).

Contributors

EDITORS

Bruce C. Kelley holds a Ph.D. and M.A. in music theory from The Ohio State University and a bachelor of music degree from Nebraska Wesleyan University. Dr. Kelley is assistant professor of music and director of music theory and composition at Shepherd University.

Mark A. Snell has a Ph.D. in history and public administration from the University of Missouri–Kansas City, a master's degree in U.S. history from Rutgers, and a bachelor's degree in music from York College of Pennsylvania. He is a former assistant professor of history at the U.S. Military Academy, West Point, New York. At Shepherd University, he chairs the Civil War and Nineteenth-Century America program and is the director of the George Tyler Moore Center for the Study of the Civil War.

CONTRIBUTORS

Eric A. Campbell has a B.A. in history from Mount St. Mary's College in Maryland and is a ranger-historian at Gettysburg National Military Park. He recently edited *"A Grand Terrible Dramma": From Gettysburg to Petersburg: The Civil War Letters of Charles Wellington Reed.*

Lenora Cuccia received her Ph.D. in musicology from Florida State University. She has taught at Mount Saint Mary College, Newburgh, New York. She enjoys participating in Civil War reenactments, as well as playing 1860s music on the fiddle. She currently resides in Italy, where her husband is stationed with the U.S. Army.

Walter L. Powell holds a Ph.D. in American literature and an M.A. in history from Kent State University. He is a past president of the Gettysburg Battlefield Preservation Association and has taught courses in historic preservation at Shepherd University.

Michael Saffle is professor of music and humanities with the Center for Interdisciplinary Studies at Virginia Polytechnic Institute. Born in Salt Lake City and a graduate of the University of Utah, he received a joint Ph.D. in musicology and humanities from Stanford University in 1977. He is a Fellow of the Center for Ulster Migrations, Cultures, and Societies.

Kirsten M. Schultz has a Ph.D. in historical musicology from the University of Toronto. Her essay is based in part on her doctoral dissertation.

Richard C. Spicer is a resident of Portsmouth, New Hampshire, and a doctoral student in the American and New England Studies Program at Boston University.

David B. Thompson is an assistant professor of music at Limestone College in Gaffney, South Carolina, and has performed as soloist and accompanist in many different venues in the United States and abroad. His interest in Civil War music is an outgrowth of a long-standing hobby, which resulted in his dissertation topic, "Piano Music in the South during the Civil War Period, 1855–1870." He holds a D.M.A. (doctor of musical arts) degree from the University of South Carolina.

Index